WRINKLIES™
BIG BOOK OF JOKES

Published in Great Britain in 2014 by Prion
an imprint of the
Carlton Publishing Group
20 Mortimer Street
London W1T 3JW

A catalogue record for this book is available
from the British Library.

ISBN 978-1-85375-915-4

Typeset by E-Type, Liverpool

Printed and bound in the UK by
CPI Group (UK) Ltd, Croydon, CR0 4YY

Previously published as *Wrinklies™ Joke Book: The Old Ones Are the Best...* and *Wrinklies™ Joke Book: The Laughter Lines.*

WRINKLIES™

BIG BOOK OF JOKES

Mike Haskins & Clive Whichelow

PRION

CONTENTS

HELLO THERE, WRINKLIES!

You're only young once, but you're older every year. Not fair is it? But then who said life was fair? And who said you're a wrinkly come to that? You're not are you? Of course you're not. Well, you're fairly sure you're not. OK, you may have a few wrinklyist tendencies, but on the whole you're in the prime of life. Aren't you? Apart from the odd laughter line (and some of them are in quite odd places for laughter lines), the odd dodgy joint (and no, we're not talking about your choice of discos here) and the occasional senior moment, you're fighting fit.

Yes, we know exactly what's happened: some joker, someone a bit younger than you naturally, has bought you this book for a laugh because you're on the wrong side of 40 and they think it will be amusing to wind you up with jokes about commodes and plastic surgery and forgetfulness, but it'll be like water off a duck's whatsit ("back", dear) because you ain't old. And if anyone says you are you can hit them with your walking stick. Only kidding!

And anyway, in this massive volume you will find mini-quizzes to determine if you are in fact a wrinkly. Perhaps you are. Someone has to be. But not you. No, OK, we hear you loud and clear, we've got the message, so now you can sit back and read it in the full knowledge that wrinkliedom is someone else's domain and, hell, you can laugh at them for a change. What's that? You've just got to go and find your reading glasses? You know you left them somewhere, but where...? OK then, whenever you're ready...

Getting Older And Wrinklier

As you get older, you will find you lose interest in sex, your friends drift away and your children often ignore you. There are other advantages, of course, but these are the main ones.

My grandmother is over 80 and still doesn't need glasses. Drinks right out of the bottle.

Henny Youngman

My grandfather will be there tonight. A marvellous old chap – you'd never think he was 104 – he looks much older.

Ronnie Corbett

When I was young I was called a rugged individualist. When I was in my 50s I was considered eccentric. Here I am doing and saying the same things I did then and I'm labelled senile.

George Burns

There are only two things we do with increasing frequency as we get older. One is to urinate and the other is to attend funerals.

Three things happen when you get to my age. First your memory starts to go and I've forgotten the other two.

Denis Healey

A man is only as old as the woman he feels.

Groucho Marx

At 65 you begin to regret the sins you did NOT commit.

I don't feel old. I don't feel anything until noon. Then it's time for my nap.

Bob Hope

The greatest problem about old age is the fear that it might go on too long.

A. J. P. Taylor

I smoke cigars, because at my age if I don't have something to hang on to I might fall down.

George Burns

It's a frightening feeling to wake up one morning and discover that while you were asleep you went out of style.

Erma Bombeck

Of course there's one way the ageing process could be slowed down: by making it work its way through Parliament.

It's scary when you start making the same noises as your coffee maker.

When you're old you think you've developed more patience, but really you're just past caring any more.

A newspaper reporter asks old Alf, "To what do you attribute your old age?" "To the fact I was born a long time ago," says Alf.

There was no respect for youth when I was young and now that I am old there is no respect for age – I missed it coming and going.

J. B. Priestley

Wrinkly's car bumper sticker: Don't worry. I drive far too fast to worry about cholesterol.

A sexagenarian? At his age? That's disgusting.

Gracie Allen

I'm looking forward to being properly old. Really old. So that I can lean over in a restaurant and say to my son, "You know what I just did? I just pissed myself... You deal with it!"

Dylan Moran

I'm going to stay in show business until I'm the last one left.

George Burns

An old man tells a friend, "I've got good news and bad news. The good news is I've finally discovered the Fountain of Youth." "What's the bad news?" asks his friend. "At my age," says the first old man, "I've forgotten what I wanted it for."

As we grow older, our bodies get shorter and our anecdotes longer.

Robert Quillen

As we grow older year by year, my husband always mourns: the less and less we feel our oats, the more we feel our corns.

At my age flowers scare me.

George Burns

Have you ever thought, in 40 years' time when they're going over all the things they had to do without when they were young, what exactly are the children of today going to moan about?

An old man is being shown round a house by an estate agent. "This house," says the estate agent, "is not only beautifully appointed and in first class decorative order, but it's a fabulous long-term investment." "Long-term?" says the old man. "You're joking aren't you? Blimey, at my time of life I don't even buy green bananas!"

I don't need you to remind me of my age. I have a bladder to do that for me.

Stephen Fry

I knew I was going bald when it was taking longer and longer to wash my face.

Harry Hill

Phrases People Use To Indicate That You Are Old – Without Actually Saying So

Past the first flush of youth

Mature

In your third age

Matronly

No spring chicken

Not as young as she/he used to be

And some less polite ones

Past it

Over the hill

Knocking on a bit

Geriatric

Senile

Old fogey/fart/bag

Crone

Coffin-dodger

Ancient

Biddy

Codger

Definitions For Wrinklies

Age always corresponds inversely to the size of your multi-vitamin tablets.

Age is not a particularly interesting subject. Anyone can get old. All you have to do is live long enough.

Don Marquis

Dorothy: Age is just a state of mind.
Blanche: Tell that to my thighs.

The Golden Girls

Age seldom arrives smoothly or quickly. It's more often a succession of jerks.

Jean Rhys

Age: that period of life in which we compound for the vices that we still cherish by reviling those that we no longer have the enterprise to commit.

Ambrose Bierce

Age is something that makes wine worth more and people worth less.

Old age is the out-patients' department of purgatory.

Lord Hugh Cecil

Old age is when you resent the swimsuit issue of *Sports Illustrated*, because there are fewer articles to read.

George Burns

To me old age is always 15 years older than I am.
Bernard Baruch

You're not old. You're chronologically challenged.

Welcome To Wrinkly World

It sounds like one of those theme parks doesn't it? Wrinkly World – a mildly enjoyable day out for all the family who are over 40! White-knuckle wheelchair rides! The ghost train – haunted by recent customers! The wall of deaf! Slow food (boiled ham burgers, toffee apples with custard, warmed-up dogs!)

Perhaps some budding entrepreneur should get on to it. Official figures show that by the year 2050, 110% of the population will be over-60, (or something like that), so there's a huge potential market, with wrinklies from John o'Groats to Lands End all raring to go – and have a nice sit down.

But before that happens we have the real world of wrinklies. And wrinklyhood is not just a state of mind or concerned with how your body is refusing to cooperate these days. It's about every aspect of your life, from the clothes you wear to the pets you keep. So, if you want to keep wrinklyhood at bay a bit longer pay careful attention to the following – and avoid behaving like a typical wrinkly.

Wrinkly World: Food And Kitchenware

Examine your kitchen cupboards and fridge. Do you possess any of the following:

Horlicks

Ovaltine

Custard powder

Camp coffee

A brown teapot

A teapot shaped like a country cottage

A tea strainer

A swear box

An apron with a picture of breasts on the front that the man of the house uses to amuse people at barbecues

A grey-looking cloth that is used for cooking spotted dick

A novelty tea towel showing London landmarks

A jokey poster detailing the "rules of the house"

A tea cosy that you or another member of your family has knitted or crocheted

A set of egg cosies

A non-fitted kitchen unit

A china toast rack

An egg coddler

Any sort of butter pat implement

Doggie choc drops

Bird seed for the wild birds in your garden

A recipe book that has actually been used and has not been purchased solely to show your hip affinity to the latest celebrity chef

Sugar tongs

A biscuit barrel

A sign above the kitchen door that reads 'Mum's The Boss'

(FYI, the more of the above you admit to possessing the more of a wrinkly you are.)

You Know You're Getting Old When...

You come out of a supermarket and spend 15 minutes looking for your car before remembering you gave up driving four years ago.

Even pensioners are looking younger.

You look back at your old love letters and find the stamps on the front have got kings on them.

You're asked to be the "before" face in a Botox ad.

Some children come to visit and you're not sure whether they're grandchildren, great-grandchildren or somebody else's great-grandchildren.

When you bend your knees everyone suddenly ducks because they think there's a sniper on the loose.

You dread one of your household appliances breaking down, because you're not sure whether you can master any more new technology.

You leave the pub before closing time – even on your birthday.

You don't look forward to birthdays any more.

The highlight of your day is putting your feet up.

Your idea of a good time is not having to do anything.

You've given up trying to keep up with the Joneses and even have trouble keeping up with the plotline of *Eastenders*.

Your idea of a workout is trying to chew a toffee.

The local paper rings to ask if you'd help them with a nostalgia piece.

The doctor tries to take your pulse and has trouble finding it.

You start planning who to cut out of your will.
A sexy young thing catches your fancy and your pacemaker opens the garage door.

A strenuous bout of weight-lifting only involves getting out of a chair.

After painting the town red, you have to take a week's rest before applying a second coat.

Middle-age
(AKA The First Age Of Wrinklydom)

Yes, it's that strange never-never land between being young and being old. You're too old for discos, but a bit young for slipped discs, too old for speed dating, but a bit young for carbon dating. You've still got some of your energy, but frankly you can't be bothered to use it. But it's also the point where you suddenly want to recapture some of your fading youth before it's too late. Men will suddenly buy large motorbikes, because they like to feel something throbbing between their legs, women will think about having a toy boy, because, well, because it makes them feel younger. Luckily it's a very loosely defined concept so no one admits to it. Being middle-aged is something that only happens to other people. Just beware that coming home with a boy's toy or a toy boy is a dead giveaway.

After 30, a body has a mind of its own.

Bette Midler

Thirty-five is when you finally get your head together and your body starts falling apart.

Caryn Leschen

Not only does life begin at 40, it also really begins to show.

Middle-age is a time of life that a man first notices in his wife.

Richard Armour

Middle-age is having a choice of two temptations and choosing the one that will get you home earlier.

Middle-age is the time when a man is always thinking in a week or two he will feel as good as ever.

Don Marquis

Middle-age is when the broadness of your mind and the narrowness of your waist swap places.

It's called middle-age because it's the time when you stop growing at both ends and start to grow in the middle.

Middle-age is when women stop worrying about becoming pregnant and men start worrying about looking like they are.

It may be true that life begins at 40, but everything else starts to wear out, fall out or spread out.

Middle-age is when you choose a cereal because of its fibre content, rather than because of its free plastic toy.

Everyone is sitting in their seats at the theatre waiting for the performance to start when suddenly a middle-aged woman at the back of the stalls stands up and shouts, "Is there a doctor in the house?" Five men stand up and the woman says, "Thank goodness for that, now if any of you are single would you like to marry my beautiful daughter?"

The really frightening thing about middle-age is knowing you'll grow out of it.

Doris Day

Middle-age is when you go to bed at night and hope you feel better in the morning. Old age is when you go to bed at night and hope you wake up in the morning.

Groucho Marx

Lying About Your Age

They say you're only as old as you feel, which is, very well until you get to 60 and you feel 80. But whatever age you are, it can always remain a secret between you and the yellowing parchment of your birth certificate.Some stars not only look magically younger every year, their age magically decreases annually too. But such devilish chicanery doesn't have to be the sole province of pop stars and actors. You, too, can fool most of the people most of the time with these simple tips on how to be economical with the truth about your advancing years.

The age of your children. One day someone suddenly realizes that your eldest child is almost 40, which puts you at 56 at the absolute minimum and more likely well into your 60s. It's at this point that you quickly say, "Look, I've never told him, but he was adopted." Just don't over-egg it by trying to pretend that he was 32 when you took him on.

Being asked directly. If someone has the effrontery to actually ask the question outright just ask them how old they think you are. Most people are polite enough to knock a few years off what they really think and then you can make them feel good by telling them they're spot on. Everyone's happy!

Inadvertent slippage. You know what it's like – someone starts talking about the war and before you can help yourself you're reminiscing about rationing, air raid shelters and all the rest while suddenly realising that everyone else is making rapid mental calculations about your age – "So, you were five when war broke out then?" It is at this point that you suddenly put them straight, "Oh yes, brilliant, wasn't it, that *Band of Brothers*? It almost made you feel like you'd lived through it yourself!" Phew!

Form filling. Next time you are confronted with the dreaded words "date of birth" simply write February 16th or whatever it is. If challenged you can quite correctly point out that they never asked the year and, to be honest, it's far too long ago for you to remember anyway.

A few pitfalls to watch out for:

If you must knock ten years off your age you will have to revise all your anecdotes. It will sound a bit odd if you talk about that time you were thrown out of the pub for fighting at the age of eight.

Do remember to hide those old pictures of you in flares, hot pants or winkle pickers. People will either assume you were extremely tall for your age and had acne at the age of three or work out that you're telling porkies.

You will be paying full fare on the buses long after all your friends are travelling free.

Unless you actually look a lot younger than you really are, people will be whispering behind your back about how old you look and how you've let yourself go, if you're trying to pretend you're 15 years younger than you actually are.

Be consistent. There's nothing worse than someone suddenly turning round and saying, "Hang on, if you were born in 1964 how come you remember where you were when Kennedy was shot? And not only that, a couple of weeks ago you said your earliest memory was watching the Coronation on your gran's telly?"

Have I Got News For You

I said to my wife, "If I ever get like that – y'know, mumbling to myself and shitting my pants – shoot me!" She said, "Better start running, monkey boy!"

Lee Evans

Everything that goes up must come down, but there comes a time when not everything that's down can come up.

George Burns

The Difference Between Quite Old And Wrinkly – And Really Old And Wrinkly

Quite old and wrinkly	Really old and wrinkly
You get puffed out when exerting yourself	You get puffed out doing the crossword
You can't put names to faces so easily these days	You can't even put a name to your own face
You start thinking about plastic surgery	You start thinking about not having any more plastic surgery as that dimpled chin is actually your belly button
You struggle to keep up with fashion	You know that pyjamas and a dressing gown will never go out of fashion
You start getting a bit grumpy now and then	Grumpy is your permanent default mode
Most of the CDs you buy these days are oldies	What's a CD?
You struggle to read small print	The only thing you read these days is the small print on medicine packaging
You feel a bit jealous of young people	You feel a bit jealous of "quite old" people
Your stomach's expanding, but your memory's shrinking	You're shrinking
You've given up worrying about what you eat	You don't care what you eat because it all tastes the same anyway
Even your children are starting to show signs of age	Your children are showing signs of popping their clogs before you do
You wake up feeling a bit achy	You wake feeling a bit surprised
You struggle with new technology	You put up with new technology as it's the only thing that's keeping you alive

You use anti-wrinkle cream	You realize that if you got rid of the wrinkles there wouldn't be much else left
Some of your views would make Alf Garnett proud	Some of your views would make Alf Garnett blush
You often talk about "the good old days"	You are pretty sure there must have been some "good old days" but can't quite remember whether you were involved in them or not
You feel you ought to be doing more exercise	You feel that any exercise at all might just finish you off
You seem to have more little aches and pains every day	You seem to have more little relatives every day
You lie about your age	You boast about your age
You're given stick by people younger than yourself	You're given a stick
You start to wonder where the years went	You start to wonder how you're still here
You're a bit sad that your kids will soon be flying the nest	You're a bit sad that your kids will soon be selling the nest and putting you in a home
You worry about losing some of your faculties	You worry about losing some of your bladder control
It only seems like yesterday when you first had your kids	It only seems like yesterday that it was yesterday
You don't seem to go out so much these days	Your joints are the only things that go out
Your trousers don't fit any more	Your trousers are suddenly loose again

And How Old Are You Really?

The problem with precise ages is that they conjure up images that somehow take over from the reality. So, if you're a slim, youthful looking person in fashionable clothes and you let slip that you're 40, the person you're talking to suddenly sees you as sad and middle-aged, despite any physical evidence to the contrary. Similarly, you see a picture of an attractive film star in the paper then notice that the caption says they're 60. Even though they look like a million dollars and they probably had to pay a million dollars to look like a million dollars, they are immediately less attractive as you scan the picture for wrinkled hands, cellulite, wig joins and other tell-tale signs of ageing. So the only answer, without outright lying, is skilful evasion. So if someone tells you they're "30-something" you can be pretty damn sure they're not a day under 39 and possibly the "30-something" they so blithely refer to is 30-12...

You're never too old to become younger.

Mae West

Forty was a difficult age for her. She took eight years to pass it.

I do wish I could tell you my age, but it's impossible. It keeps changing all the time.

Greer Garson

I refuse to admit I'm more than 52, even if that does make my sons illegitimate.

Nancy Astor

If a woman tells you she's 20 and looks 16, she's 12. If she tells you she's 26 and looks 26, she's damn near 40.

Chris Rock

I think women spend far too much money going into Boots and buying all this anti-wrinkle cream to slap on their faces to make them look younger, and it doesn't work. You might just as well slap a bit of fruit cake mix on your face, go out in the sun for two hours, then at least you've got a cake to show for it.

Jo Brand

I've known her for many years. In fact, I remember when she and I were the same age.

The woman who tells her age is either too young to have anything to lose or too old to have anything to gain.

Chinese Proverb

Two old men are talking. "You know, you're only as old as you feel," says the first. "Oh," says the second. "In that case how come I'm still alive when I'm 150 years old?"

She admitted she was 40, but she didn't say when.

She said she was approaching 40... I couldn't help wondering from what direction.

Bob Hope

Two women are discussing a mutual friend. "She's not pushing 40," says one. "No," says the other, "she's clinging on to it for dear life."

No woman should ever be quite accurate about her age. It looks so calculating.

Oscar Wilde

How old would you think you were if you didn't know how old you are?

She's approaching middle-age – for something like the third time.

Two women are talking. "I think 30 is a great age to be," says the first. "Yes," says her friend, "particularly when in reality you're 45."

A census taker knocks on an old woman's front door. She answers and goes through all his questions until he asks her how old she is. "I'm sorry," says the old woman, "but I don't believe it's ladylike to tell anyone my age." "Oh dear," says the census taker, "that does make things rather difficult." "All right. Then I'll just tell you this much," says the old woman, "I'm the same age as Mr and Mrs Hill who live next door."

"That's fine," says the census taker, "I'll just put down next to your name, 'as old as the hills'."

I never lie about my age. I just tell people I'm as old as my wife. Then I lie about her age.

A traffic policeman pulls over a lady for speeding. "Madam," he says as he goes up to her car window, "when I saw you tearing down the street, I guessed 65 as a minimum." "That's ridiculous, officer," says the woman. "I'm 54. It's these damn glasses – they put ten years on me."

She was a handsome woman of 45 and would remain so for many years.

Anita Brookner

A man asks a friend, "Did my wife tell you her age?" "Partly," says the friend.

In dog years I'm dead!

Through The Ages

From birth to the age of 18, a girl needs good parents. From 18 to 35, she needs good looks. From 35 to 55, she needs a good personality. From 55 on, she needs good cash.

Sophie Tucker

The ages of man in fruit. At 20, a man is like a coconut; he has so much to offer, but so little to give. At 30, he's like a durian; dangerous, but delicious. At 40, he's like a watermelon; big, round and juicy. At 50, he's like a satsuma; he only comes once every year. At 60, he's more like a raisin; dried out, wrinkled and cheap.

When you're three years old, success is not peeing in your pants. When you're eleven, success is having friends. When you're 17, success is having a driving licence. When you're 20, success is having sex. When you're 30, success is having money. When you're 50, success is having money. When you're 60, success is having sex. When you're 70, success is having a driving licence. When you're 75, success is having friends. When you're 80, success is not peeing in your pants.

The first 50 miles on the go all the way – your sense of direction – bowling along. Get past 60 and everything slows down to a sudden crawl and you realize you're not going anywhere any more. All the things you thought you were going to do that never came to anything. You can't turn the clock back – it's one-way traffic just gradually grinding to a halt.

Victor Meldrew / One Foot in the Grave

The ages of woman in balls. At 18, she's a football; 22 men are running after from all directions. At 28, she's a hockey ball; eight men are panting to get her. At 38, she's a golf ball; there's only one man after her now. At 48, she's a ping-pong ball; two guys are doing their damnedest to get rid of her.

What dominates the thoughts of men at different stages in their lives: Between 0-3 their bowel movements; 4-10 guns; 11-14 sex; 15-20 sex; 20-40 sex; 40-60 sex; 60-? their bowel movements…

Health Advice For Wrinklies

Most people breeze through their youth without giving their health a second thought – and why should they? They're brimming with it. Their cup runneth over with the stuff. If health were wealth they'd be millionaires. Then one by one those little gremlins start creeping in like bugs on your computer system. One day your knees start giving you a bit of trouble, your back starts playing up, you can't quite remember things you used to – like... well nothing springs to mind right now... and before you know where you are you're a walking medical dictionary of symptoms, complaints and syndromes. Then you start to take a keen interest in those articles they keep running in the newspapers about IBS, DVT, MRSA and all that other stuff which is too awful to spell out in full. Before you can say, "Nurse, the screens!" you're a fully-fledged hypochondriac – but a hypochondriac with a difference, because in your case, you've actually got every ailment going.

The definition of good health: the slowest possible rate at which you can die.

Jack Benny once said after being presented with a show business award, "I don't deserve this. But I have arthritis and I don't deserve that either."

If I'd known I was going to live this long, I'd have taken better care of myself.

Eubie Blake

I've got to watch myself these days. It's too exciting watching anyone else.

Bob Hope

An old boy goes along to his school reunion and because all his old classmates are now in advanced years they spend most of the evening talking about their failing health and comparing grisly notes. "One was on about his heart problems," the old boy tells his wife when he got home. "Another was discussing his kidney transplant, and another was banging on about his liver problems…" "Oh dear," says his wife, "it doesn't sound so much like a school reunion, more like an organ recital."

A little old lady is having a check-up from her doctor who has been treating her for asthma. He examines her, asks a few questions and notes down her croaky replies. Finally he asks, "And what about the wheeze?" "Oh they're fine," says the old lady, "I went three times last night."

A doctor begins his examination of an old man by asking him what brought him to the hospital. "Er," says the old man. "I think it might have been an ambulance."

An old man goes to see his doctor. "Well," says the doctor, "it's a long time since you've been to see me." "I know," says the old man, "I've not been well."

An old man goes for a thorough examination at the doctor's. After it's over, the old man asks, "Well, doctor, how do I stand?" "To be honest," says the doctor, "that's what's puzzling me."

A lady in her late 80s goes to the doctor's for a check-up. The doctor asks her how she's doing and receives in response a litany of complaints about her aches, pains, stiffness, lack of energy and her general increasing difficulty at doing many things. "Now come on, Mrs Siegel," says the doctor. "You have to expect things to start deteriorating at your age. After all, who wants to live to be 100?" The old lady gives him a cold look and replies, "I would have thought anyone who's 99."

Elsie goes to the doctor suffering a whole range of aches, pains, and ailments. The doctor examines her and says, "Well, Mrs Cartwright, I know you must be in some discomfort, but there's not a lot I can do. You're 75 years old and, well, I can't make you any younger you know." "I'm not bothered about getting any younger," says Elsie, "I just want to make sure I get a bit older."

An old man goes to a private practice. "I'll examine you for £100," says the doctor. "Go ahead then," says the old man, "and if you find £100, you can keep it."

Old Harry goes to see his doctor and the doctor has to give him a rectal examination. "Ooh," says Harry, "that was a bit uncomfortable." "I know," says the doctor. "I had to use two fingers rather than just one." "What was that for?" asks Harry. "I thought I better get a second opinion," says the doctor.

A man is at the doctors to hear the results of his tests. "Well, doctor," he says, "is it good news or bad news?" "Bad news I'm afraid," replies the doctor. "You've only got three months to live." "Three months!" exclaims the patient. "Is there nothing I can do?" "Well, you could try having lots of mud baths," says the doctor. "And that'll prolong my life will it?" asks the patient hopefully. "No," replies the doctor, "but at least it'll get you used to lying in dirt."

An old man hasn't been feeling well for a little while so he goes to his doctor for a complete check-over. After a while the doctor calls him in to hear the results of the tests that have been carried out. "I'm afraid I have some bad news. You're dying and you don't have much time," says the doctor. "Oh no," says the old man. "How long have I got?" "Ten," says the doctor. "Ten?" says the old man. "Ten what? Months? Weeks? What exactly?" "... nine... eight... seven... six..."

Did you hear about the old man whose health was so bad his doctor advised him not to start watching any serials.

Old Fred goes to the doctor's. The doctor examines him then says, "I'm afraid I've got some bad news for you, Fred," and hands him a small bottle of pills. "You're going to have to take these pills for the rest of your life." "That's not so bad," says Fred. "Yes it is," says the doctor. "You're not going to need a repeat prescription."

Tom, Dick and Harry are three old friends. Tom is 80, Dick is 90 and Harry is 100 years old. They all go to the doctor's together for a check-up. Tom goes in first and comes out a few minutes later and tells the others, "The doctor says I'm in extremely good health for an 80-year-old. He thinks I could live another 20 years." Dick goes into the consulting room next and emerges a little while later. He tells the others, "The doctor says I'm in fairly good health considering the fact that

I'm 90. He says I could live for another ten years." Harry goes in last and comes out an hour later. "What happened?" ask his friends. "The doctor examined me and then asked how old I was," says Harry. "And what happened when you told him?" asks Tom. "He told me to have a nice day," says Harry.

A posh old woman is talking to her friend. She tells her, "My husband is now so elderly and infirm, I have to watch him all day and night." "But I thought you'd hired a young nurse to take care of him," says her friend. "I have," says the old woman. "That's precisely why I've got to keep an eye on him."

An old man goes to the doctor and says he hasn't been feeling well. The doctor gives him an examination, and then goes to his cupboard and brings out three large bottles of different coloured pills. "Now then," says the doctor, "I want you to take the green pill with a big glass of water when you get out of bed. Then I want you to take the blue pill with a big glass of water after your dinner. Then just before you go to bed, I want you to take the red pill with another big glass of water." The old man is surprised that the doctor wants to put him on so much medication so he says, "So, doctor, exactly what it is that I've got wrong with me?" "You're not drinking enough water," says the doctor.

A pharmacist is going over the directions on a prescription bottle with an elderly patient. "Be sure not to take this more often than every four hours," the pharmacist says. "Don't worry about that," replies the patient. "It takes me four hours to get the bloomin' lid off!"

Old Alf has a very understanding doctor. Because Alf couldn't afford to have the operation he needed, the doctor touched up his X-rays for him instead.

Two old ladies are having a natter about their favourite subject, their various medical conditions. The first tells the second, "The doctor says I need another operation, but I can't afford to get it done privately and there's a 12-month waiting list on the NHS." "That's a disgrace," says her friend. "Still, never mind. We'll just have to talk about your old operation for another year."

An old man goes to the doctor. "Doctor," he says pointing to different parts of his body, "when I touch my arm it hurts. When I touch my neck it hurts. And when I touch my stomach it hurts. Do I have some rare disease?" "No," says the doctor, "you have a sore finger."

Grandma was having some stomach problems so the doctor told her to drink tepid water with a teaspoon of Epsom salts an hour before breakfast every morning. After a month she was no better so went back to the doctor. "Did you drink the water an hour before breakfast every morning?" he asked. "No, doctor," she replied. "I'm sorry but I couldn't manage more than 20 minutes."

In the waiting room at the surgery a vast crowd of people were waiting for their appointments while the doctor seemed to be working at a snail's pace. After two hours' wait, one old man slowly got up and shuffled towards the door. When everyone stopped talking to look at him, he turned and announced, "Well, I think I'll just have to go home and die a natural death."

A 90-year-old man is snoozing in the chair one day when a life insurance salesman knocks at the door. He gives him the hard sell, but the old man is a bit wary about the cost of the insurance, which at his age isn't cheap. After about 45 minutes of haggling on the doorstep, the salesman finally says, "Look, I'll tell you what, you have a think about it, sleep on it tonight and if you wake up in the morning give me a ring, OK?"

When asked in his late 90s if his doctor knew he still smoked, George Burns said, "No... he's dead."

A middle-aged man is due to have an operation and is very worried about it, so just beforehand he tells the surgeon that he's rather nervous and concerned. "You see, doctor," he says, "I've heard that only one in ten people survives this particular operation. Is that true?" "Unfortunately, yes," admits the surgeon.

"Your information is correct. But looking on the bright side you've got absolutely nothing to worry about because my last nine patients all died!"

Two little boys are talking. One says, "My grandmother is suffering from furniture disease." "What's that?" asks his friend. "It's when your chest falls into your drawers," says the first.

Signs That Your Body Isn't What It Used To Be

The doctor asks you to "take off that baggy vest" and you're not even wearing one.

When you run for the bus you're too puffed out to tell the driver what fare you want.

Your waist measurement is bigger than your leg measurement.

The last time you "got on down" at a party you couldn't get up again.

When the doctor asks you to stick your tongue out you ask him how far is absolutely necessary.

You have more replacements than original bits.

When you get to the gym the first thing you have to do is have a little sit down.

You insist on measuring your waist in inches because in centimetres it just sounds too depressing.

Combing your hair seems to take less and less time.

You get out of breath coming down the stairs.

You have hair growing on top of your nose.

Your knees creak when you bend down.

Er, What Was This Section About Again?

They say that after a certain age your brain cells start to go. Where to? And can we have them back? Of course it's infuriating when you start to forget those little things like where you left your car keys, whether you left the gas on when you went out or which house is yours when you go home. But memory loss probably has a biological function – when you look in the mirror and see a wrinkled old soul peering back at you myopically, because you can't remember where you left your glasses, you also forget that in your youth you were often mistaken for the young Marlon Brando or Sophia Loren. When you wake up in the morning full of aches and pains, and bursting to go to the loo, you forget that you used to leap out of bed like a spring lamb raring to go (and not just to the toilet). And if you can't remember stuff like that then growing old doesn't seem quite so bad. It's also pretty good news for the rest of your family who won't have to listen to you going on about "the good old days", because you won't even remember having had any.

Old Bill goes to his doctor's and says, "Doctor, my memory is terrible. I can't remember anything." "OK," says the doctor, "tell me all about it." "All about what?" says Bill.

Do you know, for as long as I can remember I've had amnesia.

A very forgetful old man goes to a singles bar and tries to pick up women by going up to them and saying, "Hello. Do I come here often?"

Two old ladies meet for a weekly game of cards. Halfway through their game one week, one of the old ladies says to the other, "I'm terribly sorry. I know we've been friends for over 60 years, but I'm afraid I just can't think what your name is. Would you remind me please?" The other old lady sits staring at her for a few moments. "I've offended you haven't I?" says the first old lady. "No," says the second, "it's just that I can't remember what it is myself at the moment."

You should try and look on the bright side when it comes to extreme memory loss. At least it means you get to meet new people every day.

A woman notices an old man sitting on a park bench sobbing his eyes out. She goes over and asks what's wrong. "I have a 22-year-old wife," says the old man. "Every single morning she insists on making mad passionate love with me before she gets up and makes breakfast for me." "OK," says the woman. The old man goes on, "She makes my lunch for me, does my washing, my ironing, keeps the house beautiful and still has the energy to make love as soon as I get home in the afternoon." "I see," says the woman. "Every evening she cooks me a delicious gourmet meal, which she serves with wine and my favourite dessert, before doing all the dishes and making love to me again until bedtime." "Fine," says the woman. "So why are you sitting here sobbing?" "I've forgotten where I live," says the old man.

Ageing men first forget names, then they forget faces. Then they forget to pull up their zips after going to the toilet and finally, worst of all, they forget to pull down their zips before they go.

Overall my memory is excellent, apart from three things: faces, names and... something else.

Three sisters aged 92, 94 and 96 all live in a house together. One night, the 96-year-old starts a bath. She puts her foot in, pauses and asks, "Was I getting in or out of the bath?" The 94-year-old yells back, "I don't know, but I'll come up and see!" She starts up the stairs and pauses. "Was I going up the stairs or down?" The 92-year-old is sitting at the kitchen table having tea, listening to her sisters. She shakes her head and says, "I sure hope I never get that forgetful." She knocks on wood for good measure. Then she yells to her sisters, "I'll come up and help both of you as soon as I see who's at the door!"

Old Bert's memory is getting worse. Yesterday he put his shoes on the wrong feet. Now he can't remember whose feet he put them on.

An old lady and her husband are always arguing over which of them has the worse memory. "OK," says the old lady, "if you want to prove your memory's not so bad, go and get me a cup of tea." Off goes her husband to the kitchen, only to return ten minutes later with a steaming bowl of porridge. "You idiot!" says the old woman. "Where the hell are my eggs?"

An old man visits his doctor and says, "Oh, doctor. I've got a terrible problem. I seem to have developed an awful memory. I can't remember where I left my car. I can't remember how I got here. I can't even remember where I live or whether I'm married or not. Can you help me, doctor?" "I can," says the doctor, "but you're going to have to pay me in advance."

In a retirement home two old men are eating breakfast one morning. One notices something in the other one's ear. "I say, old man," says the first, "did you know you've got a suppository in your ear?" His friend pulls it out and looks at it. "Thank goodness you noticed that," he says. "I wondered where that had got to. Now if only I could think where I've put my hearing aid..."

The funny thing is I never remember being absent-minded.

Thanks to the latest fertility technology, a 65-year-old woman gives birth to a baby boy. As soon as she gets home from hospital, her sister invites herself round and asks, "Can I see the new arrival?" "Not yet," says the mother. Half an hour passes and the sister asks, "Can I see him now?" "No," says the mother. The sister soon begins to get really impatient and says, "Come on! Please can I see him?" "No," says the mother. "You've got to wait until he cries." "I don't understand," says her sister. "Why have I got to wait until he cries?" "Because," says the 65-year-old, "at the moment I can't remember where I've left him."

These days the easiest way to find something lost around the house is... to buy a replacement.

Three absent-minded professors were talking together in a bus terminal. They got so engrossed in what they were saying that they didn't notice the bus had pulled in. As the driver sang out, "All aboard," they looked up startled and dashed to the bus. Two of them managed to hop on, but the third didn't make it. As he stood sadly watching the bus disappear into the distance, a stranger tried to cheer him up, saying,

"You shouldn't feel too bad. Two out of three of you got on, so that's a pretty good average." "It would be," said the professor, "except those two came to see *me* off."

Joyce tells her friend Glenda, "I'm going to divorce Harry." "Why's that?" asks Glenda. "Because," says Joyce, "he has a rotten memory." "OK," says Glenda, "but why divorce him just because he has a bad memory?" "Because," says Joyce, "Every time he sees an attractive young woman he forgets he's married to me!"

Old Sid tells a friend, "My wife has a terrible memory. She never forgets a single thing."

I have a memory like an elephant. In fact elephants often consult me.

Noel Coward

Right now I'm having amnesia and deja vu at the same time. I think I've forgotten this before.

Steven Wright

Wrinklies' Failing Faculties

And we're not talking about universities giving out Mickey Mouse degrees. No, we're talking about age's unkindest cut of all. Just when you get to the stage where you can't be bothered to go out so much and all you want to do is sit in front of the TV in the evening… you can't hear it properly. Even with the volume knob turned up to 11 you can still only just about hear the neighbours banging on the walls, so you give up and decide to read a book. But the print's a bit fuzzy. When exactly did they start printing books in a typeface called Now You See Me Now You Don't point 0000001? So you decide to go and make a cup of tea, but you can't quite remember which cupboard the teabags are in, and if you have a cup of tea too late in the evening you'll be up and down to the toilet all night, and those biscuits don't taste as good as they used to, and is it cold in here or is just me…?

A very old man, almost bent double, hobbles up to an ice-cream seller and asks for a vanilla cornet. "Crushed nuts, granddad?" asks the ice-cream man. "No," says the old man. "It's rheumatism if you must know."

For a long time old Tom's family thought he had become hunchbacked due to his advancing years. Eventually, though, they found out that it was just because he didn't know his braces were adjustable.

Three old men who are all hard of hearing are playing golf one morning. One says to another, "Windy, isn't it?" "No," says the second man, "it's Thursday." The third man then pipes up, "Yes. So am I! Let's get a beer!"

Wilt! Droop! Crack! Sag! Ever feel like the warranty on some of your parts just expired?

An old lady is waiting to go in to see the doctor. When her name is called she gets unsteadily to her feet, with the aid of a walking stick, and one of the other patients notices she is bent almost double. A receptionist helps the old lady into the doctor's room slowly and carefully, and ten minutes later the door opens and the old woman walks out completely upright. "My goodness!" says the other patient. "That's amazing! You went in there bent almost double and now you're walking out like a guardsman! What did the doctor give you, some sort of miracle cure?" "No," says the old lady, "he gave me a longer stick."

An old man tells a friend, "I just bought myself a new hearing aid. It cost me £4,000, but it's state of the art. It's perfect." "Really," says his friend. "So what kind is it?" "12.30," says the old man.

A well-known scientific conundrum: if an old lady falls over in her house when there's no one else around, does she make a sound?

An elderly gentleman realizes he has been increasingly suffering from hearing problems for a number of years. So he finally decides to go to his doctor to see if he can offer any help. The doctor fits a hearing aid, which allows him to hear extremely well once again. One month later the elderly gentleman comes back to see the doctor. The doctor says, "Yes, your hearing is pretty good once again. Your family must be really pleased at the improvement." "Oh I haven't told them about it yet," says the elderly gentleman. "I just sit around and listen to what they're all saying to each other. So far I've changed my will five times!"

An old man becomes concerned that his wife is losing her hearing. So, he walks up close to her and says loudly into her ear, "Can you hear me?" His wife doesn't answer. So the old man gets a bit closer again and says even more loudly, "Can you hear me?" Again there is no answer, so he tries once more, standing even closer and speaking even more loudly, "I SAID CAN YOU HEAR ME!!!" And his wife replies, "FOR THE THIRD TIME, YES I CAN BLOODY HEAR YOU!!!"

While it may not be entirely true to say that all the people who live in Bournemouth are getting on a bit, it is one of the few places where the shops on the high street have to have their windows made from bifocal lenses.

Two ageing nuns are talking about where they should go for their holidays. Sister Teresa has gone a bit deaf so Sister Rita has to use hand gestures in order to communicate. "I'd like to go to Florida," says Sister Rita. "You know! Florida! Where the oranges are this big and the bananas are this long." "Pardon?" says Sister Teresa. Sister Rita repeats herself, but still Sister

Teresa doesn't hear. In the end Sister Teresa speaks very slowly, with very exaggerated hand gestures. "Florida!" she says. "Where the oranges are THIS BIG and the bananas are THIS LONG." "Which priest are you talking about again?" asks Sister Teresa.

A man was sitting on a bus chewing gum and staring vacantly into space. Suddenly the old woman sitting opposite him said, "It's no good you talking to me young man, I'm stone deaf."

A flat-chested woman has problems finding a bra small enough in any of the high street chains, so eventually she tries a little backstreet lingerie shop. The woman behind the counter is a bit short-sighted and also a bit deaf, so the customer has a job explaining what she wants. After a while she simply unbuttons her blouse and shouts, "Have you got anything for these?" The old woman squints at her and says, "Try Clearasil, my granddaughter swears by it."

An old man is a witness in a burglary case. The defence lawyer asks him, "Did you see my client commit this burglary?" "Oh yes," says the old man. "But this crime took place at night," says the lawyer. "Are you sure you saw my client commit this crime?" "Yes," says the old man, "I saw him do it." So the lawyer says to the old man, "Sir, you are an elderly man now over 80 years old. Are you really going to tell this court that your eyesight was good enough for you to see my client from several feet away? Just how far do you think you are able to see at night?" "Well," says the old man, "I can see the moon. How far is that?"

An ageing snake goes to see his doctor. "Doctor, I need something for my eyes," says the snake, "I don't seem to be able to see so well these days." The doctor fixes the snake up with a pair of glasses and tells him to return in two weeks. The snake comes back as requested and tells the doctor he's very depressed. The doctor says, "What's the problem? Didn't the glasses help you?" "Oh yes," says the snake. "The glasses are fine. But I just found out I've been living with a garden hose for the past couple of years!"

An old couple are sitting at home watching a documentary programme about healthcare on the television. "I never want to end up like that," says the old man, pointing at the television. "I don't want to end up living in a vegetative state, dependent on some machine and fluids from a bottle. If that ever happens to me, just pull the plug." At which point, his wife gets up, unplugs the TV and pours away the old man's bottle of beer.

Two old men are shuffling down the street. The man on the left is dragging his right foot, the other is dragging his left foot. The man on the right says to the man on the left, "So what happened to you?" "War wound," he replies. "Normandy beach 1944. So," he says, indicating the other old man's foot, "what about you?" "I trod in some dog muck a couple of streets back," says the other.

Three old men are playing cards at home one day when they decide they should get some beer in. They draw straws and old Norman is given the money to go and buy some beer. Several hours pass and there's still no sign of Norman. One of the other old men says, "Do you know what, I'm beginning to think old Norman's run off with our money." Norman's voice is then heard from just outside the front door, "Hey! Any more comments like that and I'm not going to go at all."

At a nursing home, a group of senior citizens is sitting around talking about their aches and pains. "My arms are so weak I can hardly lift this cup of coffee," says one. "I know what you mean," says another. "My cataracts are so bad I can't even see my coffee." "I can't turn my head because of the arthritis in my neck," says a third. "I've got all those problems," says another member of the group, "plus my blood pressure pills make me dizzy all the time. I suppose that's the price we pay for getting old." The group sits silently for a few moments before an old lady pipes up. "Still, look on the bright side," she says. "At least we're all still able to drive."

Problems Of Ageing For Wrinkly Men

As if losing your hair, teeth, memory and sense of humour weren't bad enough, Mother Nature (it would be a woman wouldn't it?) has another cruel trick up her sleeve – as you get older you'll lose your libido, too. Of course, some men have led such sheltered lives that they think a libido is an open-air swimming pool, but for the rest of us libido loss is just another part of getting old. True, someone (probably a man) has now invented Viagra, but for some men it's so long since they've had sex they need a Viagram to show them where everything is. But a man losing his sex drive is a bit like a computer losing its hard drive – the memory's still there, but you can't do much with it.

Q: What's the difference between a clown and a man going through a mid-life crisis?
A: The clown realizes he's dressed in completely ridiculous clothes.

I'm getting so old that if a girl says no to me, I feel a sense of relief.

An old man sees a little boy sitting at the side of the road crying his eyes out. "What's the matter, little boy?" asks the old codger. "Why are you crying?" "I'm crying," says the little boy, "because I can't do what the big boys do." And with that the old man sits down next to him on the kerb and starts crying, too.

By the time a man is old enough to read a woman like a book, he's too old to start a library.

Q: How is a 60-year-old man like an ageing television set?
A: Both are hard to warm up, losing their colour and have difficulty maintaining their horizontal hold.

As a man gets older he realizes there are basically only three styles for his hair: parted, un-parted and departed.

Two elderly ladies were discussing the upcoming dance at the country club. "We're supposed to wear something that matches our husband's hair, so I'm wearing black," said Mrs. Smith. "Oh my," said Mrs Jones, "I'd better not go."

Old men are dangerous. It doesn't matter to them what is going to happen to the world.

George Bernard Shaw

An old man goes to a wizard to ask him if he can remove a curse he has been living with for the last 40 years. The wizard says, "OK, but you will have to tell me the exact words that were used to put the curse on you." The old man says without hesitation, "I now pronounce you man and wife."

No man is ever old enough to know better.

Holbrook Jackson

The best way to get an ageing man to do anything is to suggest he's far too old to be capable of it.

Two old women are watching their husbands. "I can't believe your husband is still chasing after women," says one. "Doesn't worry me," says the other. "Even if he catches them he wouldn't be able to remember what he wanted them for."

I'm at the age now where just putting my cigar in its holder is a thrill.

George Burns

Two old men are walking down the street together when they see a pair of teenage girls walk by. "Oh," says the first, "I wish I was 20 years older." "You stupid old fool," says his friend. "You're 90 years old. You don't wish you were 20 years older. You wish you were 20 years younger." "No," says the first. "I mean 20 years older. That way I'd be past caring."

Q: How are old men similar to bumper stickers?
A: Once you get them on they're both very difficult to get off again.

There are three ages of men: under-age, over-age and average.

It is said that at the age of 55 each man becomes what he most despised at the age of 25. I live in constant fear lest I become a badly organized trip to Bournemouth.

Simon Munnery

Have A Heart, Wrinklies

Except for an occasional heart attack I feel as young as I ever did.

Robert Benchley

An old man goes to the doctor's for an examination. On his way out of the surgery he has a heart attack and drops dead on the spot. The doctor leaps into action and tells the receptionist, "Quick! Turn him round and make it look like he was just walking in."

A man is recovering after major heart surgery. The surgeon comes to see him and gives him strict instructions, places him on a very strict diet, tells him he mustn't drink or smoke and advises him to get at least eight hours of sleep a night. Finally, the patient asks, "What about my sex life though? Will it be all right for me to have intercourse?" "Yes," says the surgeon, "as long as it's just with your wife. Nothing too exciting you understand."

A very old man went to the doctor's and was given some medicine. "This is pretty strong stuff," said the doctor, "so take some the first day, then skip a day, take some again and then skip another day, and so on." A month later the doctor saw the old man's wife in the street and asked how he was getting on. The doctor was horrified to hear that the man had died. "I didn't think the medicine was that strong," said the doctor ruefully. "No, it wasn't the medicine," said the widow. "It was all that skipping."

An old man is in hospital waiting for a heart transplant when the doctor comes to see him. "Good news!" he says. "We've found a donor. In fact, we have three so you have a choice. There's a young sportsman who was very fit. Or you can have a middle-aged doctor who never drank alcohol or smoked. Or alternatively a 70-year-old lawyer." "I'll have the lawyer's heart if that's all right," says the old man. "Did you hear me right?" asks the doctor. "I said it's from a 70-year-old lawyer." "Yes. I know," says the patient. "So it's never been used, has it?"

The trouble with heart disease is that the first symptom is often hard to deal with: sudden death.

Michael Phelps

Archie and Agnes had been married for over 60 years, so when Archie suddenly died Agnes couldn't face life without him and decided to end it all. She found Archie's old army revolver in the drawer and, just to make sure it wouldn't go wrong, she phoned her local hospital to find out exactly where her heart was. She was told it was just below the left breast. So she poured herself a large gin and fired the fateful shot. Half an hour later she was admitted to casualty with a gunshot wound to her left knee.

When she hears that her elderly grandfather had passed away, a young woman rushes to her grandmother to offer comfort. When she asks how granddad died, her grandmother tells her he had a heart attack while they were making love on Sunday morning. The young woman is shocked and says that two people aged nearly 100 should have realized the dangers of carrying on in such a way. "Oh no!" says granny. "Despite our advanced age we've managed perfectly well for years. We always used to take care by making love in time to the slow chime of the bells in the village church." She pauses and wipes away a tear before continuing, "And if it hadn't been for that ice cream van going past, your granddad would still be alive today."

Toilet Problems

An old couple are in the middle of the congregation at church one Sunday. Halfway through the service, the old man leans over and tells his wife, "I think I just broke wind. Luckily it was a silent one. But do you think I should do anything?" "Yes," says his wife. "Put some new batteries in your hearing aid."

An old lady goes to her doctor and asks what can be done about her terrible constipation. "Oh, it's awful, doctor," she says. "Do you know, I haven't moved my bowels for more than a week now." "I see," says the doctor. "And have you done anything about it?" "Oh, yes," says the old lady, "I sit there in the bathroom waiting for half an hour every morning and half an hour every evening." "No, no," says the doctor. "I mean, do you take anything?" "Yes, of course I do," says the old lady. "I take a magazine!"

Three old men are comparing ailments. "I've got problems," says one. "Every morning at seven o'clock I get up and I try to urinate, but I can never manage it." The second old man says, "You think you have problems. Every morning at eight o'clock I get up and try to move my bowels, but it never works." The third old man speaks up, "Every morning at seven o'clock I urinate and every morning at eight o'clock I defecate." "You've got no problem then," says the first man. "Yes I have," says the third man. "I don't wake up till nine."

Problems Of Ageing For Wrinkly Women

Another of nature's cruel jokes – the menopause (menopause – you just knew men would have something to do with it, didn't you?). A lot of men don't even realize their wives are going through the change of life. Yes, they see the mood swings, the odd behaviour, etc, but how are they supposed to know it's not just the usual mood swings and roundabouts? Women, of course know all about it, with the hot flushes and everything, but at least it's the end of that dreadful monthly ritual – and no we're not talking about sex with their husbands.

Q: What does a 70-year-old woman have between her breasts that a 20-year-old doesn't?
A: Her navel.

I'd love to slit my mother-in-law's corsets and watch her spread to death.

Phyllis Diller

Two old ladies are talking one day. One says to the other, "Even though I'm 75 men still look at my boobs." "Oh yes," says the second. "I bet they have to squat down a bit first though."

If you're a woman it's not any easier, you get to a certain age, you know, you've finished bearing children, all that part of your life is over, perhaps you're not quite so attractive as you once were... and then Mother Nature thinks, "What can I do to improve the quality of this woman's life? How can I help? What can I do for her? What is that magic thing…? I know, a beard!"

Dylan Moran

Have you heard about the new bra they've invented for women in later life? They call it the sheep dog. That's because it rounds them up and gets them pointing in the same direction.

If you're a woman and you get called in for a mammogram, look on the bright side. At least this is one kind of film they still want you to appear topless in.

Old age is when a woman buys a sheer nightie and doesn't know anyone who can see through it!

Two ageing ladies are long-time rivals in their social circle. One year they bump into each other at a Christmas party at their country club. "Why, my dear," says the first, noticing the other's necklace. "Don't tell me those are real pearls?" "Yes they are," says the second. "You may say that," says the first woman with a thin smile, "but of course the only way I could tell for certain would be to bite them." "Well I'd be happy for you to do that," says the second woman. "The only trouble is you'd need real teeth."

A woman is as old as she looks before breakfast.

Edgar Watson Howe

The only time a woman wishes that she were a year older is when she is expecting a baby.

An old man tells his friend, "Despite her age, my wife really doesn't seem to be growing old gracefully. Last week she took part in a wet shawl contest."

Q: How does an ageing woman manage to keep her youth?
A: By giving him lots and lots of money.

Keith asks his girlfriend Karen to marry him and she says yes, but on one condition: that he buys her a solid gold boy scout knife. He asks around, he looks on the Internet, he tries everywhere, but he can't find a solid gold boy scout knife anywhere. But because he is really keen to marry Karen he goes to a jeweller's and asks them to make one specially. He is told it will be very expensive, but he tells them to go ahead anyway. When it's ready he presents it to Karen, who then agrees to marry him. "So why on earth did you want a solid gold boy scout knife?" asked Keith. "What are you going to do with it?" "I'm going to put it away somewhere safe," Karen says, "then, when I'm old and grey, and wrinkled with half my teeth missing, and my boobs sagging and no man will look at me twice, I'll get it out. Because a boy scout would do almost anything for a solid gold pocket knife."

Q: How is a 50-year-old woman like a used tube of toothpaste?
A: They may be old and wrinkled, but if you squeeze hard enough, you'll find there's something left over.

A middle-aged woman goes to the doctor for a check-up and comes back delighted. "What are you so happy about?" asks her husband. "The doctor said I have the body of a 25-year-old," she replies. "OK," says her husband, "but what did he say about your 45-year-old arse?" "He didn't mention you at all," says the wife sweetly.

Signs That Your Brain Isn't What It Used To Be

You bend down to see if you can still touch your toes and you can't remember where they are.

When members of your family come to visit they have to introduce themselves.

When you tried one of those brain-training games your brain age was in three figures.

When you meet people you can never remember their names so constantly employ the greeting "Hello stranger!" – which is now almost literally true.

You spend ten minutes calling the cat in every night until you remember it died three years ago.

You've started counting on your fingers again.

Every TV programme you watch is a repeat – but you don't recall ever watching them before.

You tie knots in a hanky to remember things, then you can't remember where you left the damn hanky.

You still have to convert all prices to pounds, shillings and pence to understand their value and are constantly shocked to find that a packet of cigarettes is now the same price as a retirement bungalow.

You've downgraded from the "quick" crossword to the junior crossword and even then struggle a bit.

It's All In The Mind

In the town centre a slightly odd looking old man keeps wandering around yelling to no-one in particular. "Why does that man keep doing that?" asks a passer-by. "Oh, that's old Mr Jones," says a local. "He can't help it. He's just talking to himself in the street again." "Well, if he's talking to himself," says the passer-by, "why does he have to shout so much?" "He has to," says the local, "because he's deaf."

Three old men are at the doctor's to have their memories tested. The doctor says to the first old man, "What's three times three?" "Two hundred and seventy four," is his reply. The doctor worriedly says to the second old man, "It's your turn. What's three times three?" "Tuesday," replies the second old man. The doctor sadly says to the third old man, "OK, it's your turn. What's three times three?" "Nine," says the third old man. "Excellent!" exclaims the doctor. "How did you get that?" "Oh come on, doctor. That was simple," says the old man. "I just subtracted two hundred and seventy four from Tuesday."

An old man goes to see a psychiatrist. Afterwards the psychiatrist is concerned and has a word with the old man's wife. "I believe your husband may be psychotic," says the psychiatrist. "He says that when he goes to the toilet during the night God switches the light on for him when he opens the door and turns it off again when he's done." "Ah," says the old lady. "You recognize the problem do you?" says the psychiatrist. "I certainly do," says the old lady. "He's been getting up in the night and going to wee in the fridge again."

Two paramedics were dispatched to pick up a 92-year-old man who had become disoriented and take him to the hospital for evaluation. En route, with their siren going, they tried questioning the old man to determine his level of awareness. Leaning close, one asked, "Sir, do you know what we're doing right now?" The old man slowly looked up at him, then gazed out of the ambulance window. "Oh," he replied, "I'd say about 50, maybe 55 or so."

Three elderly women are talking about their grown-up sons. "My son is such a good boy," says one. "Last week he gave me an all-expenses paid trip to Europe for the summer. How nice is that?" "That's nothing," says the second woman. "Yesterday, my son bought me a new car that cost £30,000. Now there's a boy who loves his mother!" "You think so!" scoffs the third old lady. "My son goes to a top Harley Street psychiatrist, he pays him £500 an hour, he sits there all afternoon and you know the only thing he talks about? Me!"

The Wrinklies' Head To Toe Body Check (For Wrinkly Men)

If you're still not convinced that you truly are a wrinkly, take this simple body test.

Head: If you have a) a full head of skin and you are not a baby, b) "pink highlights" and you are not a baby whose hair is starting to grow, c) honest grey and you are not George Clooney, or d) jet black dyed hair and you are not a teenage goth, you are a wrinkly.

Chest: If you have a) wrinkles on your chest and are not somebody who is suffering from post-bodywax pucker, or b) grey hair on your chest and are not an after-bath child who has been over-liberal with the talcum powder, you are a wrinkly.

Stomach: If it is a) bloated and you are not a 25-year-old darts professional, or b) if it sags over your waistband and you are not an up and coming Sumo wrestler, and c) you have to tuck it in under your belt every morning when you get dressed, you are a wrinkly.

Legs: If a) your knees crack when you sit down and you are not a professional sportsman who has punished his body daily to reach the top, or b) you have varicose veins and are not a toddler playing with a blue felt tip, you are a wrinkly.

Feet: If a) your toenails are a strange yellow colour and you are not a Goth with a disgusting taste in nail varnish, or b) your ankles swell up for no apparent reason and you are not pregnant, you are a wrinkly.

So, how did you do?

Wrinklies' Health Regimes

Eat well, stay fit, die anyway.

Plenty of exercise and a healthy diet can add years to your life. Unfortunately, they're always added on at the end when you're too old to enjoy them.

The only way to keep your health is to eat what you don't want, drink what you don't like, and do what you'd rather not.

Mark Twain

A man goes to his doctor and asks him if he thinks he will live to be 100. The doctor looks him over and asks, "Do you smoke or drink?" "No," replies the man. "I've never smoked and I never get drunk." "Do you gamble, drive fast cars and fool around with women?" inquired the doctor. "Of course not," says the man. "I've never done anything like that." "Well then," says the doctor. "What the hell do you want to live to be 100 for?"

Alf is celebrating his 105th birthday and a reporter from a national newspaper is sent to interview him. "That's amazing, 105, eh?" says the reporter. "What do you think is the secret of your longevity?" Alf answers, "Well, I never drank, I never smoked, I did a five-mile run every morning, followed by a cold shower, and I always made sure I ate fresh fruit and vegetables." "Well that's fantastic, but I heard that your twin brother Jim followed exactly the same programme and he died at 55. Is that true?" "That's true," says Alf. "But you see his problem was he didn't keep at it long enough."

Two old men are talking outside the doctor's. "He's put me on the cardiologist's diet," says one. "What's that?" asks the other. "If it tastes good, spit it out," says the first.

The wrinkly's diet: forget the health food. I need all the preservatives I can get.

A little boy is sitting on a bus eating a chocolate bar, and as soon as he finishes it he produces another one from his pocket and eats that. Then he has a third and a fourth, and a fifth. When he starts eating the sixth an old man sitting nearby says, "I don't think that's a very good idea young man." "Why?" asks the boy. "It's bad for your teeth," says the old man, "it'll make you fat and give you spots, and when you're older you might even have heart problems." "Well," says the boy, unwrapping yet another bar of chocolate, "my granddad lived to be 102." "And did he eat half a dozen chocolate bars a day?" asks the old man. "No," snaps the boy. "Most of the time he just minded his own flipping business."

Agnes is celebrating her hundredth birthday and the local paper sends round a young reporter to interview her. "So, Mrs Ellis," he says, "what do you put your long life down to?" "Well," replies the old lady, "I think a bit of what you fancy does you good. I've always eaten in moderation, and I've drunk in moderation, and hardly ever smoked, and I've always done gentle exercise." "I see," says the reporter, "But your daughter tells me you've often been bedridden." "Of course I have," says Agnes, "but don't put that in your flipping newspaper, will you?"

The secret of longevity is deep breathing. Just try and keep doing it for 90 years or so.

Old Tom used to swear by a glass of liver salts. He used to drink a glass after every meal, every single day of his life. Finally he died at the grand old age of 95 and at the funeral the mourners had to beat his liver to death with a stick.

At the age of 70 Tom starts going to a local senior citizens' exercise club and the instructor says to him one day, "You know, Tom, it's hard to believe you're 70. From the shape you're in I would have said you were 55 at the most. How do you do it?" "Lack of stress," says Tom. "You see early on in our marriage the wife and I decided that if we ever started to argue she would go to the bedroom and I'd go out into the garden." "I see," says the instructor, "and how do you think that has helped?" "Well for the past 50 years," says Tom, "I've been living almost permanently out in the fresh air."

You will always stay young if you live honestly, eat slowly, worship faithfully – and lie about your age.

An elderly lady sends her husband out to the local market to buy some organic vegetables. The old man asks one stallholder, "These vegetables are for my wife. Have they been sprayed with any poisonous chemicals?" "No," says the market trader. "You'll have to do that yourself."

A man asks his elderly father what his secret was for living such a long life. "I'll tell you, son," says the old man, "every morning I sprinkle a little bit of gun powder on my cereal." The man follows this advice to the letter. Amazingly it works and, when he finally dies at the age of 100, he leaves 14 children, 28 grandchildren, 35 great-grandchildren and a 15-foot diameter hole in the wall of his local crematorium.

A woman notices a little wizened old man rocking in a chair in his back garden. "I couldn't help noticing how happy you look," she calls across to him. "What's your secret for a long happy life?" "What? Me?" the little man croaks back. "I just enjoy life to the full. I smoke three packets of cigarettes a day. I also drink a case of whisky a week. I don't worry about what I eat at all and I never do any exercise." "That's amazing," says the woman. "So how old are you?" "Twenty-six," says the man.

The Wrinklies' Head To Toe Body Check (For Wrinkly Women)

Head: If your hair is a) a strange shade of blue and you are not a Chelsea football supporter, b) of a rigidity that would be immoveable in a tsunami and you have not had a no.1 razorcut, or c) white and you are not an albino, you are a wrinkly.

Chest: If it is a) heading south and you are not a frequent flyer to sunny climes, or b) it needs more support than the England football squad and you are not Jordan, you are a wrinkly.

Stomach: If you a) have the profile of Alfred Hitchcock in one of his famous cameos and you are not actually pregnant, or b) wear a figure-squashing girdle and are not some young pop star saucepot trying to attract attention, you are a wrinkly.

Legs: If a) your calves resemble sides of mutton and you are not an all-in wrestler, or b) you wear dark-coloured tights and you are not the principal boy in your local pantomime, you are a wrinkly.

Feet: If they: a) have to be put up and rested after walking and you are not Ian Botham raising money for charity, or b) you haven't actually seen them for some time and you are not extremely short-sighted, you are a wrinkly.

There, how did you do?

Exercise Your Wrinklies

Look after your body and your body will look after you. Rubbish! You've given your body everything it has wanted or craved over the years – chocolate, alcohol, big fat juicy burgers, chips, the finest cigarettes, supersized doughnuts, a permanent holiday from any strenuous exertion; in short, you've spoiled it rotten and how does it repay you? By packing up when you need it most! Call that gratitude? And now, just when you feel old enough to really indulge yourself and shy away from any arduous work, you've got doctors, nurses, health "gurus", the government and the rest of the blinkin' nanny state telling you to get on your bike and cut down on all the things you enjoy most. Typical!

"You know I exercise every single day," says an old man to his friend. "So you know what that means." "Yes," says his friend. "When we die you'll be much healthier than I am."

An old lady decides her body has got out of shape, so she joins a fitness club to do some exercise. She signs on to do an aerobics class for senior citizens. On her first day she bends, twists, gyrates, jumps up and down, and perspires for an hour. But, by the time she manages to get her leotard on, the class has finished.

A little old lady tells her friend, "I've just bought myself one of those treadmills so I can do a bit of exercise." "What's it like?" asks her friend. "Oh, it's quite hard work," says the old lady. "So at the moment I'm just doing widths."

An old lady of 95 goes to a gym and asks if she can join the aerobics class. "Ooh, I don't know," says the instructor. "I'm not sure whether that's a very good idea." He looks her up and down and asks, "How flexible are you?" "Oh, very," replies the old lady. "But I can't do Wednesday mornings."

Old Ned says his doctor told him to take up jogging and it would add ten years to his life. He's only been doing it two weeks and it's worked. He already feels ten years older.

"My husband's taken up jogging," says an old woman to her friend. "He says he thinks it's the only way he'll ever hear heavy breathing again."

Two old women are chatting over coffee one morning and Mildred says, "How's your husband doing in the bedroom department these days?" Ethel replies, "Ooh, Mildred, I tell you what, he makes me feel like an exercise bike. Every day he climbs on and starts pumping away, but we never seem to get anywhere."

You can take up jogging and it will help you live longer. Unfortunately it will feel absolutely awful. So that way it will help your life seem to last even longer again.

You have to stay in shape. My grandmother started walking five miles a day when she was 60. She's 97 today and we don't know where the hell she is.

George Carlin

Old John decides to start doing some exercise to get his weight down so he joins his local health club and has a go on the running machine. He does very well on his first day and manages to lose one and a half stone. Unfortunately he manages this because the machine tears his leg off.

Gentle Exercise For Wrinklies

When you get to a certain age you get out of the habit of doing exercise. You don't run for the bus anymore and, quite frankly, just running for secretary of your local gardening club would puff you out. But you shouldn't give up! No, exercise doesn't have to involve pulling on running shorts, trainers, track suits, body warmers and all that stuff. You can get all the exercise you need at your age by simply adapting your daily routine slightly, as follows:

If you're too lazy or too old to change channels on the TV without the remote control at least press the buttons with your toes to give your feet a bit of exercise. Come on, tone up those toes!

Even combing your hair can give much-needed exercise to ageing arms. And if you're bald, there's absolutely no excuse, simply comb the hair under your arms or sprouting out of your ears.

Replace all your zips with buttons – that extra finger twiddling will help keep your digits young!

Have a cold bath now and then – the shivering will shake off those extra pounds in no time.
If you must eat sweets make sure they're nice and chewy – those really gluey toffees will give your face muscles a first class workout.

Read the paper without your glasses – the constant backwards and forwards motion when attempting to alternate between large and small typefaces will tone up those flabby arm muscles.

Buy a large, energetic and thoroughly disobedient dog, and the constant tug of war you have when taking him out for walks will have your biceps looking like Arnold Schwarzenegger's in a couple of weeks.

Keep those hands supple by varying which finger you use for punching in phone numbers, scratching head, pushing glasses up nose, etc.

With advancing age the knees are one of the first things to go, so stop using them so much – cut down on stroking cats, crouching down to talk to small children or bothering to pick up any coin you've dropped that's under a pound. And the good news is it'll get you out of cleaning the toilet!

But Mother Nature has her own way of keeping you wrinklies moving about and this is why your memory goes. You get so much exercise hunting round the house looking for mislaid glasses, keys, teeth, etc, that you hardly need to go to the gym.

Not Long For This World!

A 60-year-old woman is getting some test results at the hospital and the consultant says, "I'm sorry, Mrs Arbuthnot, but you haven't got long to live. I give you twenty-four hours at the most." Distraught, the woman goes home and says to her husband, "Come on, you! I've only got twenty-fours to live! I want you to take me upstairs and make wild passionate love to me all night!" Her husband looks at her tetchily and says, "It's all right for you, you haven't got to get up in the morning."

A woman accompanied her husband to the doctor's surgery. After his check-up, the doctor called the wife into his office alone. He said, "Your husband is suffering from a very severe disease, combined with horrible stress. If you don't do the following he will surely die. Each morning, make him a healthy breakfast. Try to be pleasant, and make sure he stays in a good mood. For lunch make him a nutritious meal. For dinner prepare something nice and healthy again. Don't burden him with chores, as he has probably had a hard day. Don't discuss your problems with him, it will only make his stress worse. And most importantly, make love with your husband several times a week and satisfy his every whim. If you can do this for the next one to two months, I think your husband will regain his health completely." On the way home, the husband asked his wife, "What did the doctor say?" "You're going to die," she replied.

An old dying man is lying in bed. One day he feels his senses begin to slightly revive as the smell of home baking comes wafting up the stairs and sets his mouth watering. With his last remaining strength he manages to pull himself out of bed and slowly clambers down the stairs to the kitchen. There he finds his wife has been busy baking a delicious looking chocolate cake. "Oh look," says the dying old man, "isn't that lovely? You've gone to the trouble of making me my very favourite cake." Just as he's about to cut himself a slice, his wife suddenly whacks his hand with a wooden spoon. "What's the matter with you?" asks the dying man. "Get your hands off that!" his wife tells him. "That's for the funeral!"

At 50, everybody gets the face they deserve.

George Orwell

Just remember, when you're over the hill, you begin to pick up speed.

Charles M Schulz

What The Doctor Says And What You Hear

When you get to a certain age you're naturally more concerned about your health and when you get to be a bit older than that you're more than likely getting very paranoid about your health. So when a doctor makes a passing observation you might find that you're reading more into it than you should:

What the doctor says	**What you hear**
Can you pass urine into this tube?	Are you still capable of actually passing water at will at your age?
Do you suffer from any allergies?	You are covered from head to foot in giant purple spots
Breathe in	Just checking to see if you're still alive
Breathe out	Just checking in case that was a fluke or possibly a death rattle
What's your name?	Next I'll ask him/her who the Prime Minister is to see if he's doolally
Can you come back and see me in two weeks?	With a bit of luck he/she will be dead by then and I'll have a quiet life
Does this hurt?	Poor old soul probably hasn't got any feeling left at his/her age
Take your clothes off	I haven't had a good laugh all day
I'm going to refer you	I don't want you keeling over in my surgery and scaring the other patients
You're remarkably fit for a man of your age	You can't expect your luck to last for much longer can you?
Are you a bit hard of hearing?	I'm just about to mumble some very bad news
Your blood pressure's a bit on the high side	You are about to spontaneously combust

Well I don't think you need to come back and see me	You'll be dead by the end of the week
You're amazing for your age	It's amazing you're still alive
It's nothing to worry about	It's fatal, so worrying won't help
I can't seem to find anything wrong with you	Let's just say you're very very old and you're bound to feel terrible
Let's have a listen to your chest	I can hear this funny creaking sound and I'm not sure where it's coming from
Lie on the couch please	It'll be so much easier to get you to the mortuary later

You Know You're Getting Old When...

You find yourself taking pleasure in comparative shopping for cemetery plots.

You find yourself telling people what a loaf of bread used to cost.

You get out of the shower and find you're glad the mirror is all fogged up.

You get the same sensation from a rocking chair that you used to get from a roller coaster.

You get tired just watching the fish swim around in the aquarium.

You get two invitations to go out on the same night... and you pick the one that will get you home the earliest.

You get up at night, go to the bathroom, then can't remember why you're there.

You get your full share of exercise acting as a pallbearer for healthy friends who spent all their spare time exercising.

You give up all your bad, unhealthy habits, and you still feel crappy.

You go into a record shop and wonder why you don't see any records.

You go to a garden party and you're mainly interested in the garden.

You go to a museum and find most of your favourite childhood toys are on display.

You go to a restaurant and complain that the butter is too tough for your teeth.

You go to your local barber's and your local barber asks why.

You have breakfast in bed as a necessity rather than as a luxury.

You have delightful dreams about mouth-watering prunes.

You have stopped counting freckles and started tabulating age spots.

Things To Avoid When You're Older

Botox on forehead – unless you can have your entire face and body Botoxed it's going to look a bit odd with a completely smooth bit shining out like a sandy island in a sea of wrinkles.

You often read about those plucky grannies or granddads who suddenly decide at the age of 90 that they're going to do their first bungee jump, parachute jump or some other wildly adventurous exploit. But remember, you only tend to hear about the ones that survive...

Giving up drinking. It's hardly worth it now is it? And with your liver pickled in enough alcohol to launch the Queen Mary it would be too much of a shock to your system and might just finish you off anyway.

Ditch those youthful nicknames like "Spider", "Babs", "Tiger" etc – you're going to feel a bit of a fool when you get that 100th birthday message from the Queen addressed to Bert "Kid" Smythe, aren't you?

Getting drunk. Yes, you've spotted a possible contradiction here, but a little of what you fancy and all that is fine, though if you find yourself getting paralytic you will forget that you're actually knocking on a bit and the sight of you stripping off and dancing on the table will not be welcomed – even at the day centre.

Toy boys/girls. They'll only accentuate how old you actually are with their smooth skin, shining hair and well-toned bodies, and not only that, you just won't be able to keep up with them. Mind you, what a way to go!

Living in a bungalow. This is the ultimate indicator that you are officially old. Before people even knock on your door they'll know you're old. "Ah, bungalow!" the prospective charity collector/conman/burglar will say, "Here lives a soft touch/mug/easy target." Mind you, the upside is that they may think you're too poor to be worth bothering with.

Other old people. Before you know where you are you'll all be sitting around having a moan-a-thon about the "kids of today", "political correctness gone mad" and the price of walking sticks.

Wrinklyspeak

Elsewhere in this book you will find a section in which you can determine your wrinkly age through the language that you use, i.e. you can find out whether you're quite old or *very* old. But some phrases will be used by all wrinklies. If you find yourself using any of the following phrases regularly, congratulations, or possibly commiserations – you are now officially a wrinkly:

Question/statement	Wrinkly response
How are you?	Mustn't grumble
Did you have a good Christmas?	It was very pleasant
Did you have a nice holiday?	It was very pleasant
Would you like a cup of tea?	Only if you're making one
See you	Not if I see you first
Goodbye then	Don't do anything I wouldn't do

Other useful wrinkly phrases include:

(At bedtime) "I'm off up the wooden hill to Bedfordshire"

"The country's going to the dogs"

"It's political correctness gone mad"

"It's health and safety gone mad"

"Let's agree to disagree shall we?"

"Ta muchly"

"Thanks ever so"

"A bit of what you fancy does you good"

"Not at my age"

"Giving me gyp"

"She's no spring chicken"

"Food doesn't seem to taste like it used to"

"There's too many TV channels, and never anything good on"

"You can't go out dressed like that"

I'm A Senior Citizen And...

I'm awake hours' before my body lets me get out of bed.

I'm a walking storeroom of facts... Unfortunately I seem to have lost the key to the storeroom.

I'm anti-everything now: anti-fat, anti-smoke, anti-noise, anti-inflammatory.

I'm having trouble remembering simple words like... er...

I'm not grouchy, I just don't like traffic, waiting, children, politicians...

I'm so cared for: long-term care, eye care, private care, dental care.

I'm sure everything I can't find is in a secure place somewhere.

I'm sure they are making adults much younger these days.

I'm the first one to find the toilet wherever I go.

I'm the life of the party... even when it lasts till 8pm.

I'm usually interested in going home before I get to where I'm going.

I'm very good at opening childproof caps with a hammer.
I'm walking more (to the toilet) and enjoying it less.

I'm wrinkled, saggy and lumpy, and that's just my left leg.

The real reason I have to smile all the time is because I can't actually hear a word you're saying.

I'm a Senior Citizen and I think I am having the time of my life... Aren't I?

Songs For Swinging Wrinklies

"Hit Me With Your Walking Stick" – Ian Dury and the Blockheads

"Bifocal Race" – Queen

"Pick Me Up Before You Go-go" – Wham!

"It's a Beautiful Day Centre" – U2

"Cocoa" – The Sweet

"Bus Pass the Dutchie" – Musical Youth

"Old" – Spandau Ballet

"My Degeneration" – The Who

"Papa's Got a Brand-New Colostomy Bag" – James Brown

"Stairlift to Heaven" – Led Zeppelin

"I'm So Retired" – The Beatles

"Sunny Afternoon Nap" – The Kinks

"Ovaltine-age Kicks" – The Undertones

"Don't Make Me Over The Hill" – Dionne Warwick

"I Can't See Clearly Now" – Jimmy Cliff

"Saturday Night's Alright (For Napping)" – Elton John

"Knockin' On Devon's Door" – Bob Dylan

Things You Spend More Time Doing As You Get Older And Wrinklier

Well, to be honest, pretty much everything you do takes longer as you get older, whether it's climbing the stairs or remembering what you went up there for in the first place. But that's OK, you wouldn't want to use up what little energy you have on racing around like some daft youngster, would you? Oh, you would? But isn't it nice to take your time, stop and smell the roses – even if it is at yet another funeral – and just relax a bit? Of course it is, though you don't want to relax so much that you sleep past your bus stop, drop off in mid-conversation or look so comatose that the rest of the family start making your funeral arrangements. But it's true, you will find as you get older that you spend more time:

Thinking about the good ol' days, and the good thing is that the older you get the more good ol' days there are to look back on.
Trying to remember where you left things – such as your passport, or husband or wife when out shopping.

Getting out of bed – one foot, then the other, ooh! Little rest. Up onto elbows. Another little rest. Swivel body slowly round... oh, sod it, I'll have another five minutes...

Getting your shopping. Parkinson's Law states that work expands to fill the time available for doing it and the same goes for shopping. If your weekend isn't a non-stop melee of partying and debauchery, then choosing just the right thing to have for your dinner can take the best part of a Saturday morning – leaving the afternoon free to choose what you have for pudding.

Moaning. Yes, it's an easy target and a bit of a cliché, but when you're old you need a hobby. The good news is that the older you get the more there is to moan about: everything's changing, you don't understand anything about the world anymore, young people are so damn young, your body won't do a thing you tell it to, your mind's got a mind of its own, and it's bloody raining again.

Talking to yourself. For a start you're the only one who listens and, secondly, you're the only one talking any blooming sense so it stands to reason, doesn't it?

Trying to look younger. Even if you haven't actually booked a session with Dr Plastic, you'll find that you're now getting more than your money's worth out of the NHS, clocking up zillions of points on your Boots loyalty card and spending a large percentage of your day rubbing in creams, taking potions and vitamins, teasing your last few strands of hair into something approaching a style, and generally indulging in some extreme body maintenance. Though when you get to the further extremities of wrinklyhood you may well say, "Oh bugger it, they can take me as I am." You will then be regarded as a charming old eccentric – who whiffs a bit.

Wrinkly Pets

A vicar goes to visit a little old lady who lives in his parish. She shows him into her living room and there sitting on a perch is her pet parrot. "I can't help noticing," says the vicar, "that you seem to have tied a ribbon to each of your parrot's legs. What are they for?" "Well," says the old lady, "if I pull the left ribbon he sings 'Abide With Me'. And if I pull on the right ribbon he sings 'All Things Bright and Beautiful'." "Oh my goodness!" chuckles the vicar. "I wonder, though, what happens if you pull both ribbons at the same time?" "I fall off the flipping perch," says the parrot.

A lady had a beautiful cat that she adored. One evening as she sat stroking it by the fireside, she dreamed of her cat turning into a handsome prince. Suddenly there was a flash of light and, lo and behold, there stood before her the most handsome prince anyone could possibly imagine. The prince took her hand in his and murmured, "Aren't you sorry now that you took me to the vet last week?"

An old lady orders a new carpet for her living room and a man turns up to fit it for her. After he's put the carpet down, the man feels in his pocket for his packet of cigarettes and finds they're missing. He then notices a lump in the middle of the old lady's new carpet. "Oh no!" he says to himself. "I've dropped my fags and laid the carpet on top of them." In the end he decides the easiest thing is to get a hammer and gently tap the lump until it's completely flat. Just as he's got the bulge level, the old lady walks in with his pack of cigarettes in her hand. "Look!" she says. "You must have dropped these in the hall. Now I wonder if you could help me to find something. My pet budgie seems to have gone missing somewhere..."

An old man tells his wife he thinks their dog is getting a bit long in the tooth. "I think Rover is getting a bit old," he says, "he seems to be going deaf." "Absolute nonsense!" says his wife. "Just watch this! Rover sit!... Oh dear, maybe you're right. Fetch the shovel and clean that up!"

Wrinkly World: Pets

Do you possess any of the following:

A little dog with a tartan coat

A budgie

A cat with a very unoriginal name, such as Tiddles

A dog with a human name – e.g. Timothy, or Ian

A cat wearing a collar with a bell on it

A cat that weighs four stone

A sad and solitary goldfish in a lonely bowl

Framed pictures of all your deceased pets

A chair that your cat or dog has all to itself

A tortoise

If you answered 'yes' to any of the above then welcome to Planet Wrinkly.

The Wrinklies' Daily Routine

Get up

Go to toilet

Go back to bed because it's only 2.30am

Get up

Go to toilet

Go back to bed because it's still only 4.45am

Get up

Go to toilet

Take handful of pills for various ailments

Have bath/shower, then rub on various creams, lotions, embrocations for various other ailments

Eat breakfast (no more than one cup of coffee allowed)

Read paper and have rant about "the world going mad", "political correctness gone mad" and people becoming celebrities despite being totally devoid of talent

Go to work, complain about the weather, the traffic, the useless bloody public transport system; swear at anyone who dares to invite you to "have a nice day"

Arrive at work and have audience-enhanced rant about the blooming weather, the blooming traffic and anything else you can blooming well think of

Go home – complain about young people to the wife/husband; swear at the TV; smear on a boatload of creams for various ailments

Get into a bed and read your book. At 7.30pm.

Go to toilet

Christmas Test

If you're still not sure whether you qualify as a wrinkly then take this simple test:

Before Christmas you:

Moan about the fact that it's coming earlier every year

Complain about the fact that everything's too expensive

Say you'll be glad when it's all over

During Christmas you:

Moan about the house being full of relatives, with the older ones getting on your nerves, the little ones getting under your feet and the teenagers getting under the influence

Complain that all this rich food is giving you heartburn

Say you'll be glad when it's all over

After Christmas you:

Moan that it's gone on far too long (even though it was exactly the same length as last year)

Complain that the council still hasn't collected all the discarded Christmas trees and that the shops are already selling Easter eggs

Say you're glad it's all over

If you have found that you agree with at least three of the above statements you are officially a wrinkly. You may well be only 35, but your attitude screams 65 – you miserable old git!

A Wrinklies' Guide To The Modern World

iPod – a portable gramophone crossed with a hearing aid.

iPhone – A portable desktop computer that nobody uses as a phone.

Rocket salad – lettuce that tastes funny.

Reality TV – home movies of people you've never met.

Celebrity – anyone who has appeared on the television more than once. This now comprises about half the population.

WAGs – the wives and girlfriends of footballers who achieve celebrity in their own right by... well, by being photographed a lot. Not to be confused with the "kiss and tell" girls who sell their "I slept with a footballer" stories to the Sunday papers and are known as "Sexual Liaisons And Gold-diggers" or SLAGS.

HDTV – a useful new type of TV that shows pin-sharp pictures that will enable you to read the letters on *Countdown* more easily.

MRSA – the proof that you will finally get something out of the NHS after paying for it for all those years.

Jeremy Clarkson – one of the very few people under 70 whose views you agree with.

Email – a marvellous new way of sending messages, but when will they finally invent a stamp that will stick to the computer screen without falling off?

Blog – a bit like one of those round-robin letters people send at Christmas – without the interesting bits. May possibly stand for Boring, Long Or Godawful.

Texting – after a hundred years of technology and telecommunications and all those "it's good to talk" BT ads we have finally reached the stage where you can communicate with one another by telephone without talking. And they call it progress.

The Wrinklies' Guide To Modern Technology

It's a sure sign of ageing when you can't cope with new technology. In the Stone Age there were probably old people struggling with the wheel. "How do you work this thing again? I just can't get my head round it. It's all right for you youngsters with your new-fangled ideas – what's wrong with the bison for goodness sake?" And when Alexander Graham Bell unveiled his new telephone there were probably oldsters galore refusing to have any truck with it. "If I wanted to talk to my sister in Wales I wouldn't have moved to East Anglia, now would I? What excuse have I got now?" And even when TV came along there were probably people who just couldn't get the hang of it. "That there announcer told me he'd be bringing me the news at six o'clock; I waited in especially and did the bugger turn up?"

A company has just brought out a new mobile phone specially adapted for older users – it has a bigger keypad, rotary dialling and, best of all, less memory.

An old lady receives a computer for her birthday. Her son tells her he is keen to teach her the advantages of the World Wide Web. He sets up the computer and sits his mother down in front of it. He demonstrates how to switch it on, how to access the internet and how to search for information. "I'm not sure about this," says the old lady. "It's easy, Mum," says her son. "Just pretend the search engine is a person you're talking to. Just ask it a question, press return and it'll answer anything you want." The old lady reaches for the keyboard and types into Google: "Hello. How are Auntie Ginnie's varicose veins?"

For the first time in many years, an old man leaves his house out in the countryside and travels into the nearest town to go to see a film at the cinema. After buying his ticket, he stops at a kiosk to buy some popcorn. He is astonished at the price he is charged and tells the popcorn seller, "Do you know what? Last time I came to the cinema, a bag of popcorn only cost sixpence!" "Well, you're certainly going to enjoy the film this evening," says the popcorn man. "They've got sound now and everything."

Ways To Tell If You Are A Wrinkly

OK, you've taken the wrinkly test, but you're still not convinced that you're a member of the grey brigade. You imagine somehow that you've been tricked or conned into outing yourself as a budgie-fancier. In short, you think those tests have been rigged, don't you? You scored highly, but you aren't having any of it. You are in denial. All right then, let's get specific. Do you recognize any of the following?

When you open your bathroom cabinet you realize that the cosmetics are outnumbered by the medicines.

You find it easier to sit down than to stand up.

When the binmen ask for a tip at Christmas you say, "Here's a tip – don't drop half the flaming rubbish in the road on your way to the dustcart, then you might get a Christmas box!"

You fondly reminisce about the days when there were "proper" programmes on the telly and not all this "How Clean Is Your Big Brother Supernanny Get Me Out Of Hell's Kitchen Love Island" so-called reality TV (it's all fixed anyway) and if that's reality I'm glad I'm not long for this world.

You have one or all of the following on your front door: "No junk mail", "Callers will be asked for ID", "Neighbourhood Watch", "Bugger off", a security chain, a picture of a ferocious looking dog with the quite transparent porky "I live here" emblazoned underneath.

You don't need to listen to the weather forecast, because you can predict the climate by the noise your joints make as you get out of bed in the mornings.

You can't understand why Radio 2 is playing so much rubbishy modern music and has young upstarts like Jonathan Ross presenting shows – disgraceful!
When it's time to go to bed you have the totally irrational wish that the bed could come down to you instead.

You are constantly shocked to find that policeman, politicians and other figures of authority appear to be fresh-faced youths who don't look like they've even started to shave yet.

You find it impossible to read a newspaper without your blood pressure rising to dangerously high levels.

Wrinkly World: Wrinkly Menswear

Do you possess any of the following:

An off-white or olive green windcheater

A green tartan or grey flat cap

A blue blazer with silver buttons

A collection of ties that your wife won't let you wear

A trouser press

A tie hanger

Hush Puppies

A hand-knitted scarf

Spectacles on a string round your neck

A trilby with a little feather in the band

A grey or olive green cardigan with brown buttons that look like footballs chopped in half

A boater that you wear semi-ironically in the summer

Grey flannels

Shoe trees

Cuff links that you haven't worn for 30 years, but haven't quite got round to throwing away

Striped pyjamas

A tartan dressing gown

Tartan or "comedy" slippers

An old leather belt / Braces

A proper hanky

A walking stick that is not a mobility aid, but a fashion statement (e.g. one with a carved animal head on the top)

If you have answered 'yes' to any of the above you are well on the way to being a wrinkly.

Films For Wrinklies

Gran Theft Auto

Butch Cassidy and the Tea Dance Kid

The Big Snooze

The Pipe, The Slippers and The Rose

Granny Hill

Four Funerals and Another Funeral

Saving Private Pension

Stairlift Express

Grandchildren of the Damned

Saga Holiday

Senior Citizen Kane

Retirement Home Alone

Oldfinger

Grumble Fish

The Pruning of the Rose

Help! The Aged

A Gran Day Out

Loo Stop

Old Git Carter

Speak Up Pompeii

The Mild Bunch

Moaner Lisa

The Droopy Dozen

Gone With the Wind

The Wizard of Snooze

9 1/2 Warts

Some Like It Hot Chocolate Before Bed

Snore Wars

It's A Wonderful Lie-in

Good Will Writing

The Old Dear Hunter

Being Nice To Older People

If you're one of the younger people reading this book who seems to be always putting their foot in it with the older generation, then here are a few tips on being more diplomatic.

Old people are not DEAF AS POSTS, they are A LITTLE HARD OF HEARING

Old people are not AS BLIND AS BATS, they are SLIGHTLY MYOPIC

Old people are not OLD GITS, they are IMBUED WITH THE WISDOM OF AGE

Old people are not SENILE, they have MEMORY RETENTION ISSUES

Old people are not STUCK IN THEIR WAYS, they GOT IT RIGHT FIRST TIME

Old people are not BIGOTS, they have FIRM VIEWS

Old people are not TECHNOPHOBES, they are DIFFERENTLY COMPETENT

Old people are not OVER THE HILL, they are OUTASITE!

Old people are not WRINKLY, they have CHARACTERFUL FACES

Old people are not SLOW, they just like to TAKE THEIR TIME

Old people are not JUDGEMENTAL, they TELL IT LIKE IT IS

Old people are not MOANERS, they like to EXPRESS THEIR INNER EMOTIONS

Old people are not DANGEROUS DRIVERS, they just like to MIX IT UP A BIT

Old people are not FORGETFUL, they are MENTALLY SELECTIVE
Old people are not DODDERY, they MOVE IN MYSTERIOUS WAYS

Old people are not LIVING IN THE PAST, they EXPERIENCE TEMPORAL SHIFT

Old people are not GRUMPY, they have A HAPPINESS DISCONNECT

Old people are not PENSIONERS, they have ALTERNATIVE WAGE ARRANGEMENTS

You Know You're Getting Old When...

All the cars behind you turn on their headlights.

All your midnight oil is all used up by 9.30pm.

Christmas starts to piss you off.

Strangers feel comfortable calling you "old-timer".

Conversations with people your own age usually turn into a bout of "ailment duelling".

Even dialling long distance makes you feel tired.

When you're just visiting a friend in hospital, a member of staff comes toward you with a wheelchair.

Every time you suck your belly in, your ankles balloon out.

Everything that works hurts and what doesn't hurt doesn't work.

Fortune tellers offer to read your face instead of your palm.

Funeral directors call and make idle conversation about how you're feeling.

Getting a little action in the bedroom means you don't need to eat any fibre today.

Getting lucky means you take less than ten minutes to find your car in the supermarket car park.

Half the stuff in your shopping trolley has the words "for fast relief" printed on the label.

Happy hour is a 30-minute nap.

You start having dry dreams and wet farts.

It gets harder and harder for them to make those sexual harassment charges stick.

Lawn care has become a highlight of your life.

It takes longer to rest than it did to get tired in the first place.

It takes you a couple of tries to get over a speed bump.

Wrinkly Appearance

Age brings with it some difficult wardrobe choices. On the one hand you're not going to want to look old before your time with flat caps, headscarves and tweedy clothes; people will either think you're ancient or you've suddenly become a member of the Royal Family. On the other hand you don't want to look like old hen dressed as spring chicken. Think how embarrassing it must be for the children of certain rock stars to see their wizened old parents tottering around in high heels and make-up – and yes, we mean you female rock stars, too. You need to strike just the right balance between dignity and fashion. So if you must dye your hair, do it properly otherwise you'll end up looking like a patchwork Cruella De Ville; if you insist on having a tattoo make sure it's one that's out of sight and won't look too weird when it's stretched or shrunk dramatically over the years; and if you absolutely can't help yourself wearing a thong, a tiny swimsuit, tight jeans or way too much make-up, please take this simple and kindly meant tip – don't leave the house!

Time may be a great healer, but it's a lousy beautician.

As you get older you learn that beauty comes from within... from within bottles, jars, phials, compacts...

Two ageing ladies are talking in the beauty parlour one day. "Of course I've always had a nice firm chin," says one. "Yes," says the other one, "in fact now I see the firm has taken on a couple of partners."

A man goes to a reunion of all his old classmates from school. The next day his friend asks him how it went. "It was OK," he says, "but unfortunately all my old friends had become so old and overweight, hardly any of them seemed to recognize me."

Two old men are talking. The first says, "Back in the 1960s my wife used to spend all her time and money trying to make herself look like Elizabeth Taylor." "What about now?" asks his friend. "Now," says the first old man, "she spends all her time and money trying NOT to look like Elizabeth Taylor."

She doesn't show her age, but if you look under her make-up it's there.

I've only got one wrinkle and I'm sitting on it.

Jeanne Calment

Of course older people say they don't have wrinkles, they have laughter lines. So we must all do a hell of a lot more laughing once we pass 50.

She's thinking of having her hair dyed back to its original colour. The only problem is now she's got to try and remember what that was.

An old man tells his friend, "You know, my wife is still as beautiful today as she was the first time I saw her." "That's nice," says his friend. "Yes," says the old man, "it takes her a couple of hours in the morning to get there, mind."

Grey hair is God's graffiti.

Bill Cosby

A husband and wife are getting ready for bed. The wife is standing in front of a full-length mirror, taking a long hard look at herself. "You know dear," she says, "I look in the mirror and I see an old woman. My face is all wrinkled, my hair is grey, my shoulders are hunched over, I've got fat legs and my arms are flabby." She turns to her husband and says, "Tell me something positive, to make me feel better about myself." He studies hard for a moment, thinking about it, and says in a soft, thoughtful voice, "Well, there's nothing wrong with your eyesight."

His face is so wrinkled it's capable of holding three whole days' worth of rain.

Two old ladies are chatting at a day care centre. Alice says, "You know I like that man who brings round the tea; he said I've got the skin of a 20-year-old." "Hmm," replies Gertrude, "Well I think you'd better give it back to her then – look how wrinkled you've got it!"

Saffy: Mountaineers have died falling in to shallower ravines than your wrinkles!

Absolutely Fabulous

A little boy watches as his grandmother applies a face mask and asks, "What's that for?" "To help make me more beautiful," says the grandmother as she removes the mask. "Hmm," says the boy. "Doesn't seem to have worked, does it?"

A middle-aged woman goes off to a health centre for a week and has a series of beauty treatments, including waxing, facials, a special diet, saunas and more. When she gets back home fully revitalized and glowing with health, she asks her husband, "So, if you'd never met me before, just on the way I look now, how old would you say I was?" Her husband looks her up and down and says, "I'd say from your skin, 26. From your hair about 20. And from your body..." The woman giggles girlishly and says, "You old flatterer, don't you think you're overdoing it a bit?" "Hold on," says the husband, "I haven't added them up yet."

An old couple are getting ready to go out one night. The old man admires his wife. "Wow," he says, "you look great." "Thank you," she says. "Yes," says the old man, "it must have taken you ages."

Old Albert is complaining to his mates in the pub: "Every night before she goes to bed my missus puts curlers in her hair, a mudpack on her face and slices of cucumber over her eyes. It's a waste of time if you ask me, I can still tell it's her."

An old man tells his friend, "My wife tried putting on a mudpack to make herself attractive." "Did it work?" asks his friend. "It did for a bit," says the old man, "but then it fell off."

A woman says to her husband, "I don't look 38 do I?" "No," he says, "but you did when you were."

I have flabby thighs, but fortunately my stomach covers them.

Is it really a coincidence that the Roman Numerals for 40 are "XL".

Sally: Remember: Every morning your face has slipped a little bit more. Since I turned 30 I've had to put a daily limit on facial expressions. I only ever smile at single men, so I can justify the loss of elasticity.

Coupling

Old Mavis has got lovely sleek black hair all the way down her back. It would be nice if she had some on her head as well but you can't have everything.

People who knew him 20 years ago say he looks the same now as he did then – old.

Artificial De-Wrinkling: Cosmetic Surgery

You know how when some people, as they get older, fail to recognize others – even members of their own family? Well now, due to the wonders of modern cosmetic surgery, you can even forget what you used to look like yourself! How fabulous is that? Despite being on the wrong side of middle-age you can wake up in the morning, go into the bathroom and be confronted by a gorgeous, fresh-faced thing with perfect teeth, beautiful hair and a youthful body. Yes, you forgetful old fool, you've forgotten that one of your grandchildren is over to stay!

I don't plan to grow old gracefully. I plan to have face-lifts until my ears meet.

Rita Rudner

A man tells his friend, "Now my wife's getting a bit older, she's getting into all this cosmetic surgery and beauty treatment business. Yesterday she was at the beauty clinic for over two hours. And that was just for the estimate."

An ageing woman is worrying about the cosmetic surgery she has booked. "Is it going to hurt?" she asks her doctor. "Yes," he says, "but not until you receive my bill."

Advice for wrinklies trying to get rid of the wrinkles: I don't know much about plastic surgery but a good rule of thumb is that you know it's time to stop when you look constantly frightened.

A definition of unhappiness: a woman who has her face lifted only to find an identical one lurking underneath.

A middle-aged man goes to his wife's plastic surgeon to complain. "You've given her a face lift, a bottom lift, a breast lift and a tummy lift," he says. "So what's the problem?" asks the surgeon. "What's the problem?" splutters the man. "She's 18 inches off the flipping ground now!"

A 60-year-old man decides to have a face-lift for his birthday. He spends £10,000 and is really happy with the results. On his way home, he stops at a newsagent and buys a paper. While he's there, he asks the sales assistant, "I hope you don't mind me asking, but how old do you think I am?" "About 40," says the sales assistant. "I'm actually 60," says the man feeling very pleased with himself. After that, he goes into a chip shop for some lunch and asks the assistant there the same question. The assistant says, "I'd say about 35." "Thanks very much," says the man, "I'm actually 60." Later, while he's waiting at a bus stop, he asks an old woman the same question. She replies, "I'm 85 years old, and my eyesight is going. But when I was young, there was a sure way of telling a man's age. If I have a feel in your pants for a minute, I will be able to tell you your exact age." As there is no-one around, the man lets her slip her hand down his pants. Ten minutes later, the old lady says, "Right. You're 60 years old." "That's incredible," says the man, "you're exactly right. How do you do that?" "I was behind you in the chip shop," says the old lady.

A woman with terrible bags under her eyes finally decides to do something about it, so she goes to a plastic surgeon and asks him to get rid of them. He performs the operation and tells the woman afterwards that to save her from having to keep coming back in years to come he has fixed a discreet handle to the back of her neck. "If those bags start coming back," he says, "just turn the handle a bit and it'll tighten up your skin and the bags will just disappear like magic." "Well thank you," says the woman, delighted. Every so often, when the bags under her eyes begin to show she turns the handle and they disappear, but after many years two bags appear which are just impossible to remove, however much she turns the handle so she goes back to the surgeon. He takes a look and says, "Madam, those aren't eye bags – they're your breasts. You've been turning that handle too hard." "Oh my goodness!" exclaims the woman. "I suppose that'll explain the goatee as well."

A famous old actor was bemoaning his lot on a chat show: "Some women get their good looks from their mothers. Mine gets hers from the plastic surgeon – and it's costing me a fortune!"

A man tells his friend, "My wife went in for a face lift operation last week." "Did it work?" asks the friend. "Not really," says the man. "When they saw what was under it, they dropped it again."

Two women are sitting in the old people's home bitching about the other inmates. One old lady says to the other, "Look at her, she's had her face lifted so often, when she raises her eyebrows her bedsocks shoot up her legs."

The best way to prevent sagging: just eat till the wrinkles fill out.

Edna is a 45 year-old woman. One day she has a heart attack and is taken to hospital. While on the operating table she has a near death experience. Seeing God she asks, "Is this it? Is my time up?" God replies, "No, Edna, my child. You have come here too soon. In fact you have another 43 years, two months and eight days to live." Upon recovery, Edna decides to stay in the hospital and have a face lift, liposuction, breast implants and a tummy tuck. She even has someone come in and change her hair colour and brighten her teeth! Well, she thinks to herself, since I have so much more time to live, I may as well make the most of it. After all her cosmetic surgery and treatment, she gets out of hospital, but, while crossing the street on her way home, she is run over by an ambulance and killed. She arrives up in Heaven in front of God and is completely furious. "What's going on?" she asks God. "I thought you said I had another 43 years? Why didn't you pull me from out of the path of the ambulance?" "Oh, sorry, Edna," replies God, "I didn't recognize you!"

Two men are sitting in a pub and opposite them is an attractive, young looking woman sitting on her own sipping a glass of wine. One of the men indicates the woman and says, "I reckon that woman has had a face lift you know." The other one says, "How can you tell?" And the first man replies, "Every time she crosses her legs her mouth suddenly closes."

Wrinkly World: Fashions For The Wrinkly Woman

Do you possess any of the following:

A tweed skirt

Toffee-brown stockings or tights

Stocking or tights that show extensive repairs
A collection of hats

Spectacles on a string round your neck

Sensible shoes

A light summer headscarf that holds several megawatts of static electricity

Various items of clothing in a variety of tartans

A bra that looks as though it could double as a comfy hammock for two

A selection of pastel-coloured "woollies"

An off-white or pale pink nightie

A brown dressing gown

Fluffy slippers

An ancient suspender belt the colour of a sticking plaster

A perfume that smells as though it may well kill 99% of all known household germs

A proper hanky

A ballgown that hasn't see active service since 1972

A selection of pale pastel blouses with mother-of-pearl buttons

A hairnet

Curlers

A large collection of cheap toiletries given to you by family that you don't want

All your clothes smell of pot pourri.

A few old hatpins that even you don't use any more

An extensive collection of floral frocks

If you have answered 'yes' to any of the above then, welcome to the Grey Brigade!

You Know You're Getting Old When...

You remember the days when you could get tired legs from using a sewing machine.

You remember when service stations actually gave you service.

You start repeating all the stupid, irritating things your mother used to say to you as a child.

You sink your teeth into a juicy steak and they stay there.

You start to answer questions with the phrase, "Because I said so!"

You start to appreciate the attractions of accordion music.

You start to clean out your ear with a cotton bud, then realize you forgot to take out your hearing aid.
You step off a curb and look down one more time to make sure the street is still there.

You suddenly find you are proud of your lawn mower.

You take a metal detector to the beach.

You tap your feet and hum along to the music in lifts.

You think you know all the answers, but nobody will ask you the questions.

You throw a wild crazy party and none of your neighbours even notice.

You wake up looking like the photograph on your passport.

You walk around barefoot and get compliments about your new alligator shoes.

You wonder how you could be over the hill when you don't even remember getting on top of it.

You wonder why you waited so long to take up macramé.

Your back goes out more than you do.

Your birthday cake can no longer support the weight of the candles.

Your chemist offers to carry the bag of medicines to the car for you.

Out And About With The Wrinklies

An old couple arrive at the airport just in the nick of time to catch the plane for their summer holiday. "Do you know what?" says the old lady. "I wish I'd brought the piano with us." "What on earth are you talking about?" says her husband. "Why would you want to bring the piano with you." "Because," says the old lady, "I've left our tickets on top of it."

At the seaside there are two old men on their annual holidays standing in the sea with their trousers rolled up, smoking their pipes and watching the boats go by. One of them glances down at the other one's feet and says, "Blimey, mate, look at the state of your feet, they're absolutely filthy!" The other one looks down and agrees. "Yeah, I know," he says, "we couldn't come last year."

Cliff and his wife Esther go to their local county fair every year and every year Cliff tells his wife, "You know what I'd really like to do. I'd like to ride in that helicopter they've got over there." And every year Esther replies, "Cliff, you know very well that they charge

£50 a ride. That's a lot of money to us pensioners." Finally Cliff tells Esther, "Esther, look, I'm 85 years old. If I don't get a ride in that helicopter this year, I might never get another chance." "Cliff," says his wife, "I've told you, £50 is a lot of money to pensioners like us." The helicopter pilot happens to hear the old couple's conversation and says to them, "OK, I'll make a deal with you. I'll take the both of you for a ride. If you can stay quiet for the entire trip and not say a word I won't charge you! But if you say one word, I'll have to charge you £50." Cliff and Esther agree and up they go in the helicopter. The pilot does all kinds of fancy manoeuvres, but doesn't hear a word from the couple. He does some daredevil tricks over and over again, but still not a word from the back. When they land, the pilot turns to Cliff and says, "Goodness me, I did everything I could to get you to scream back there, but you didn't. I'm impressed!" Cliff replies, "Well, to tell you the truth, I almost said something when Esther fell out, but you know... £50 is a lot of money to pensioners like us."

An old man is trying to get his reluctant old friend to come out for a walk. "What happened to your get up and go," he asks. "It got up and went without me," says his friend.

Two old men are looking round a National Trust property when one says to the other, "You know, visiting these historical sites isn't so much fun when they all turn out to be younger than you are."

Albert and Henry are taking a stroll along the sea front one day when a seagull flies over and drops a blob of excrement right on the top of Albert's bald head. Henry is horrified at what has just happened and says in great concern, "Wait right there. I'll be back in a moment." Henry waddles off as fast as he can go to the nearest public convenience and returns a few minutes later with a length of toilet paper. "It's a bit too late for that," says Albert. "That seagull will be miles away by now."

One night, at the lodge of a hunting club, two new members were being introduced and shown around. The man guiding them said, "See that old man asleep in the chair by the fireplace, he's our oldest member and can tell you some hunting stories that you'll never forget." They woke the old man up and asked him to tell them a hunting story. "Well, I remember back in 1944," said the old man, "we went on a deer hunt in Canada. We were on foot and hunted for three days without seeing a thing. On the fourth day, I was so tired I had to rest my feet. I found a tree that had fallen, so I laid my gun down, propped my head on the tree and fell asleep. I don't remember how long I slept, but I remember the noise in the bushes that caused me to wake up. I was reaching for my gun when the biggest buck that I had ever seen jumped out of the bushes at me like this WHOOOOHHHHHH!!!!!!!!!!!... I tell you, I just filled my pants." The young men looked astonished and one of them said, "I don't blame you, I would have filled my pants too if a huge buck jumped out at me." The old man shook his head and said, "No, no, not then, just now when I said WHOOOOHHHHHH!!!!!!!!!!"

Two old ladies were sitting in the park enjoying some music. "I think it's a minuet from Mignon," said one. "I thought it was a waltz from Faust," said the other. So the first old lady got up and shuffled over to a nearby notice board. "We were both wrong," she said. "It's a Refrain from Spitting."

A plane has a rough flight over the ocean. Suddenly a voice comes over the intercom: "Ladies and gentlemen, please fasten your seat belts and assume crash positions. We have lost our engines and we are trying to put this baby down as gently as possible on the water." "Oh stewardess! Are there any sharks in the ocean below?" asks a little old lady, terrified. "Yes, I'm afraid there are some. But not to worry, we have a special gel in the bottle next to your chair designed especially for emergencies like this. Just rub the gel onto your arms and legs." "And if I do this, the sharks won't eat me any more?" asks the lady. "Oh, they'll eat you all right, only they won't enjoy it so much," answers the stewardess.

Solly, an old Jewish man, gets on a train. The second class compartments are full, so he takes a peek into first class and sees an empty seat temptingly close to the door. The train is about to leave, so Solly reckons it's a safe bet the seat won't be taken. He slips inside the carriage, sits down and gets out his copy of the *Racing Post*. He happily spends the next half hour reading his paper while munching on a salt-beef sandwich and dipping into a jar of pickled herrings. Suddenly he's tapped on the shoulder by a steward. "Excuse me, sir," says the steward. "But this seat is reserved for the Archbishop of Canterbury." "So?" says Solly. "Who says I'm not the Archbishop of Canterbury?"

Two old golfing partners are at the airport, booking a flight. One of them says, "Do you think we should take out any insurance?" "No," replies the other one. "I never bother any more. I used to, but it never seemed to make the slightest bit of difference."

The Wrinklies' Holiday Test

All right, you're still not sure whether you're a wrinkly. You're borderline. OK, we believe you, but are you brave enough to take this test to find out whether you are winging your way to Planet Wrinkly? Go on, we dare you! Unless you're too old for such things of course...

Before going on holiday

You moan that there aren't any proper travel agents anymore and why should you have to book online when you know all computers hate you, but you suppose if you really must then you'll have to get your 12-year-old nephew to help you...

You complain that converting to the Euro has taken all the romance out of foreign travel and you hark back to the days when you could wander around the Dordogne with a pocket full of Francs and, yes, you would take a holiday in England but it's more expensive than Spain and the weather's so unpredictable...

You say it's costing you a fortune and in two weeks what will you have to show for it apart from sunburnt arms and a gyppy tummy?

During the holiday

You moan that it' s too hot or too wet (if you did take that holiday in England) and you can't sleep at night because of British hooligans lowering the tone of the place and...

You complain that the food is too greasy/spicy/bland/ foreign and they can't make a decent cup of tea, and, oh, you'd murder anyone for a good old British fry-up...

You say you're going to try and bloody well enjoy it because you're bloody well paying enough for it, but you won't be sorry to see a good old bit of British rain and have a decent cuppa...

After the holiday

You moan that, typical (!), the whole time you've been away the weather at home has been glorious, and the bank is ripping you off by charging you to change back your currency that you've got left over, and someone (not you, naturally) forgot to cancel the flipping papers.

You complain that you're exhausted and you've got to be back at work in two days and you really need another holiday to recover from your holiday and that's it for another year, 50 weeks of saving before you can afford to go again…

You say you had a great time, but you can't work out how to download your holiday pics from your digital camera, and you certainly didn't vote for getting rid of proper films, but then nobody asks your opinion about anything do they…?

All right, admit it. Be honest. Have you found yourself agreeing with at least three of those statements? We thought so. Welcome to Oldsville.

Wrinklies At The Wheel

With age comes experience – or is it the other way round? Anyway, this truism doesn't seem to apply to driving. Probably because they keep changing the rules. It's not your average senior citizen's fault is it?

One decade you're driving down a perfectly normal road quite happily, then next decade it's become a one-way street! No-one told you did they? Old habits die hard. And motorways? Don't even start on motorways. Now, if I'm not meant to drive slowly, why do they call it the "slow lane"? Yes, all right, three miles an hour is pretty slow, but when your eyesight's as bad as mine and your reaction speeds make a tortoise look a bit nippy, it's the only safe way to drive. If only some of these hot-headed youngsters took a leaf out of my book...

Two old women, Millie and Dolly, are out driving in a large car. Both can barely see over the dashboard. As they cruise along they come to a junction and go through a red light. Millie, in the passenger seat, thinks to herself, "I must be losing my mind. I swear we just went through a red light." After a few minutes they come to another junction and go through another red light. Millie is almost sure that the light was red, but is concerned she might be mistaken. At the next junction they go through another red light. Millie turns to Dolly and says, "Millie! Did you know we just ran through three red lights in a row! You could have killed us!" Millie looks around and says, "Oh! Am I driving?"

Being 55 years old is like driving at 50 miles an hour. Everybody seems to pass you.

An old lady decides one day that she really should learn to drive. So after many attempts she passes her test and tells her husband that to celebrate she's going to drive him over to France for a holiday. But then a week before the trip she suddenly announces the holiday is off. "Why did you change your mind?" he asks. "Well," says the old lady, "it's this business of driving on the right. I've been practising round town for three weeks now and I just can't get used to it – in fact, I've nearly killed three people."

A police officer is driving along one day when he sees an old lady in her car, driving along while knitting at the same time. The police man attempts unsuccessfully to get her attention, but to no avail. Finally he drives right alongside her, winds down his window and calls out, "Pull over, madam!" At which points the old lady turns to him and says, "No. Socks actually."

A dilapidated and ancient Ford pulls into a petrol station. "Could you let me have two litres of petrol?" asks the old fellow at the wheel. "Why don't you fill her up, now that you're here?" asks the attendant. "Well," says the old man, "she might not run that far."

An elderly couple are driving around the M25 in their ancient Skoda with the wife at the wheel. A police car pulls them over onto the hard shoulder. "Do you realize you were speeding back there?" says the policeman. The woman being slightly deaf, turns to her husband and asks, "What did he say?" The old man shouts back, "He says you were speeding." The policeman says, "May I see your licence?" The old woman turns to her husband and asks, "What did he say?" The old man shouts, "He wants to see your licence." The woman hands over her licence. The officer says, "I see you're from Farnborough. I spent a bit of time there once. Do you know what? I had the worst sex I've ever had in my life with a woman in Farnborough. Oh she was a dreadful, unresponsive old bag!" The woman turns to her husband and asks, "What did he say?" The old man yells back, "He thinks he knows you!"

An old man is driving slowly round the supermarket car park, looking for a space, when finally he spots one in the corner. He carefully and gingerly tries to reverse into it, but as he does so a young man in a zippy hatchback swerves in front of him and pinches the space. The old man gets out to remonstrate with the youngster, but the young man says, "Tough luck, mate, that's what you can do when you're young and quick." So the old man climbs out of his car, lifts up his walking stick and starts bashing in the bonnet of the young man's car. "And that's what you can do when you're old and rich," says the old man, walking off.

An old man is out driving on the motorway when his mobile rings. It's his wife calling. She says she's just heard a news report about a car that's driving the wrong way up the motorway. "I know," says the old man. "But it's not just one car. It's hundreds of them."

The Wrinklies' Driving Test

Even if you've passed all the other wrinklies' tests, perhaps one of the surest ways of finally establishing whether you're one of life's elder statesmen/women is the way in which you drive.

Before going out in the car do you:

Moan about the fact that you have to go out on the roads with all those other lunatics

Complain that you're taking your life in your hands and it's going to cost you a fortune in car parking charges when you get wherever you're going

Say nobody under the age of 30 should be allowed on the roads anyway

During a car journey do you:

Moan that you're the only one observing the speed limit and not chatting on a mobile phone while you're driving

Complain about all the blooming road works, confusing one-way systems and the gaps between toilet stops on motorways

Say half these kids don't look old enough to drive anyway

After a car journey do you:

Moan about the state of the roads/the volume of traffic/the rudeness of other drivers

Complain you don't know why you bother taxing and insuring your car when no one else seems to bother

Say that if young women want to drive tanks why don't they join the army

So how did you do? If you found yourself agreeing with at least three of the above statements then congratulations, you have entered the magical realm of Wrinkliedom!

Wrinkly World: Furnishings And Household Accessories

Do you possess any of the following:

A shiny three-piece suite that is not meant to be shiny

A card table

A tallboy

A proper old-fashioned free-standing wooden wardrobe

A cake stand

Artexed ceilings

A set of occasional tables

A tablecloth "for best"

Curtains hanging on rings

A bureau

A set of doilies

Little cloths that go over the arms of the sofa

A set of fire accessories such as tongs, shovel and poker on a little stand

A draught excluder (possibly made to look like a snake or a dachshund)

A clothes horse

A Teasmade

A radio alarm permanently set to Radio 2
A fan heater

A two-bar electric fire

A Formica-topped kitchen table

A tin bath for soaking your "poor old feet"

A tin of toffees with a picture of one of the royal castles on it

A pouffe

Anything made from "leatherette"

An umbrella stand

A hatstand

Net curtains

A woolen toilet roll cover

Eating Out

An elderly couple go to a trendy restaurant, but are turned away because it's full. They return the next night, but again it's full and they go home disappointed. The next night the same thing happens again. "Look," says the maître d', "to save you time, why don't you make a booking?" The old couple agree this would make sense, but discover that the restaurant is booked solid for the next three weeks. "Tell you what," says the maître d', "try phoning tomorrow. There might be a cancellation." The old man rings the next day and discovers that there haven't been any cancellations and now the restaurant is booked solid for the next five weeks! The old man complains bitterly. "You know," he says, "your restaurant would do a lot more business if you weren't so bloody full all the time!"

A rich old man goes to a dating agency and ends up going to have dinner with an elderly dowager. The next day at his London club a friend asks him if he enjoyed himself. "Well, I would have done," says the man. "Would have done?" asks the friend. "What do you mean?" "Well," says the old man, "I would have done if the melon had been as cold as the soup, and the soup had been as warm as the wine, and the wine had been as old as the chicken, and if the chicken had been as young as the maid, and the maid had been as willing as the old dowager then, yes, I would have had a very good time indeed."

Wrinkly Birthday To You...

It's a sure sign of wrinkliehood when you stop looking forward to your birthdays. Remember how proud you were when you first become a teenager or turned 18 (or 21 for you older folk)? You may have even felt slightly proud of the fact that you reached the grand old age of 30 with all your own hair, teeth and fashion sense intact. But then what your friends joshingly referred to as the "big four O" loomed and as it got closer the feelings of dread, queasiness and slight panic began to take over. With all the enthusiasm of going to have your teeth pulled you celebrated your 40th with wry and rueful jokes, and self-deprecating remarks, and then relaxed a bit, because, frankly, 41 or 42 isn't a whole lot different from 40. But when the "big five O" starts looming wheezily and wizened on the horizon, that's when you start to use subterfuge, evasion and downright lying. Just one tip – people usually notice if they're asked to attend your second 40th birthday party.

Keith tells Harry, "We've recently had a terrible tragedy in our family. My grandmother died on her 99th birthday." "Oh no," says Harry. "That's sad." "I know," says Keith. "And we were only halfway through giving her the bumps at the time."

A man asks his wife what she'd like for her 40th birthday. She says she'd like to be six again. Next day the man buys his wife a party hat and a big sticky cake, and hires a clown to show her some magic tricks, and sings songs. The wife looks at her husband as if he's crazy. "But I thought you'd be happy," says the husband. "You said you wanted to be six again." "You idiot," she fumes. "I meant my dress size."

People ask me what I'd most appreciate getting for my 87th birthday. I tell them, a paternity suit.

George Burns

There is still no cure for the common birthday.

John Glenn

A newspaper reporter visits a very old man on his birthday. "Have you lived in this town your whole life?" asks the reporter. "Obviously not, you young fool," says the old man. "I haven't died yet, have I?"

It's a terrible thing having to grow old by yourself. My wife hasn't had a birthday for the past five years.

Old Bill is known as the most boring man in his neighbourhood. He spends his days constantly bragging to anyone who will listen about how fit he is, how active he is and how young he feels despite his advanced years. "Look at that!" he says to a group of other elderly people as he pats his well-honed stomach. "That's the result of 100 sit ups a day – and I can still do them," "How else do you keep so fit?" asks one of his audience. "I don't smoke," says Bill, "I don't drink, I never eat unhealthy processed foods or snacks, and I've never chased loose women! And tomorrow – guess what! I'm going to be celebrating my 95th birthday." "Really?" says another old man. "How?"

Old age is like everything else. To make a success of it, you've got to start young.

Theodore Roosevelt

Wrinklies' Party Games

Sag – You're It!

Pass the Paracetamol

20 Questions followed by 20 "Eh?"s

Pin the Toupee on the Bald Wrinkly

Kick the Bucket

Simon Says Something Incoherent

Doc, Doc, Grouse

Hide and Sleep

Musical Wheelchairs

Cup of Char-ades

What Was That Simon Said Again?

Spin the Bottle of Sanatogen

Monotony

Short-sighted Man's Buff

Postman's Knock-knees

Shakes and Bladders

Blimey! Is That The Time Already Mr Wolf?

Ring a Ring an Ambulance

Here We Go Round the Flipping Mulberry Bush Again

Pass The Kidney Stone

It's Murder In the Dark When You're Trying To Find the Toilet at 3am

Chinese Whispers – What's Wrong With English Whispers Then?

Wrinkly Antiques And Artworks

A wealthy old dowager goes to the National Gallery one day and tries to impress one of the attendants with her knowledge of art history. "Oh, look!" she says. "Now correct me if I'm wrong, but isn't this a Goya?" "Er, no, madam, it's a Gainsborough actually," corrects the attendant. "Ah," says the old woman, "but that one over there... now that is definitely a Renoir isn't it?" "Sorry madam," says the attendant, "actually it's a Seurat." "Oh," says the woman, glancing around hastily to find one she definitely knows. "Now that horrible, ugly scary looking one;

I know that for certain. It's The Scream by Edvard Munch." "No, madam," says the attendant. "That is in fact a mirror."

A man tells a friend, "You know, I am a keen collector of antiques." "I know," says his friend. "I've seen your wife."

Two old ladies are visiting an art gallery one day and walk through the sculpture section. A few minutes later they emerge looking rather shocked and shaken. "Blimey!" says the first one. "Did you see that statue of that feller?" "What the feller with the big doodah hanging out for everyone to see?" says her friend. "Yes I did see that. Absolutely enormous wasn't it?" "I know," says the first one, "and it was so cold in that art gallery as well."

I'm very proud of my gold pocket watch. My grandfather, on his deathbed... sold me this watch.

Woody Allen

They're Not Wrinkles, They're Smile Lines: Looking On The Bright Side

Psst! Do you want to know a secret? Getting older isn't as bad as you think. Oh people like to make jokes about false teeth, grey hair, hearing aids, corsets, impotence, forgetfulness, stairlifts, Zimmer frames, loss of brain cells and all the rest, but unless you're extremely unlucky it won't all happen to you. And, if the loss of brain cells comes first you won't realize that the rest of it is happening to you! Sorry, cheap shot. But the good news is that people are staying healthier longer, they're living active lives and showing the youngsters a thing or two. But enough about the Rolling Stones; with the oldies of this world due to outnumber youngsters any time soon it's going to be a wrinkly world – everyone else will just have to live in it.

Looking on the bright side, when you're in your 40s the glass is still half-full. On the down side, pretty soon your teeth will be floating in it.

Don't forget: being "over the hill" is a lot better than being underneath it!

If things get better with age, then I must be approaching "magnificent".

It feels great to be nearly 100. I mean, for those parts of me that still have feeling.

Bob Hope

Nice to be here? At my age it's nice to be anywhere.

George Burns

The good thing about being over the hill is that you then start to pick up speed.

God put me on earth to accomplish a certain number of things. Right now I'm so far behind I will never die.

There are some nice things about old age, like I can sit here and think how it's great that wrinkles don't hurt.

The older you get, the better you realize you were.

Whenever I begin to feel a little blue, I remember to start breathing again.

You know that inside every old person there's a young person trying to work out what the hell happened.

I intend to live forever. So far, so good.

I'm not confused, I'm just well-mixed.

Another good thing about being poor is that when you're 70 your children will not have declared you legally insane in order to gain control of your estate.

Woody Allen

Here's something you won't want to live to see. Do you realize that in about 40 years we'll have hundreds of thousands of elderly men and women running round covered with shrivelled old tattoos?

One of the nice things about being senile is you can hide your own Easter eggs.

I used to dread getting older, because I thought I would not be able to do all the things I wanted to do, but now that I am older, I find that I don't want to do them.

Lady Nancy Astor

A reporter goes to interview a 104-year-old woman. "What do you think is the best thing about being 104?" asks the reporter. "Very little peer pressure," says the old woman.

The Perks Of Getting Older And Wrinklier

If you've never smoked, what the hell? Why not start? What's the worst that can happen?

In a hostage situation they're more likely to keep the young, pretty ones.
Nobody will expect you to run a marathon.

Nobody will expect you to run into a burning building.

You can buy things now and know they will never wear out.

You can eat your dinner at four in the afternoon and not feel ridiculous.

You can enjoy heated arguments about pension plans with your friends.

Men can stop trying to hold their stomachs in, even if a supermodel walks into the room.

You get to hear all about other peoples' operations.

You no longer have to think of a speed limit as a challenge.

Your doctor will no longer immediately dismiss you as a hypochondriac.

Your eyes won't get much worse.

You've finally got your number of brain cells down to a manageable size.

You've got nothing left to learn the hard way.

Nostalgia

It's hard to be nostalgic when you can't remember anything.

Old Tom tells Old Bert, "I was young once you know." "Cor!" says Bert. "You must have a good memory."

Nostalgia is a longing for a place you'd never think of moving back to.

After the age of 80, everything reminds you of something else.

Lowell Thomas

Two old men are talking over some sad memories. "You know it's 40 years today I lost my wife and children," says one. "Is it really?" says the other. "That's terrible." "Yes it is," says the first. "I'll never forget that poker game."

Nostalgia isn't what it used to be.

Then And Now

Then: "Whatever".
Now: "Depends".

Then: dreaming of moving to California because it's cool.
Now: dreaming of moving to California because it's warm.

Then: Getting out to a new, hip joint.
Now: Getting a new hip joint.

Then: Growing pot.
Now: Growing a pot belly.

Then: How high are you?
Now: Hi! How are you?

Then: Long hair.
Now: Longing for hair.

Then: Parents begging you to get your hair cut.
Now: Children begging you to get their heads shaved.

Then: Passing the driving test.
Now: Passing the vision test.

Then: Screw the system.
Now: Upgrade the system.

Then: Seeds and stems.
Now: Roughage.

Then: the Rolling Stones.
Now: the kidney stones.

Then: Peace, Love and Understanding
Now: Quiche, Maltloaf and Lots of sitting

A little nonsense now and then is relished by the wisest men.

Roald Dahl

Old age is no place for sissies.

Bette Davis

Wrinkly World: Outside The House

Does your property "boast" any of the following:

Stone cladding

Pebble-dashing

Crazy paving

A wooden letterbox on a pole

A house name such as "Dunlivin"

Overshoes in the porch

A "Please shut the gate" sign

A boot scraper

A hedge shaped like a bird

Any instruction sign headed "Polite notice"

Traffic cones for "reserving" your parking space when you're out

A coal bunker

A dustbin with your house number painted on it

A handrail to help you up and down the front step

A birdbath

A wishing well

If you answered "yes" to three of more of the above you now have one foot in the grave. Sorry.

Crafty Old Wrinklies

They say there's no fool like an old fool, but that's exactly what wrinklies want you to think. When you get to a certain age you suddenly have a whole armoury of tricks and ruses to keep you one step ahead of those grasping and demanding young whippersnappers, otherwise known as your family.

"Eh? What's that? You want to borrow how much? Sorry, you'll have to speak up..." "Ooh with my knees/heart/arthritis I can't carry the shopping on my own/clean the house/take the dog for a walk...", "All my money's tied up in investments, but as soon as I go it'll be left to the son or daughter who's done the most for me....", "What's that officer? Shoplifting/speeding/reckless use of mobility scooter? Oh, take pity, I'm only a poor old pensioner..."

An elderly man bought a large farm in Florida and fixed it up with walkways, orchards, tennis courts and a pond at the furthest edge of the property. One evening he decided to go down to the pond and took a bucket with him to bring back some fruit. As he got nearer, he heard voices shouting and laughing with glee. As he came closer he saw a bunch of young women skinny-dipping in his pond. He made the women aware of his presence and they all went into the deep end. One of the women shouted to him, "Hey, you old pervert! We're not coming out of here until you leave!" "That's OK," said the old man, "I didn't come down here to watch you ladies swim naked or make you get out of the pond naked." Then he held up his bucket and said, "I'm just here to feed my alligator!"

An old man calls his son on the other side of the country and tells him, "Your mother and I have something to tell you, but we don't really want to discuss it over the phone. We're just telling you because you're our oldest son and we thought you ought to know. We've decided to split up and get a divorce." "What do you mean?" asks the son, horrified at this news. "You've been married for over 50 years." "Sorry, but there it is," says the old man. "I don't understand," says the son. "Why would you want to get a divorce after all this time?" "We don't want to talk about it, because it's far too painful. We've made our minds up and that's it," says the old man. "We just want you to call your brothers and sisters, and pass on the news to spare us any further grief." The son insists on talking to his mother, but the old man tells him there's nothing he can do. "Just hold on, Dad," says the son, "don't do anything rash!

Next week is Christmas and I'll be taking time off work anyway, so I'm going to come straight over to you and help you get this whole thing sorted out." Over the next hour all the other children call saying they too are going to come over to help sort things out as well. After all this the old man turns to his wife and says, "Well, there we are. It worked like a charm. But what are we going to do to get them to come over to us again next year?"

One night an old woman is horrified to see a police car pull up outside her house, even more so when she sees her husband brought out of the back and led up to the door. "What happened?" the old lady asks the policeman. "I'm sorry, madam," says the policeman, "we found this elderly gentleman at the local shopping centre. He was lost and couldn't remember how to get home." "Oh no!" says the old woman. After the police have gone she turns to her husband and says, "The shopping centre's only half a mile away. How could you have forgotten your way home? You're not losing your marbles are you?" "Of course not," says her old husband. "I wasn't lost. I was just too tired to walk."

An old man goes up to a young man at the Post Office and says, "Excuse me, would you address this postcard for me?" The young man gladly does so and then says, "Would you like me to write a short message on here for you as well?" "Yes, please," says the old man and dictates what he would like to say. Finally the young man, feeling very pleased with himself for his good deed, asks, "Now, is there anything else I can do for you?" The old man thinks a moment and says, "Yes, please. At the end could you just add, 'Please excuse the sloppy hand writing.'"

An elderly gentleman walks into a West End furriers with his young lady and says he wants to buy her a mink coat costing £15,000. "Will a cheque be OK?" asks the man. "Certainly, sir," says the sales assistant. "But we'll have to wait a few days for it to clear. Can you come back on Monday to take delivery?" "Certainly," replies the old man, and he and his girlfriend walk out arm in arm. Next Monday the man returns. The sales assistant is furious, "You've got a nerve coming back here. It turns out there's hardly a penny in your bank account and your cheque was worthless." "Yes, sorry about that," replies the man. "I just came in to apologize... and to thank you for the greatest weekend of my life."

Ancient Wisdom

A rambler in the country sees old farmer sitting on his porch, holding a small length of rope and studying it intently. "Good afternoon," says the rambler. "Tell me, what's that piece of rope for?" "I can use it to tell the weather," says the old farmer. "Really?" says the rambler, impressed. "How does it work?" "Well," says the farmer, "when the rope shifts slightly from side to side, that means it's windy. And when it feels wet, that means it's raining."

An old Cherokee chief sat in his reservation hut, smoking a ceremonial pipe, eyeing the two US government officials sent to interview him. "Chief Two Eagles," one official began, "you have observed the white man for many generations, you have seen his wars and his products, you have seen all his progress and all his problems." The chief nodded. The official continued, "Considering recent events, in your opinion, where has the white man gone wrong?" The chief stared at the government officials for over a minute and then calmly replied: "When white man found the land, Indians were running it. No taxes. No debt. Plenty buffalo. Plenty beaver. Women did the work. Medicine man free. Indian men hunted and fished all the time." The chief smiled and added quietly, "White man dumb enough to think he could improve system like that."

You Know You're Getting Old When...

The pharmacist has become your best friend.

The reason you walk around with your head held high is you're trying to get used to your trifocals.

The twinkle in your eye is the reflection of the sun on your bifocals.

The waiter asks how you'd like your steak... and you say, "pureed".

Those issues of Reader's Digest just can't come fast enough.

"Tying one on" means fastening your Medic Alert alarm.

When you do the "Hokey Cokey" you put your left hip out... And it stays out.

When you look in the mirror, one of your parents is looking back at you.

You and your teeth have given up sleeping together.

You buy a compass for the dashboard of your car.
You answer to Bill, or George, or Mary… in fact, anyone's name but your own.

You are cautioned to slow down by the doctor instead of by the police.

You are on a first name terms with the chief nurse at your local hospital.

You have become obsessed with the price of petrol.

You begin every other sentence with the word "Nowadays…"

You begin to lose hope of ever finishing that Green Shield Stamp book you've had on the go since 1973.

You begin to outlive enthusiasm.

You bought your first car for the same price you paid for your kid's new trainers.

You buy a compass for the dashboard of your car.

You call the ambulance service and they're able to tell you your address.

You can clean your teeth in the dishwasher.

You can go out with someone who is a third of your age without breaking any laws.

Wrinkly Wisdom

In some cultures the elders are revered for their sagacity (No kids, sagacity is not a theme park for wrinklies!) and wisdom. In our culture they are revered for how much money they might leave you when they die. The rest of the time wrinklies are marginalized, ignored and otherwise discarded by a culture obsessed with youth. But if you take the trouble to sit down and listen to what a wrinkly has to say you might learn something, such as the fact that the world's gone mad, a state pension is hardly worth walking down to the post office for and they don't write decent songs anymore. But no, that's just cynical and patronising stereotyping. George Burns was still cracking great gags in his 90s, and at a similar age George Bernard Shaw was still writing plays, Pablo Picasso was still painting and Bertrand Russell continued to be an active philosopher and campaigner. True, they may also have thought the world had gone mad, pensions were lousy and nobody was writing songs like they used to, but just consider this: they may have been right.

People say that age is just a state of mind. I say it's more about the state of your body.

Geoffrey Parfitt

Age is a very high price to pay for maturity.

Age is important, but only if you are a cheese or a fine wine.

Old age comes at a bad time.
By the time a man is wise enough to watch his step, he's too old to go anywhere.

By the time you're 80 years old you've learned everything. You only have to remember it.

George Burns

Now you're finally able to make ends meet, someone seems to have moved the ends.

Anyone who tells you that he can do the same things at 40 as he did when he was 20 probably didn't do much at 20.

Don't let old age get you down. It's too hard to get back up again afterwards.

One of the many things no-one tells you about ageing is... that it is such a nice change from being young.

Don't complain about getting old. A lot of people are denied the privilege.

Don't forget, age is largely a matter of mind over matter. If you don't mind it, it won't matter.

Life is like riding a bicycle; you won't fall off unless you stop pedalling.

Don't worry about avoiding temptation. As you grow older, it will avoid you.

What most persons consider as virtue, after the age of 40 is simply a loss of energy.

Voltaire

When you're old you love giving people the benefit of your advice. It compensates for your inability to set a bad example any more.

Growing old is mandatory. Growing up is optional.

Half our life is spent trying to find something to do with the time we have rushed through life trying to save.

Just when you've learned to make the most of your life, you realize most of your life has gone.

Everything that goes up must come down. But there comes a time when not everything that's down can come up.

George Burns

Opportunities always look bigger going than coming.

Remember: don't ever let anyone tell you you're getting old. If they do just run over their toes with your mobility scooter.

Remember: never ask old people how they are. At least, not if you have anything else to do that day.

There comes a time when you should stop expecting other people to make a big deal about your birthday. When you turn 11…

I'll never make the mistake of being 70 again.

Casey Stengel

The older we get, the fewer things seem worth waiting in line for.

People never seem to get too old to learn new ways of being stupid.

Maturity means being emotionally and mentally healthy. It is that time when you know when to say yes, when to say no, and when to say WHOOPEE!

By the time you're older you should have learnt that the real art of conversation is not only to say the right thing in the right place, but also to not say the wrong thing at the tempting moment.

If you live to the age of 100 you have it made because very few people die past the age of 100.

George Burns

Experience is a wonderful thing. It enables you to recognize a mistake when you make it again.

Experience is what causes a person to make new mistakes instead of the same old ones.

Experience is what you get when you didn't get what you wanted.

The secret of growing old is having lots of experience you can no longer use.

Wisdom is the comb that life gives you shortly after all your hair has fallen out.

Children are a great comfort in your old age. And they help you reach it faster, too.

Lionel Kauffman

Remember to be nice to your kids. They're they one who will choose your nursing home.

Remember that age and treachery will always triumph over youth and ability.

Blessed are the young, for they shall inherit the National Debt.

Herbert Hoover

The only truly consistent people are dead.

The secret of longevity is to keep breathing.

Sophie Tucker

You're only young once – but you can be immature forever.

Wrinkly World: In The Garden

Would an unsuspecting visitor find any of the following in your back garden, or worse, allotment:

Gnomes

Cherubs

Men made out of flower pots

A little pond (possibly with gnomes fishing in it)

Grey stone ornaments with amusing messages emblazoned on them

A bird table

A complex sprinkler system (with 10+ settings)

A little windmill

Stone birds, squirrels or rabbits

A vegetable patch

Fairy lights

Garden chairs with holes in the arms to put your drinks

A selection of footballs, tennis balls, frisbees and other paraphernalia that you refuse to throw back, because they'll only bloody well chuck them back again as soon as your back's turned

Wind chimes

A lawn mower that you don't have to plug in

His 'n' hers sun loungers

A swinging chair

A hammock (possibly constructed from one of the wife's bras)

If you answered "yes" to any of the above then welcome to Wrinkly World. Admission is free for the over 65s!

The Wrinklies' Guide For Putting The World To Rights

The trouble with the world today, according to wrinklies, is that it's run by young people. And young people, as most wrinklies will tell you, don't know anything. Not even the fact that they're born. If only they'd consult their wiser elders occasionally they'd soon start putting things right. So here, for the edification of youngsters and the gratification of wrinklies are a few tips on getting the world into shape – and boy, does it need it!

Crime

Lock 'em up and throw away the key – yes, even for parking in the "disabled" bay at the supermarket.

Bring back the birch/tawse/cat o' nine tails/rack/thumb-screw/Dixon of Dock Green/Hanging, drawing and quartering/national service (it never did me any harm).

Put more bobbies on the beat – proper ones, ones with moustaches, not four-foot high women with "equality and gender awareness" training.

Education

Go back to the three Rs – reading, writing and arithmetic (yes, I know that's one R, a W and an A, but that's how we were taught so it must be right).

Bring back the cane – it'll instil a bit of discipline into the little blighters and teach them never to do it again, and I should know, I was caned every day when I was at school.

Go back to chalk and talk – none of this new-fangled computer nonsense. Where did computers get anyone? Well, apart from the Moon obviously... all right, and Mars, and yes, OK, making Bill Gates the richest man in the world, and....

Global Warming

If all this global warming stuff is true how come my flat's so cold? Eh? I could do with a bit of global warming round my chilblains, let me tell you...

OK, if London is under water in 50 years who cares? I won't be around to see it and Venice seems to manage all right, so what's the problem?

If the icebergs had melted 100 years ago the *Titanic* would never have sunk so think on...

Why they have to put those energy-producing windmills in the middle of the sea beats me – have the fish got TV down there or something?

The Environment

We didn't have an environment in my day; we had indoors and outdoors – load of nonsense if you ask me.

Cardboard in this bin, glass in that bin, tins in the other one – it's a load of rubbish isn't it? Ah! Aha! "Load of rubbish!" Get it? All right, suit yourselves. At least it was clean, not like half the so-called comedy on TV these days.

They ruined the atmosphere when they started firing all those rockets into space if you ask me. Yuri Gagorbachov or whatever his name was. And as soon as the Cold War ended global warming started. Whichever way you look at it, it's obviously the Russians' fault isn't it?

Health

They should close down these mixed-sex wards straightaway. They shouldn't be having sex in hospital in the first place.
Bring back matron!

Let's go back to the days when you had trust in the hospital and not the hospital in a trust.

When I was a nipper the hospital staff were super and the bugs were nowhere to be seen. Now it's the other way round!

Give It Up For The Wrinklies!

As you get older you give up some things and some things give you up. You start getting a bit wheezy so you give up smoking, you find it difficult to concentrate so you cut down on your drinking. You begin to begin to get a spare tyre so you cut down on the Michelin star meals. You start to find pleasure in the simple things, like your spouse. You enjoy walking in the fresh air – especially since you had to give up driving due to being a menace to other road users (in the humble opinion of the local magistrates) and you don't even watch so much TV because of the terrible language – i.e. you swearing at the telly every time there's yet another reality show instead of a proper Wednesday play or something sensible.

You can live to be 100 if you give up all the things that make you want to live to be 100.

Woody Allen

And you find you're no longer a slave to fashion, because it's moved on so much that you don't know whether your clothes are retro, ironic or just simply a bit naff, so you give up and refuse to have anything to do with it. Similarly, your senses suddenly turn into nonsenses and your body goes on strike, refusing to do what you tell it. Suddenly you go from life in the fast lane to life in the "five items or fewer" lane – and that's just your brain cells.

An 80-year-old man is having a check up at the doctor's. As the doctor listens to the man's heart, he mutters, "Uh oh!" "What's the problem?" asks the old man. "Well," says the doctor, "you have a serious heart murmur. Do you smoke?" "No," says the old man. "Are you a heavy drinker?" asks the doctor. "No," says the man. "Do you have much of a sex life?" asks the doctor. "Yes," says the old man. "That's my sole remaining pleasure in life." "OK," says the doctor, "but now you've got this heart murmur, you're going to have to give up half your sex life." "OK," says the old man, "but which half do you want me to give up? The looking or the thinking?"

An old man sits reminiscing and says, "Do you know, I can remember the time I gave up both booze and sex at the same time. Dear me, that was the worst half hour of my life."

Your Wrinkly Age – Language

You might not think you're old, but one of the giveaways is the language you use, and no, we're not talking about the cursing under your breath as you try to extricate yourself from the armchair at bedtime.

No, we mean those everyday words and phrases that mark you out as a wrinkly, even though you may still be dressing like a teenager. For example:

If you're young you refer to the radio, if you're quite old you might call it the wireless, and if you're very old you can't quite remember off the top of your head what it's called and refer to it as "the thingy".

If you're young and wish to convey to somebody that you find the winter weather inclement you might refer to it as "freezing", if you're quite old you may make reference to "brass monkeys", but if you're very old, and made of sterner stuff you will merely say "it's a bit parky".

If you're young you will probably download your musical entertainment from the internet, if you are quite old you may seek out what is quaintly known as a "record shop", if you are past the first few flushes of youth you will pick up your Fifty Golden Oldies or the *Best of Paul Anka* at the supermarket or possibly a petrol station.

Similarly, on reading in the paper of some crazy bureaucratic decision you will start spouting off that the world has "gone mad" and that thank goodness, you won't be long for this Earth, etc etc.

And you may find as you get older that certain phrases spring to your lips, seemingly unbidden. For example, if a young child shyly refuses to speak to you, you may find the celebrated wrinkly phrase "What's the matter, cat got your tongue?" spouting from your saggy lips.

You'll find you can't help yourself, and it is just another indicator that you have reached wrinkliehood, or what is sometimes known as World of Leather Features.

But sometimes this wrinklyspeak is tinged with an ironic wrinkly humour. So when you don't quite hear what somebody has said to you, you may respond with "You'll have to speak up a bit, I'm deaf in one eye!" And when the other person does indeed raise their voice you may find yourself shouting, "All right! I'm not deaf you know!"

And as the years advance and you find yourself at the mercy of unyielding joints, unsympathetic petty officials and other travails of senior life, you may find that you tend to swear a bit more than you used to. Following any such choice language you will wittily quip "Pardon my French!" Tres amusant of course, but it will mark you out as a wrinkly, because no one under the age of 45 has ever been heard to use this off-the-peg bon mot.

You Know You're Getting Old When...

You lose an argument with a phone answering device.

You nod off and other people in the room fear you may have died.

You realize you can't find your glasses without having your glasses on in the first place.

You realize that a postage stamp now costs more than a cinema ticket did when you were 14.

You recall when milk came in glass bottles and they were recycled automatically.

You regularly get into arguments with your friends about which denture adhesive is better.

You have to get up from a couch in stages.

You have an airbag fitted onto your walking frame.

You have too much room in the house and not enough room in the medicine cabinet.

You hear snap, crackle and pop at breakfast time as you sit down at the table – and it's not your cereal, it's your joints.

You know your way around, but you don't feel like going.

Everything either dries up or starts to leak.

You know you're getting old when the candles cost more than the cake.

Bob Hope

You know you're getting old when your wife decides to give up sex for Lent and you don't notice the difference until the August bank holiday.

You like sitting in a rocking chair, but you can't get the damned thing started.

You look at the celebrity birthdays and don't have a clue who they are.

You look both ways before crossing a room.

You look forward to a dull evening.

You light the candles on your birthday cake, and a group of campers form a circle round it and start singing "Kumbaya".

You turn up the volume on the TV so loud you end up going deaf. Again.

You select the largest font size possible on your eBook device. And it's still too small.

Lessons In Life That Wrinklies Should Have Learnt By Now

A penny saved is worthless.

A person who is nice to you, but rude to the waiter, is not a nice person.

Going to church doesn't make you a Christian anymore than standing in a garage makes you a car.

Friends may come and go, but enemies accumulate.

Artificial intelligence is no match for natural stupidity.

Don't worry about what people think – they don't do it very often.

If you look like your passport picture, you probably need the trip.

If you're too lazy to start anything, you may get a reputation for patience.

My father was a very wise old man. He once told me, "Son, don't worry about trying to understand women. If you ever do manage to eventually understand them, you won't believe it anyway."

Never, under any circumstances, take a sleeping pill and a laxative on the same night.

One-seventh of your life is spent on Monday.

There is always one more imbecile than you counted on.

If there really is a God who created the entire universe with all of its glories, and He decides to deliver a message to humanity, He will not use, as His messenger, a person on cable TV with a bad hairstyle.

If you had to identify, in one word, the reason why the human race has not achieved, and never will achieve, its full potential, that word would be: "meetings".

No matter what happens, somebody will find a way to take it too seriously.

Nobody cares if you can't dance well. Just get up and dance.

People who feel the need to tell you that they have an excellent sense of humour are, in fact, telling you that they have no sense of humour whatsoever.

People who want to share their religious views with you almost never want you to share yours with them.

The badness of a movie is directly proportional to the number of helicopters in it.

The main accomplishment of almost all organized protests is to annoy people who are not involved.

The most powerful force in the universe is gossip.

The one thing that unites all human beings, regardless of age, gender, religion, economic status or ethnic background, is that, deep down inside, we all believe that we are above-average drivers.

There is a very fine line between "hobby" and "mental illness".

When trouble arises and things look bad, there is always one individual who perceives a solution and is willing to take command. Very often, that individual is crazy.

You should never say anything to a woman that even remotely suggests you think she's pregnant unless you can see an actual baby emerging from her at that moment.

You should not confuse your career with your life.

You will never find anybody who can give you a clear and compelling reason why we observe "Daylight Saving Time".

Nobody is normal.

The Wrinklies' Visitor Test

If you've passed any of the other wrinklies' tests and still consider yourself just about on the right side of wrinkliehood, but there's still a little cloud of doubt in your mind, try this one:

Before visitors are due to come do you:

Moan that they always come at the most inconvenient time and you've got nothing in common with them and you're only inviting them because your other half wants them round

Complain that you've got to clean the house from top to bottom especially and cater to their faddy dietary requirements and put up with their blooming dog/ flipping kids/irritating habits

Say that if you had your way you wouldn't bother keeping up with all these people and could enjoy a quiet life instead

During the visit do you:

Complain in general about blooming dogs/flipping kids/irritating habits in the hope that the visitors will take the hint

Say how lovely it is to see them again whilst stifling a yawn and glancing at your watch

After visitors have been do you:

Moan that they outstayed their welcome/bored the pants off you/couldn't take the hint when you started putting on your pyjamas

Complain that they hardly touched the food you got in specially and never once complimented you on your new Jack Vettriano print/pine coat stand/novelty doorbell chimes

Say that you can't really see the point in having them over just for the sake of it and why don't we just keep it to Christmas cards and have done with it?

If you have found yourself agreeing with at least three of the above statements, then welcome to the one club where you won't be turned away by a bouncer with a youth-biased door policy!

Married For Ever Such A Long Time

When you take your wedding vows you are signing up for the long haul, the full Monty, the whole "till death us do part" thing. Though these days a lot of people seem to have slightly rewritten that last phrase to "till divorce us do part". But if you're one of those who has stuck at it through thick and thin, in sickness and in health, from a roll in the hay to a roll in the café, then congratulations! Of course you've had your ups and downs, well at least until you moved into that retirement bungalow, and the lust may have been lost, but these days you prefer companionship, loyalty and affection – which is precisely why... you bought a dog.

A wife asks her husband, "How do you think we should celebrate our 60th wedding anniversary?" "How about a two minute silence?" he suggests.

We've just marked our tenth wedding anniversary on the calendar and threw darts at it.

Phyllis Diller

Henry's wife tells him, "Henry, for our 40th wedding anniversary I want you to take me somewhere I've never been before." "OK," says Henry under his breath, "how about the blooming kitchen?"

Bryan says to Dave, "It's your 20th wedding anniversary soon, isn't it, Dave? What are you going to buy the missus?" "A once-in-a-lifetime trip to Australia," says Dave. "Wow!" says Bryan. "I'm sure she'll be absolutely thrilled, but how on earth will you top that on your 25th anniversary?" "Well," says Dave, "I was thinking maybe then I could send her the money to pay for her ticket back."

Q: What's the definition of a cheapskate?
A: A man who buys his wife a pack of cards on their diamond wedding anniversary.

On their 30th wedding anniversary a couple go back to the resort where they spent their honeymoon. On the way, they are driving through the countryside when the man says, "Look! Remember that field? Remember what we did on the way to our hotel 30 years ago?" The wife smiles and says, "Oh yes!" So they get out of the car and make love right up against the wire fence. When they get back in the car the husband says, "Wow! That was amazing! I think if anything you were even more animated this time round than you were 30 years ago!" "I know I was," says the wife, "because 30 years ago that bloomin' fence wasn't electrified!"

An old couple have gone back to their honeymoon hotel every year on their wedding anniversary. One year, when they're shown to their room, they find they've been given a whole suite rather than the usual double room. "Excuse me," says the old man to the hotel porter. "I think there's been a mistake. This is the bridal suite." "That's all right sir," says the porter. "There's no need to perform. If we'd put you in the kitchen we wouldn't be expecting you to knock up dinner."

Joe says to Pete, "On our silver wedding anniversary the wife and I went back to the same little country hotel where we spent our wedding night." "And was it all just the same?" asks Pete. "Almost," says Joe, "except this time I was the one crying my heart out in the bathroom."

The old farmer and his wife are getting ready for their 50th wedding anniversary dinner. The farmer's wife says, "Albert, should I go out in the yard and kill a chicken?" Albert says, "Oh come on Phyllis, why blame a chicken for something that happened 50 years ago?"

A married couple are celebrating their 60th wedding anniversary. At the party everybody wants to know how they've managed to stay together so long in this day and age. The husband tells them, "When we were first married we came to an agreement. I would make all the major decisions and my wife would make all the minor decisions. Well, can you believe it? I'm able to tell you today that in 60 long years of marriage, we've never needed to make a single major decision."

Every week, in church, the vicar notices one old couple who are always sitting in the same pew holding hands. Thinking that at their age this is rather charming he stops them one week on their way out to remark on it. "I can't help noticing," says the vicar, "how close you both seem even after all these years, holding hands and so on." "Close! Don't be so ridiculous!" says the old woman. "I'm just trying to stop the old bugger cracking his knuckles all the way through the service!"

A 60-year-old couple are celebrating their 40th wedding anniversary. During the celebration a fairy appears and says that since they've been such a loving couple she'll give them each one wish. The wife wishes to travel around the world. The fairy waves her wand and poof! She has a handful of plane tickets. Next, it's the husband's turn. He pauses for a moment, then says, "I'd like to have a woman 30 years younger than me." So the fairy picks up her wand and poof! He's 90!

A married couple have been together for years. One night the husband is reading the newspaper when his wife tells him, "I wish I was your newspaper. Then you'd give me your full attention for hours every evening." "Oh that's nice, darling," says the man. "You know I wish I could have a wife like a newspaper as well." "Oh yes," says the woman. "Because then you'd be able to put your hands all over me every night?" "No," says the husband. "Because then I could throw the old one out each night and pick up a nice, fresh, new one every morning."

On their 40th wedding anniversary a man says to his wife, "Whatever you want, just name it and I'll buy it for you. It doesn't matter how much it costs. Just say what you'd like for our anniversary." She replies, "A divorce." "To be honest," he says. "I wasn't thinking of spending quite that much."

A couple are celebrating their 40th wedding anniversary. A friend asks them, "What's your secret for such a long marriage?" "We take the time to go out to a restaurant twice a week," says the husband. "You know the sort of thing. A candlelight dinner, soft music and a slow walk home." "That's lovely," says the friend. "Yes it is," says the husband. "My wife goes on Tuesdays and I go on Fridays."

A 95-year-old man takes his 92-year-old wife to the solicitors and says they want a divorce. "But why?" asks the solicitor, "You've been married for over 70 years, why do you want a divorce now?" "We haven't been getting on for quite a few years," says the wife, "but we wanted to wait until the children had died before we split up."

Married Lots Of Times

My grandmother was a very tough woman. She buried three husbands and two of them were just napping.

Rita Rudner

He's been married so often, he signs the wedding certificate in pencil.

He's been married so often, his wedding certificate says "To whom it may concern..."

He's been married so often, they don't issue him with a new marriage licence now. They just punch the old one.

Marriage is the triumph of imagination over intelligence. A second marriage is the triumph of hope over experience.

She's been married so many times she has rice marks on her face.

Zsa Zsa Gabor was once asked, "How many husbands have you had?" She replied, "Do you mean apart from my own?"

Mixed Marriages Between Old Wrinklies And Young Non-Wrinklies

For some older people it's the ultimate achievement – to marry someone much younger than themselves. But what does the young person get out of it? If their sole aim was to go to bed with something wrinkly they could simply stop ironing their pyjamas. But by some strange coincidence the older half of these unlikely marriages is often rich or famous, or both. Of course, there are exceptions, such as... well, there must be some exceptions, but the older person also has to adjust when they marry someone much younger. No going to bed early with a cup of cocoa when the younger half wants to go out clubbing and then suffering the embarrassment of everyone laughing at them when they attempt to do the Twist to the latest hot dance floor track.

An 82-year-old man goes to his doctor for a check up. A few days later the doctor sees the old man walking along the road with a gorgeous young woman on his arm. The doctor calls the old man in again and says, "I saw you with your new girlfriend, but I'm not sure that's a good idea after what I told you last week." "What do you mean?" says the old man. "I'm doing exactly what you told me to do. You said I should get a hot mama and be cheerful." "No I didn't," says the doctor. "What I actually said was, 'You've got a heart murmur. Be careful.'"

Old Alf is 80 years old when he marries a 20-year-old woman and after a few months she is pregnant. "Are you sure this is a good idea?" Alf's doctor asks him. "It seems a bit late in life to be having another child." "I think it's the perfect time for me to have a baby," says old Alf. "After all I have to get up 12 times during the night now anyway!"

An ageing man marries a beautiful young bride many years his junior. On their honeymoon night they climb into bed and the old man asks his new bride, "Tell me, did your mother tell you what to do on your wedding night?" "Oh yes," she says. "She told me everything I needed to know." "That's handy," says the elderly gentleman as he turns out the light. "Because I seem to have forgotten."

An 80-year-old man marries a 20-year-old girl. After a few months of marriage the young woman goes into hospital to give birth. The nurse comes out to congratulate the ageing husband and says, "This is amazing. How do you do it at your time of life?" "Well," says the old man, "you've got to keep that old motor running." The following year the young bride gives birth again. The nurse comes out again to congratulate the old man and says, "You really are amazing. How do you do it?" "Well," he says again, "you've got to keep the old motor running." The third year of marriage, the same thing happens once again. Out comes the nurse to congratulate the old man saying, "Well, well, well! You certainly are quite a man!" "Yes, well," says the old fellow, "you've got to keep that old motor running." "Yeah," says the nurse, "actually if I were you I'd consider getting an oil change. This one's come out black!"

An old farmer gets married to an 18-year-old. A few weeks after the service, the vicar decides to call round at the farm to ask the old boy how things are going with his new young wife. "Oh," says the old man, "I can't keep my hands off her." The vicar mumbles his approval and goes on his way. A few weeks later he calls round again and asks the same question. "I still can't keep my hands off her," says the old man. "I suppose that's good," says the vicar. "Not really," says the old farmer. "She's gone and run off with one of them."

A 90-year-old man tells his doctor that he is planning to get married to a woman 65 years his junior. "Under the circumstances, do you have any suggestions for me?" asks the old man. "Yes," says the doctor thinking the old man's not going to be able to keep a young woman like that satisfied. "I think it might be an idea for you to take in a lodger." A year later the old man comes back for a check up. The doctor asks him how his marriage to the 25-year-old is going. "Oh fine," says the old man. "In fact, she's going to have a baby in a few weeks." "Oh yes," says the doctor knowingly. "So you took my advice and took in a lodger did you?" "Yes I did," says the old fellow. "The only problem is that she's pregnant now as well."

An ageing multi-millionaire gets married to a beautiful 19-year-old model. His friend tells him, "You're an old devil. How did you manage to marry a beautiful young girl like that when you're 60?" "It was partly the money," says the old man, "and partly the fact that I told her I was 95."

Ross: I would date her, but there is a big age difference.
Joey: Well think about when you're 90...
Ross: I know, she'll be 80 and it won't be such a big difference.
Joey: No. What I was gonna say is when you're 90 you'll still have the memory of what it was like to be with a 20-year-old.

Friends

A 90-year-old man gets married to an 88-year-old woman. At the church door the guests don't throw rice, they throw vitamin tablets.

People's Manners Today!

An old couple are sitting at their dinner table when the old man sneezes very loudly. "Well," says the old woman, "I notice that you've finally learnt some manners and have started to put your hand in front of your mouth when you sneeze." "I have to, don't I?" says the old man. "It's the only way I can catch my teeth."

Things older people don't want to hear from cheeky young whippersnappers: Hey, I know! Let's all play getting older! OK! You go first!

Old Alf says people spoke a lot more politely in the old days. In fact when he was young he says he was a member of a gang called Heck's Angels.

A feminist woman gets on a bus one day and all the seats are taken, so an old man stands up and offers her his seat. "No thank you!" says the woman, pushing him back in his seat. "I think the world has moved on a bit." At the next stop a woman gets on and again the old man stands up and offers his seat. Now angry, the feminist pushes him back down. "We sisters don't need your patronising gestures!" she fumes. At the next stop a third woman gets on and again the old man stands up. "You just don't get it, do you, granddad?" screams the woman. Now it's the old man's turn to be angry, "Look, you old boiler, just let me off the bloody bus will you! I've missed three stops already!"

Things older people don't want to hear from cheeky young whippersnappers: Hey! Want some onions to go with those liver spots?

I was told to always respect my elders. Unfortunately it's getting harder and harder for me to find any.

A Wrinkly And His Money

Remember when you wished for the income you can't live on now?

Sign outside a Scottish cinema: "Free admission for old age pensioners, but only if accompanied by both parents."

Sophia: I'm settling my estate.
Dorothy: What estate? Your bus pass and loofah sponge?

The Golden Girls

The Golden Girls

A reporter asks a rich old American man how he made his money. The old man replies, "Well, son, it was 1932. The depth of the Great Depression. I was down to my last nickel and I invested that nickel in an apple. I spent the entire day polishing the apple and, at the end of the day, I sold that apple for ten cents. The next morning, I invested those ten cents in two apples. I spent the entire day polishing them and sold them for 20 cents. I continued this system for a month, by the end of which I'd accumulated a fortune of $1.37. Then my wife's father died and left us two million dollars..."

A pretty young girl walks up to the fabric counter in a large department store and says, "I want to buy some material for a new dress. How much does it cost?" "To a pretty little thing like you, miss," says the unctuous male counter assistant, "it's one kiss per yard." "OK," says the girl. "I'll take ten yards." With expectation and anticipation written all over his face, the clerk hurriedly measures out and wraps the cloth, then holds it out teasingly. The girl snatches the package. "Thanks," she says and points to a little old man standing beside her. "My granddad says he'll pay the bill."

Harry gets to the age of 65 and decides to go and get his bus pass. When he gets to the council office he is asked to produce his pension book and other documents. He then realizes he's left them at home, but the woman on the desk feels sorry for him and says, "Don't worry about your documents; just let me have a look at your chest." "My chest?" asks Harry. "Why?" "Do you want a bus pass or not?" says the woman. So Harry opens his shirt to reveal grey chest hair. "OK," says the woman, "that's fine. I'm sure you're old enough to qualify." And with that she gives him his bus pass. When he gets home Harry tells his wife what happened. "You idiot!" she exclaims. "What's the matter?" asks Harry. "Well," says his wife, "if you'd dropped your trousers as well, she'd have probably said you were also entitled to disability allowance!"

Wrinklies In Retirement

With more and more people taking early retirement these days there's no reason that "retirement" should conjure up images of bus passes, rose pruning and church hall bingo, but it does. And even if your retirement is filled with exotic cruises, luxury hotels and playing Chemin de fer in Monte Carlo, it's difficult to escape the image that the word brings to mind. Perhaps it needs rebranding? Now there's a challenge for those young advertising execs – make retirement seem cool and youthful. Retirement – it's the new work!

Retirement must be wonderful. I mean, you can suck in your stomach for only so long.

Burt Reynolds

An ageing human cannonball goes to tell the circus ringmaster that, after 50 years in the job, he feels he's had enough and he wants to retire after tonight's performance. "Oh no," says the ringmaster, begging him to reconsider. "Where else will I find a man of your calibre?"

Retirement at 65 is ridiculous. When I was 65 I still had pimples.

George Burns

Now I'm retired I can do whatever I want. As long as it's not too far from a public convenience.

Why do they give you a watch when you retire? Don't they realize it's the first time in your life you don't care what time it is?

The bad thing about retirement is that it means you get twice as much of your spouse on half as much money.

At his retirement presentation old Tom was told by his boss, "We don't know how we'll manage without you. Mainly because we're not sure exactly what it was you did here."

It is time I stepped aside for a less experienced and less able man.

Scott Elledge

Albert's boss is making a speech on the occasion of Albert's retirement. "Today we would like to thank Albert for his service to our company," says the boss. "Albert has always been someone who does not know the meaning of 'impossible task', who does not know the meaning of 'lunch break' and who does not understand the meaning of the word 'no'. So we have all clubbed together and bought Albert... a dictionary."

There's one thing I always wanted to do before I quit... retire!

Groucho Marx

You can always tell the guest of honour at a retirement dinner. He's the one who keeps yawning after the boss's jokes.

When you're retired you wake up in the morning with nothing to do and go to bed at night with it still not done.

When old Bill retired from his job, his boss made a little speech to all his colleagues and told them they weren't so much losing a worker as gaining an extra car park space.

The best time to start thinking about your retirement is before the boss does.

What The Comments In The Retirement Speech Really Mean

Active socially: drinks heavily.

Character above reproach: still one step ahead of the law.

Excels in the effective application of skills: makes a good cup of coffee.

Shows tremendous flair and imagination: some of those expenses claims could qualify for the Booker prize.

Has the energy of a man half his age: he's worn out 14 young secretaries so far – and that's just this year.

Has the respect of all his staff: he scares the living daylights out of them.

His honesty is beyond reproach: covers his tracks extremely well, and he even bunged me a few quid to say that.

Has enjoyed a long career: that's "career" as in "going down hill extremely fast".

Fitted in well with the rest of the team: he doesn't understand what's going on either.

Has helped turn this company round: from one of the most profitable firms in the sector to the basket case it is today.

Popular with colleagues: shows them all the ways to fiddle their expenses too.

His departure will be a great loss: to all the local pubs, wine bars and betting shops.

Great communication skills: can yabber away on the phone at the company's expense for hours.

A born leader: a little Hitler.

Has made great personal sacrifices for the company: keeps his lunch break down to two and a half hours.

Has a good relationship with his superiors: a right little creep.

Shows initiative: has set up a private business fully equipped with office machinery and stationery nicked from the company.

Will never be forgotten: we will pursue him through the courts until every last penny he embezzled has been repaid.

Never misses an opportunity: to get out of working.

Possesses people skills: is a person.

Visionary thinker: spends most of the day looking out of the window.

Irreplaceable: thank God!

Internationally known: likes to go to conferences and trade shows in Las Vegas.

Is well informed: knows all the office gossip and where all the skeletons are kept.

Tactful in dealing with superiors: knows when to keep his mouth shut.

Willing to take calculated risks: doesn't mind spending someone else's money.

A Wrinkly Looks Back At His Career

My first job was working in an orange juice factory, but I got canned ... couldn't concentrate.

Then I worked in the woods as a lumberjack, but I just couldn't hack it, so they gave me the chop.

After that I tried to be a tailor, but I just wasn't suited for it... mainly because it was a so-so job.

Next I tried working in a car spares factory, but that was too exhausting.

Then I tried to be a chef – figured it would add a little spice to my life but I just didn't have the thyme.

I attempted to be a deli worker, but any way I sliced it, I couldn't cut the mustard.

My best job was being a musician, but eventually I found I wasn't noteworthy.

I studied a long time to become a doctor, but I didn't have any patience.

Next was a job in a shoe factory... I tried but I just didn't fit in.

I became a professional fisherman, but discovered that I couldn't live on my net income.

I managed to get a good job working for a pool maintenance company, but the work was just too draining.

So then I got a job in a workout centre, but they said I wasn't fit for the job.

After many years of trying to find steady work, I finally got a job as a historian, until I realized there was no future in it.

My last job was working at a coffee shop, but I had to quit because it was always the same old grind.

So I retired and I found I am perfect for the job!

Homes For Retired Wrinklies

An old people's home gets a celebrity visit from Cliff Richard. Cliff arrives and before he leads them all in a sing-along, he goes round saying hello to all the elderly residents. Unfortunately no-one seems to recognize him, so Cliff says to one old lady, "What about you? Do you have any idea who I am?" "No, sorry, dear," says the old lady. "But let's call one of the nurses over. I'm sure they'll be able to tell you."

The old people's home next gets a special visit from Bruce Forsyth. Bruce tells the residents a series of funny jokes and they all seem to find his act extremely amusing. Afterwards Bruce says to the matron, "That seemed to go well, dear. A couple of the audience laughed so much they wet themselves." "Don't kid yourself, Bruce," says the matron, "they'd have done that whether you were here or not."

A man finds a place for his elderly mother at a care home. All the residents are given a wristband on which can be written details of any food allergies they have. Unfortunately the man is not told about this and, when he comes to visit his mother the next day, he is furious when he finds the staff have stuck a wrist band on her on which is written the single word, "Bananas".

A man goes to visit his elderly mother who is in a retirement home. When he gets there he is told his mother is asleep at the moment, but if he wishes he can sit by her bed and wait until she wakes up. As he sits there he looks through her newspaper and magazines, and eats his way through a packet of peanuts on her bedside cabinet. When she wakes up, he apologizes, "I'm terribly sorry, Mum. I think I've just eaten your entire packet of peanuts." "That's OK, dear," says his mum. "I'm not very keen on nuts. That's why I always just nibble the chocolate off and put them back in the packet."

Two very old men are sitting outside the Sunnyglades rest home watching the world go by when one asks the other how he's feeling today. "Oh," he says, "do you know what, I feel just like a little baby." "What happy and healthy and full of energy?" "No," says the other one, "bald and toothless, and I think I've just filled my nappy."

A charity organized a special Christmas lunch for elderly people in the area and a couple of weeks after the event they were charmed to receive a thank you letter from one of the guests. She wrote: "I am just writing to thank you for your kindness in inviting me to the Christmas lunch, where I was lucky enough to win a lovely portable radio in the raffle. In my retirement home I share a room with another elderly lady who would occasionally allow me to listen to her radio when she was feeling generous, until it broke recently. Now I have my own radio and when she asks if she can listen to it I can say, 'No, you can't you old cow!'"

The manager of an old people's home decides to hire an animal act to entertain everyone at the home's annual tea-party. He calls a theatrical agent and asks what sort of acts he has to offer. "I've got a tiger," says the agent. "It does a high wire act and juggles plates." "Too dangerous!" replies the manager. "It might fall on someone or bite them." "How about a performing seal?" says the agent. "It can play a variety of musical instruments." "Too noisy," replies the manager. "The old folk won't like it. What we need is something unusual, but nice and sedate, so it won't upset them." "I know," says the agent. "How about Morris the gibbon? He's very quiet. All he does is card tricks." "Perfect," replies the manager. "So... Let's try a mellow gibbon round the old folk's tea..."

The Wrinklies' Guide To Understanding The Modern World

The modern world can be a confusing and bewildering place for people who grew up with fewer than 200 TV channels. Some of these new-fangled terms, such as "user friendly" or "balsamic vinegar" are simply lost on folk who can still remember when all mail was first class. So here, for the help of you third-agers, are a few translations you might find handy:

Gender issues – when women think that they get a raw deal, but quite like being women when blokes buy them a drink, pay for them to get married, etc.

Internet chat room – where you can talk to complete strangers without ever meeting them – a bit like being cold-called by a telephone banking salesman.

Gay marriage – you've heard of the gay divorce? Well this is what immediately precedes it.

Pensions time bomb – something you hope will go off after you've gone off.

Biodegradable carrier bags – ones that will fall apart after a few years, unlike the unbiodegradable ones that fall apart as soon as you start lugging your shopping home from the supermarket.

Call centre – a place where British people can still indulge in their favourite hobby of queuing, even when they're housebound.

Supermodel – a model who can tell people to get stuffed.

Celebrity chef – just like a normal chef, but with swearing.

Farmers' market – where you can buy fresh produce without going to the supermarket, though for some reason they usually hold them just outside the supermarket, so you have to go there anyway.

Skinny latte – a glass of hot milk for three quid.

Rogue trader – just like an ordinary trader, but one who gets caught.

Virtual reality – like ordinary reality just after you've taken a couple of those little green pills the doctor gave you.

Hoodie – item of clothing that disguises the wearer's face – or, in other words, a cheap alternative to plastic surgery.

Second life – an alternative life in cyberspace where you can take on a new persona and live in a world divorced from reality – very similar to dementia.

Love In Old Age

I don't date women my own age – there are no women my own age.

George Burns

An 85-year-old widow goes out on a blind date with a 90-year-old man. When she gets home later that night, she seems to be rather upset. "What happened?" asks her daughter. "Oh it was terrible," says the old widow. "I had to slap that man's face three times." "Oh no," says the daughter. "You don't mean he got fresh with you?" "I wish he had," says the old widow. "No, I kept thinking he was dead."

An old man and an old lady are sitting in their garden one evening. "I remember," says the old lady, "when we were first courting you used to kiss me every time we were alone." And so the old man stretches over and kisses her. Then she says, "And I remember when we were first courting you used to hold my hand whenever you could." And so the old man reaches over and takes her hand. Then the old lady says, "And I remember when we were first courting you used to love to nibble my ears all the time." With this the old man groans, gets up and starts hobbling towards the house. "Where are you going?" asks the old lady. "I'll be back in a minute," says the old man. "I've just got to get my teeth."

An old man and an old woman have been dating for a little while and decide to get married. As part of the preparations for the wedding they visit their local chemist's shop. Inside the old man asks the chemist, "Tell me, do you supply a range of heart medicines here?" "Oh yes," says the chemist. "What about vitamin supplements?" asks the old man. "Of course," says the chemist. "Lumbago ointment?" "Yes." "Pills for arthritis." "Yes." "Viagra." "Yes." "Incontinence pants." "Yes." "Excellent," says the old man and then calls over to his bride to be, "Darling, I think we've found just the place to do our wedding list."

Old Bert falls in love with old Ethel and decides to propose. As a stickler for tradition, Bert takes Ethel's hand, gets down on one knee and tells her there are two things he would like to ask her. "What's the first?" asks Ethel. "Will you marry me?" says old Bert. "Oh yes," says Ethel. "What's the second?" "Can you help me back up?" says Bert.

Senior Citizens' Personal Ads

BEATLES OR STONES? I still like to rock, still like to cruise in my Camaro on Saturday nights looking for rock gods to fiddle with my g-string. If you were a groovy stag, or are now a groovy bull, let's get together and listen to my boss collection of eight-track tapes. No baldies, please.

FOXY LADY: Sexy, fashion-conscious blue-haired beauty, 80s, slim, 5'-4" (used to be 5'-6"), searching for sharp-looking, sharp-dressing companion. Matching white shoes and belt a plus.

LONG-TERM COMMITMENT: Recent widow who has just buried fourth husband looking for someone to round out a six-unit plot. Dizziness, fainting, shortness of breath not a problem.

MEMORIES: I can usually remember Monday to Thursday. If you can remember Friday, Saturday and Sunday, let's put our two heads together.

MINT CONDITION: Male, 1932, high mileage, good condition, some hair, many new parts, including hip, knee, cornea, valves. Isn't in running condition, but walks well.

SERENITY NOW: I am into solitude, long walks, sunrises, the ocean, yoga and meditation. If you are the silent type, let's get together, take our hearing aids out and enjoy quiet times.

WINNING SMILE: Active grandmother with original teeth seeking a dedicated flosser to share rare steaks, corn on the cob and caramel toffee.

READY TO SHINE: Smooth male (i.e. bald), 60s, GSOH, looking for a head wax, buff and polish.

Wrinkly Sex

Wrinkly sex. Hmm, doesn't sound very attractive does it, but that's what light switches are for. Anyway, the older people get the less they are interested in sex, or possibly, the less sex is interested in them. When was the last time you saw anyone with grey hair in the *Playboy* centrefold? No, people find that they are more interested in things like gardening as they get older. Gardening is the new sex. And why not? It lasts longer, gives you more exercise and you don't have to expose your ageing body to the ridicule of your partner. And if you think about it maybe older people aren't supposed to be having sex. Nature generally only allows women to have babies up to the age of about 40-ish, anything after that is for the purposes of recreation rather than procreation. Mother Nature is basically saying, "All right, if you will insist on having sex even when you are not trying to have babies then I'm going to do my utmost to stop anyone wanting to go to bed with you" – and this is where the wrinkles come in.

An old couple are sitting on their sofa watching television one night. During one of the commercial breaks, the old woman asks, "Whatever happened to our sexual relations?" After a long thoughtful silence, her slightly deaf husband replies, "I don't know. We didn't even get a Christmas card from them last year did we?"

Sex for an old guy is a bit like shooting pool with a rope.

George Burns

An old couple are sitting in the local park on a beautiful spring day. "Spring days like this really take me back," says the husband. "Do they?" says his wife. "Tell me, do you remember the first time we ever made love?" The old man sits and thinks for a moment and then says, "No. In fact to be honest with you, I can't remember the last time."

Two old soldiers are watching young girls walk by in the park one day when one says to the other, "You remember how when we were young servicemen, they used to put Bromide in our tea to stop us thinking about girls." "Yes," says his friend. "Well," says the first, "I think mine's finally begun to work."

An old man was passing a group of giggling teenagers in the park. "What's the joke, lads?" asked the old man. "Oh nothing," said one boy, "we were just seeing who could tell the biggest lie about their sex life." "You young boys just disgust me!" exclaimed the old man. "Do you know, when I was your age, I never even thought about sex." After a pause the boys all cried in unison, "OK, granddad! You win!"

Three middle-aged women are talking about their love lives. Daphne says, "My husband is like a Rolls-Royce convertible; smooth, sleek and sophisticated."

Beryl says, "Mine is like a Ferrari. Fast, furious and incredibly powerful." Blanche, the oldest one of the group, says, "Mine's like an old Morris Minor: needs a hand start and you have to jump on quick once you've got it going."

One afternoon, an elderly couple are relaxing in front of the television. Suddenly, the woman is overcome with lust and says to her husband, "Let's go upstairs and make love." "Which would you prefer?" asks her elderly husband. "I'm not sure I can do both."

An old man shuffles very slowly into the doctor's surgery and says, "Doctor, I need you to give me something to lower my sex drive." "How old are you?" asks the doctor. "Ninety-six," says the man. "Ninety-six and you want to lower your sex drive!" says the doctor. "I would have thought at your age, it's all in your head." "It is," says the old man. "That's why I want you to lower it."

Two ageing married men are talking. "So, how's your sex life?" says the first. "I'm having old age pension sex," says the other. "Old age pension sex? What's that?" asks the first. "Oh, you know," says the second, "I get a little each month, but it's not really enough to live on!"

Old Bernard gets talking to a young man at his local pub. When the conversation turns to the young man's sexual conquests, Bernard tries to impress him by telling him how he has managed to keep sexually active himself, despite his advancing years. "So how often do you sleep with a woman?" asks old Bernard. "A few times a week," says the young buck. "Huh!" says Bernard. "My wife and I make love nearly every day." "Nearly every day!" says the young man. "But you must be nearly 80 years old." "It's true. We make love nearly every day," says Bernard. "We nearly made love on Monday. We nearly made love on Tuesday..."

An 87-year-old woman comes home from bingo one night and finds her 92-year-old husband in bed with their home help. The old woman becomes violent. She attacks her husband and pushes him off the balcony of their 20th floor flat. At her trial she pleads not guilty. "What do you mean 'not guilty'?" asks the judge. "You were seen doing it." "I know," says the old woman, "but I thought it was a reasonable assumption that if he was able to get up to that kind of thing at his age, he'd be able to fly as well."

A famous sex expert worked out that people usually lied about how often they had sex. So he devised a test to tell for certain how often a person made love. To prove his theory, he filled a lecture theatre with volunteers and went round them all, asking each of them to smile. By looking at the size of the person's smile, the expert was able to accurately assess the truth about the frequency of their sexual relations. When he came to the last volunteer, an elderly gentleman, who was grinning from ear to ear, the expert guesses he must have sex twice a day. "Oh no," said the old man. The expert was surprised at this so he tried again and suggested, "Once a day then." "No, no," said the old man. "Twice a week?" "No." "Twice a month?" "No." "Once a month?" "No." Eventually the expert got as far as once a year and the old man said, "Yes!" "I can't believe it," said the sex expert. "This completely disproves my theory. So if you only have sex once a year what are you looking so damn happy about?" "Tonight's the night," said the old man.

A man decides to surprise his elderly grandfather by hiring the services of a call girl to visit him on his 90th birthday. The girl turns up on his doorstep and tells him, "Hi, I'm here to offer you super sex." "Oh really?" says the old man. "OK. I think I'll have the soup then please."

A senior citizen shuffles painfully into a house of ill repute and asks how much it will cost him for a night of pleasure. "Two hundred pounds," replies the madam. "Two hundred pounds!" splutters the old man. "Are you putting me on?" "We can if you want," says the madam, "but that will be an extra ten quid."

Albert Grimshaw was about to reach the grand old age of 100 and he decided to celebrate the event by making love for the first time in many years. When the happy day came the Queen sent him a telegram and the Duke of Edinburgh sent him a diagram.

One evening in the retirement home 90-year-old Elsie came downstairs in a see-through negligee and approached three old men sitting on the sofa. "Now then, boys," she announced, holding up a clenched fist, "whoever can guess what I'm holding in my hand gets to spend the night with me making wild passionate love!" "An elephant?" suggested one appalled old man. "That's close enough, dearie!" she said, grabbing him by the hand and leading him away.

An old lady goes to a specialist and tells him that she's obsessed with sex and believes she might even be a nymphomaniac. "I might be able to help you," says the psychiatrist. "But I better tell you, I charge £200 per hour." "I see," says the old lady. "How much would it be for the whole night?"

An old man and wife go to see their doctor and ask if they can have an AIDS test. The doctor is shocked and surprised. "But why?" he asks, "You've been together for 45 years, you've not had other partners." The old man replied, "No, but they said on the radio this morning that you should go for a test after having annual sex."

Two old widows in their 80s are sitting in their chairs in their retirement home. "Tell me," says one to the other, "when you were married, did you and your husband have mutual orgasms?" The second old widow thinks for a few moments and then says, "No, I think we were with the Prudential."

Two old soldiers, Bert and Tom, are sharing a glass of malt in the corner of their club one evening. "Tell me," says Bert to Tom, "when was the last time you made love to a woman?" Tom considers this for a minute and says, "1947." "Good Lord!" says Bert. "That's an awfully long time ago." "No it's not," says Tom. "It's only a couple of minutes past eight o'clock now."

An elderly man hobbles into a brothel and tells the madam he would like a young girl for the night. Surprised, she looks at the ancient wizened creature and asks how old he is. "I'm 90 years old," gasps the old fellow. "Ninety years old!" replies the madam. "Sorry, pop. I think you've had it." "Oh, have I?" says the old man, fumbling for his wallet. "So how much do I owe you?"

Q: How does an ageing car mechanic make love?
A: He attaches jump leads to his nipples and gets a start from a younger man.

Tips On Lovemaking For Wrinklies

Create that special mood by adjusting the lighting. SWITCH THEM ALL OFF!

Don't worry about making all the noise you want. Your neighbours are probably deaf too.

Keep extra Polygrip close by to avoid the embarrassment of losing your teeth under the bed.

Make sure you put 999 on your speed dial before you begin. Maybe call ahead?

Put on your glasses and have a quick double check that your partner is actually in bed with you.

Set your bedside alarm for three minutes' time in case you happen to doze off halfway through the proceedings.

Write your partner's name on a pad at the side of the bed in case it slips your memory.

If it works, call everybody you know and tell them the good news.

And remember, whatever else you do, don't think about trying to do it a second time.

Remember to record your favourite TV shows that evening, just in case you get stuck on top of each other and don't make it down in time.

Ask a neighbour to come and check in on you in 20 minutes. Just in case.

Open a window. You may need to shout for help.

Signs You May Be Going Through The Menopause

The Phenobarbital dose that wiped out the Heaven's Gate Cult is the only thing that gives you four hours of decent rest.

You change your underwear after every sneeze.

You have to write post-it notes with your kids' names on them.

Your husband jokes that instead of buying a wood stove, he is using you to heat the family room this winter. Rather than simply saying you are not amused, you shoot him.

You're on so much oestrogen that you take your Brownie troop on a field trip to see the Chippendales.

Oooh, Young Man!

Three little old ladies are sitting on a park bench when a man in a raincoat jumps out from a bush and flashes at them. Two of the women have a stroke, but the other one can't quite reach.

A little old lady walks into a police station. "I want to report something, officer," she tells the desk sergeant. "I was walking through the park when a great big beast of a man leapt out of the bushes and molested me all over my body." "Oh yes," says the policeman, "and did this happen this morning?" "No," says the old lady. "It was in 1957." "That's quite a long time ago," says the policeman, "why are you telling me about it now?" "Oh, you know," says the old lady, "it's nice just to reminisce occasionally."

An old lady calls the police round to her house. She tells them she is shocked and appalled because the man who lives in the house opposite keeps wandering around his bedroom completely naked. The policeman looks out of her window to check and says, "But you can't see into his bedroom from this window." "No," says the old lady, "but you can if you climb on top of the wardrobe and look out of the skylight."

An old maid gets held up in a dark alley. She says she has no money on her, but the robber insists that she's lying and that she's got her cash hidden somewhere about her person. He then starts feeling all over her trying to find the money. After a few minutes of squeezing and fiddling with every bit of her body, the old lady says, "I told you, young man, I haven't got any money. But… ooo-er… if you keep doing that I could always write you a cheque!"

Two old dears go to the zoo and visit the elephants' enclosure. One male elephant seems to be in a bad mood and is rampaging around with a large erection. "Oh my goodness!" says Ethel. "Do you think he'll charge?" Her friend replies, "By the look of him, love, I think he'd be entitled to, don't you?"

An old lady calls the emergency services in a desperate state. "Send someone over quickly!" screams the old woman into the phone. "Two naked men are climbing towards my bedroom window!" "This is the Fire Department, lady," says the voice at the other end of the phone. "I'll have to transfer you to the Police Department." "No, no," says the old lady. "It's YOU I want! They need a longer ladder!"

Wrinkly Nudity

An old lady goes to the Chelsea Flower Show, where she whips off all her clothes and streaks through the judges' enclosure. In the end they decide to award her first prize for Best Dried Arrangement.

Two ageing university lecturers are sunbathing on the veranda of their apartment at a nudist resort. "So tell me," says one, "have you read Marx?" "Yes I have," says the other, "I think it must be this wicker chair I'm sitting on."

A little old lady goes out shopping on a windy day and as she's walking along the high street her hat blows off. She tries to grab it and her skirt is blown up over her head, revealing that she's not wearing any underwear. A passing policeman then books her for indecent exposure. When she gets to court the magistrate asks why she didn't use her hands to hold her skirt in place rather than trying to grab her hat.

"Well," she says, "Everything under my skirt is 87 years old, but my hat was brand new!"

Two old men are sitting in the garden of a home for retired gentle folk. Suddenly one of the elderly female residents runs past them, streaking. "My goodness!" says the first. "Wasn't that Elsie Clitheroe?" "I think it was," says his friend. "She's 98, you know," says the first. "Yes," says the other. "What was that she was wearing?" "I don't know," says his companion. "But it looked like it could do with a good iron."

Viagra

If you're depressed and think you might need Viagra, see a professional. If that doesn't work, see a doctor.

Two old men are talking. "My doctor's refused to give me Viagra," says one. "Why?" asks the other. "Because," says the first, "he said it would be like sticking a new flagpole on a condemned building.

The marketers of Viagra have a new slogan, "Let the Dance Begin". This is better than the original, "Brace Yourself, Grandma!"

Jay Leno

An old couple are sitting at home one day when the old lady asks her husband, "So, granddad are you going to take any of those Viagra tablets I got for you?" The old man looks at her and says, "No, I'm not." "Why not?" asks the old lady. "Because," says the old man, "there's no point putting lead in your pencil if you haven't got anyone worth writing to."

I started my new diet this morning. It consists of Viagra and prune juice. Now I can't tell if I'm coming or going!

An ageing couple are in bed one morning in an amorous embrace when the wife says: "Darling, our love life is wonderful again now that you've started taking Viagra, but I think I'd better go and make us a full English breakfast." "Oh no," says her husband. "I'm not hungry at all. The Viagra takes away my appetite." Later in the day, the wife says: "Darling, I want to make you a nice wholesome lunch." "No, no," says the husband. "I'm just not hungry after using that Viagra." At dinner time, the wife tries again, "Are you hungry yet? I can make us a steak and kidney pie." "No," says the husband, "I'm telling you for the last time, Viagra seems to kill my appetite." "OK," says the wife, "but I need to get myself something to eat, so for the last time, will you just get off me so I can get out of bed!"

An old man goes to his doctor and gets his prescription for Viagra. The doctor tells him to take the tablet now and then in an hour's time he'll be able to give his wife a nice surprise. When the old man gets home from the doctor's surgery he discovers that his wife has gone out shopping and won't be back for some time. He phones the doctor and tells him, "I've already taken the tablet and now it's going to be wasted." "That's a bit of a shame," says the doctor. "Do you have a housekeeper? If you do you could occupy yourself with her instead." "That's no good," says the old man. "Why not?" says the doctor. "Well," says the old man, "I don't need Viagra with the housekeeper."

Did you hear about the old man who made an appointment with an impotence clinic? He had to cancel because something came up.

An old man is telling his friend about his Viagra tablets. "It's the greatest thing I've ever known," he says. "It's the Fountain of Youth! It makes you feel like you're young again." "Can you get it over the counter in the chemist's?" asks his friend. "You can if you take six," replies the first.

An old man walks into a chemist's and asks for a bottle of Viagra. The pharmacist says, "Do you have a prescription?" "No," says the old man, "but here's a picture of my wife."

An old man goes to the chemist to get himself some Viagra, but is horrified by the price. "I can't believe it, £40 for two tablets," says the old man. "That's a disgrace!" "It's not too bad," says his wife. "After all, it works out at only £20 a year."

An old man goes on holiday, but falls asleep on the beach and ends up with terrible sunburn. Wincing in pain, the old man hobbles off to the local doctor for help. The doctor takes one look at him and says, "There's not much I can do about sunburn this bad, but here's some Viagra for you." "What?" says the old man. "How is Viagra going to help my sunburn?" "It's not," says the doctor. "But it will help keep the sheets off you in bed tonight."

An elderly man goes to his chemist and asks for a prescription of Viagra. "OK," says the pharmacist. "How many do you want?" "I want 12 tablets," says the old man, "and I want you to cut each of them into quarters for me." "Why do you want me to do that?" asks the pharmacist. "A quarter of a tablet won't do much for you." "Look, son," says the old man, "I'm over 90 years old. I don't need the tablets for sex. I just need them to make sure that when I go to the toilet it's sticking out far enough so it doesn't go all over my shoes."

An old man is at his dentist's. The dentist examines him and says, "I'm going to have to take one of your teeth out. I'm going to give you a shot of Novocain and I'll be back in a few minutes." The old man grabs the dentist's arm. "No! Please," he says, "I hate needles!" "OK," says the dentist. "Then I'll have to give you gas." "That's no good either," says the old man. "The gas always makes me sick for days." "In that case," says the dentist, "you'd better take this

Viagra tablet." "Viagra?" says the old man. "Will that kill the pain?" "No," says the dentist, "but it will give you something to hang on to while I'm pulling your tooth."

Some nursing homes are giving their elderly male patients Viagra in their night time mug of cocoa. Apparently the cocoa helps them sleep, while the Viagra helps stop them from rolling out of bed in the night.

Viagra claimed its first victim last week after an old man took an overdose. It wasn't the old man who passed away, however. It was his wife who died of exhaustion.

Did you hear about the boatload of Viagra that went down on Loch Ness? A few minutes later the monster came up.

Q: What do you get if you mix Viagra and Prozac?
A: An old man who is ready to go, but doesn't really care where.

A truck carrying a load of Viagra slid off the road and fell into the Ohio River. Now none of the lift bridges will go down.

Q: What happens to men who take Viagra at the same time as being on a course of iron supplements?
A: Every time they get an erection, it points north.

Q: What's the difference between Niagara and Viagra?
A: Niagara Falls.

An old man tries Viagra for the first time, but when he swallows the tablet it gets stuck in his throat. The next morning he wakes up with a stiff neck!

Q: What's the similarity between Viagra and Alton Towers?
A: They both involve an hour's wait before a two-minute ride.

Q: What do you get when you smoke pot and take Viagra?
A: Stiff joints!

Old men don't need Viagra, because they're impotent. Old men need Viagra because old women are very, very ugly.

Jimmy Carr

They May Be Wrinkly But They've Still Got It

An old man is celebrating his 100th birthday. The local newspaper sends a reporter to cover the story. "Well," says the reporter, "you seem in remarkably good shape. What's the secret of living so long?" "There's no secret," says the old man. "It's probably just because I've never messed around with women and I've never touched a drop of alcohol." Just then there's a crash and a scream from a room upstairs. "Oh my goodness," says the reporter, "what was that?" "Don't worry about that," says the old man, "it's just my dad. He's pissed again and chasing the home help round the bedroom."

A 90-year-old man has been married four times, but appears at his doctor's to announce that he is getting married again, to a highly sexed 18-year-old girl. "Are you mad?" says the doctor. "You realize that if you start having frequent sex again it could prove fatal." "Ah well," says the old man, "if she dies, she dies."

An old man goes to his doctor's and says he is worried about his failing sex drive and that his wife might stray if he is no longer able to satisfy her. "Hang on!" says the doctor to the old man. "How old are the pair of you?" "I'm 82," says the old man. "And my wife is 79." "OK," says the doctor. "And when did you notice this problem with your sex drive?" "Twice last night," says the old man, "and once again this morning."

An ageing spinster is sitting on a park bench one day all on her own. A rough looking man walks over and sits at the other end of the bench. After a few moments, the woman asks, "Are you a stranger here?" "I used to live here years ago," says the man. "Oh," says the woman. "So, where were you all these years?" "In prison," he says. "Oh," says the woman. "What did they put you in prison for?" And the rough man looks at her and very quietly says, "I got into a wild drunken rage one night and I killed my wife in the most violent terrible way imaginable." "Oh," says the woman. "So you're single then..."

An old man says to his friend, "You know, even though I'm old, I've definitely still got it." "Oh yes," says his friend. "Yes," says the old man. "The problem is nobody wants it any more."

Taking Precautions

An old lady goes to her doctor and asks for contraceptive tablets, claiming they help her sleep at night. "Why would contraceptive pills make you sleep any better than normal?" asks the doctor. The old lady replies, "Because I put them in my granddaughter's coffee."

Eighty-year-old spinster Miss Jones was the organist in her local church and was admired for her sweetness and kindness to all. One afternoon the vicar visited her at home and she showed him into her old fashioned living room. She invited him to take a seat while she made them some tea. As he sat facing her old Hammond organ, the vicar noticed a glass bowl sitting on top of it. The bowl was filled with water and in the water floated a condom! When Miss Jones returned with their tea and biscuits, the vicar couldn't help but ask about the condom floating in the glass bowl. "Oh, yes," Miss Jones replied, "isn't it wonderful? I was walking through the park a few weeks ago and I found this little package on the ground. The directions said to place it on the organ, keep it wet and that it would prevent the spread of disease. And do you know I haven't had a cold all winter?"

Two old ladies are standing outside their nursing home so they can have a smoke. The sky darkens and it begins to rain. Feeling the patter of raindrops, one of the old ladies reaches into her handbag and pulls out a condom. She cuts off the end, slides the rubber tube over her cigarette and continues smoking. "What are you doing?" says the old lady standing with her. "These things are really handy," says the other old lady, showing her packet of condoms. "If it starts to rain, you put them over your cigarette and it doesn't get all wet and spoilt." "What a good idea," says her friend. "Where can I get a packet of these miniature cigarette Pac-a-macs?" "You can get them at any chemist," says her companion. So the old lady hobbles off to the local chemist and announces loudly to the young man behind the counter that she wants to purchase a box of condoms. The pharmacist is rather taken aback by this, but asks her if there is any particular brand that she prefers. "No, that doesn't matter, young man," says the old lady, checking the pack of cigarettes in her bag, "just as long as they're big enough to fit a Camel."

Things That Make You Feel Old (Even When You're Not)

We all get old eventually – if we're lucky. But what about when you're not actually that advanced in years, but certain things make you feel old very suddenly and bring you down to earth with a shuddering jolt? For example:

Bald Punks

It doesn't seem five minutes ago that the nation was being shocked and horrified, largely via some lurid tabloid reportage, by those spitting, swearing, snarling punks. Maybe you were even a punk yourself, but now, thanks to all those TV documentaries about the 1970s or rock music, we suddenly find ourselves confronted by fat, bald, middle-aged men who apparently once used to be punk rockers. Suddenly they seem as threatening as suet puddings, but even worse they make you feel ancient.

Documentaries About the 80s

If punk seems five minutes ago, then the 80s are a mere nanosecond back in time. It's probably a sign that TV executives are getting younger and they want to trawl over the ashes of their recent youth, but for goodness sake, some of us are still wearing ripped jeans and playing with Rubik cubes. Nostalgia it ain't.

Rock Star Children

Just when you thought you'd heard the last of certain rock stars from the 60s and 70s, who should start popping up in the gossip columns but their flipping children! Spoilt brats with silly names falling out of nightclubs or launching their own doomed careers in a haze of cocaine and their own celebrity scent. And when their children hit the front pages you know it's time to apply for your bus pass – and hope that it will take you away from all this.

Fashion Revivals

If you're past 50 then your flared trousers alone have probably necessitated you fitting a revolving door to your wardrobe. Those loons have been in and out more often than the cuckoo in your granny's favourite clock. And each time one of the fashions from your youth is revived you realize another decade has slipped by. Why can't these overpaid fashion designers think of something new instead of making you feel old?

Culture Shift

Remember when you used to listen to Radio 1 because it had all your favourite music on it? Then you woke up one morning to find that they were playing modern stuff and all your faves had been relegated to Radio 2? Then you found all your favourite DJs had gone there too, or to oldies stations. Then there was the first time you heard one of your all-time favourite records being used as background music at your bank, or worse still in a lift, or on a TV advert for toilet rolls or something. It's almost as if they're trying to tell you something.

Troublesome Wrinklies

An old man comes out of the newsagents and crosses over to the car parked opposite where a traffic warden is writing a ticket. "Oh come on!" says the old man. "I'm a pensioner. I can't afford to pay that, can I?" The traffic warden ignores him and continues writing the ticket. The old man becomes more abusive. "You fascist!" he says. "You slimy piece of I don't know what. You've got no heart. You pathetic, jumped up stupid little man!" The traffic warden proceeds to write another ticket and then another as the old man keeps ranting at him about his lack of consideration. The car ends up with five tickets on the windscreen. "You should have spoken to him a bit more nicely," says a passer by to the old man, "and then he might have let you off." "I don't care," says the old man. "This isn't my car."

An old man is making a long distance call in the USA when all of a sudden he gets cut off. He hollers, "Operator, giff me beck da party!" She says, "I'm sorry, sir, you'll have to make the call all over again." He says, "What do you want from my life? Giff me beck da party." "I'm sorry sir," says the operator, "you'll have to place the call again." "Operator, ya know vat?" says the old man. "You can take da telephone and shove it in you-know-vere!" And with that he hangs up. Two days later he opens the door and there are two big, strapping men standing in his way telling him, "We've come to take your telephone away." "Vy?" asks the old man. "Because," they say, "two days ago you insulted operator number 28. But if you'd like to call up and apologize, we'll leave the telephone here." "Vait a minute," says the old man, "vat's da rush? Vat's da hurry?" He goes to the telephone and dials. "Hello? Get me operator 28. Hello, operator 28? Remember me? Two days ago I insulted you? I told you to take da telephone and shove it in you-know-vere?" "Yes?" says the operator. "Vell," he says, "get ready… they're bringin' it to ya now!"

An old lady from a remote village in Cornwall goes to stay with her niece in Surrey. Nearby is a very well known golf course. On the second afternoon of her visit, the elderly lady goes for a walk. Upon her return, the niece asks, "Well, Auntie, did you enjoy yourself?" "Oh, yes, indeed," says the old lady. "Before I had walked very far, I came to some beautiful rolling fields. There seemed to be a number of people wandering around them, mostly men. Some of them kept shouting at me in a very eccentric manner, but I took no notice. There were four men who followed me for some time, uttering curious excited barking sounds. Naturally, I ignored them, too. Oh, by the way," she says holding out her hands, "I found a number of these curious little round white balls, so I picked them all up and brought them home hoping you could explain what they're all about."

Two guys left the bar after a long night of drinking, jumped in the car and started it up. After a couple of minutes, an old man appeared in the passenger window and tapped lightly. The passenger screamed, "Look at the window. There's an old ghost's face there!" The driver sped up, but the old man's face stayed in the window. The passenger rolled his window down part way and, scared out of his wits, said, "What do you want?" The old man softly replied, "You got any tobacco?" The passenger handed the old man a cigarette and yelled, "Step on it!" to the driver, while rolling up the window in terror. A few minutes later they calmed down and started laughing again. The driver said, "I don't know what happened, but don't worry; the speedometer says we're doing 80 now." All of a sudden there was a light tapping on the window and the old man reappeared. "There he is again," the passenger yelled. He rolled down the window and shakily said, "Yes?" "Do you have a light?" the old man quietly asked. The passenger threw a lighter out of the window, saying, "Step on it!" They were driving about 100 miles an hour, trying to forget what they had just seen and heard, when all of a sudden there came some more tapping. "Oh my God! He's back!" The passenger rolled down the window and screamed in stark terror, "WHAT DO YOU WANT WITH US?" The old man gently replied, "I just wondered if you wanted any help getting out of the mud?"

Three old men are chatting about their ancestors and boasting about what they had done in the forces. The first one says, "My great grandfather was in the First World War trenches and survived." The second one says, "Well my great grandfather was in the Boer War and he survived." Not to be outdone the third one says, "Well, if my great grandfather was alive today he'd be internationally famous." "Really?" say the other two, leaning forward. "Why's that?" "Because he'd be 153 years old," says the third old man.

An avid young golfer finds himself with a few hours to spare after work one day. He works out that if he hurries and plays as fast as he can, he could get in nine holes before he has to go home. Just as he is about to tee off an old gentleman shuffles onto the tee and asks if he could accompany the young man as he is golfing alone. The young golfer doesn't like to refuse and lets the old gent to join him. To his surprise the old man plays fairly quickly. He doesn't hit the ball far, but nevertheless plods along consistently without wasting much time. Eventually they reach the ninth fairway, and the young man finds himself with a tough shot. A large pine tree stands right in the direct line of his shot, between him and the green. After several minutes of debating how to hit the shot the old man finally tells him, "When I was your age I was able to hit the ball right over the top of that tree." With this gauntlet thrown down, the youngster swings as hard as he can and hits the ball right smack into the top of the tree trunk, where it thuds back on the ground less than a foot from where it started. "Damn it!" says the young golfer. "How on earth did you manage to hit the ball over that tree?" "Well," says the old man, "of course in those days the tree was only three feet tall."

A granddad is talking to his grandson. "How many miles do you walk to school?" asks granddad. "About half a mile," says the boy. "Huh!" snorts granddad. "When I was your age I walked eight miles to school every day. What grades did you get in your last report?" "Mostly Bs," says the boy. "Huh!" says granddad in disgust. "When I was your age I was getting all As. Have you ever been in a fight?" "Twice," says the boy, "and got beaten up both times." "Huh!" says granddad. "When I was your age I was in a fight every day. How old are you anyway? "Nine years old," says the boy. "Huh!" snorts granddad. "When I was your age I was 11."

An old man is finding it increasingly difficult to get around so he asks his similarly aged neighbour if he would mind popping into town to the post office to see if a package he is expecting has turned up yet. His old neighbour says he was going into town anyway to get his groceries. So off he totters, all the way down the street and into the town. The old man sits watching for several hours until eventually his elderly neighbour re-appears, slowly plodding all the way back down the street again. "So?" says the old man to his neighbour. "Was my package there?" "Oh yes," says the neighbour. "It's there all right."

An old man is telling his grandson about how he used to work in a blacksmith's when he was a boy. "Oh yes," says the old man, "I had to really toughen myself up to work in that place. Do you know I would stand at the back of my house, get a five-pound potato sack in my right hand and a five-pound potato sack in my left hand, and then raise my arms up and extend them straight out from my sides. I'd then stand there holding them out like that for as long as I could. After a while I moved onto ten-pound potato sacks, then 20-pound potato sacks. Finally I was able to do it with a pair of fifty pound potato sacks." "Wow, granddad," says the little boy. "That must have been hard." "Oh yes," says the old man, "it was. And it was even worse when I started putting potatoes in the sacks."

Wrinklies And The Law

A little old lady is in court for stealing a tin of peaches after absent-mindedly popping them into her bag rather than her trolley. Under the circumstances the judge decides to be lenient and asks her how many peaches there were in the tin. "There were three peaches," she replies. "Very well then," says the judge, "in that case I sentence you to three days in prison." Just then her husband pipes up and says, "She stole a tin of peas as well!"

An elderly lady calls 999 on her mobile phone. In a panic she calls for the police to come quickly, because her car has been broken into and a number of items have been stolen. "What exactly has been taken, madam?" asks the operator at the other end of the line. "Oh it's terrible, officer," says the old lady. "They've taken my car stereo. They've taken the steering wheel, the gear stick, the brake pedal and even the accelerator!" "My goodness," says the operator, "I've never heard of anything like this before. I'm sending someone out straightaway." A few minutes later the operator gets a call from the policeman attending the scene. "Case solved!" says the policeman. "The stupid old woman climbed into the back seat by mistake."

Old Tom and Old Ned used to meet in the park every day. One day Tom didn't turn up, but Ned presumed his friend must have caught a cold or something. A week passed by and Tom still didn't appear, so Ned began to worry. However, since the only time they ever met was at the park, Ned didn't know where Tom lived, so he couldn't check whether his friend was all right. A month passed by and Ned presumed he must have seen Tom for the last time, but then suddenly one day he reappeared. "Where have you been?" asked Ned. "I've been in prison," said Tom. "Prison!" said Ned. "How on earth did that happen?" "Well," said Tom, "you know the pretty waitress in the café I go to sometimes? One day she filed charges against me saying that I tried to molest her. I was taken to court and because I'm 89 years old, I was so proud that when I got in the dock I pleaded guilty and the judge gave me 30 days for lying under oath."

An elderly gentleman came home one night to find a homeless girl of about 18 ransacking his house. He grabbed her by the arm and was just about to call the police when the girl dropped down on her knees and begged him, "Please don't call the police! I'm in too much trouble already. In fact, if you don't call the police, I'll let you make love to me and do all the things you've ever wanted to do!" The old man thinks about this for a minute and finally yields to temptation. Soon the pair are in bed together, but despite the old man's very best efforts he finds he no longer has what it takes. Finally he gives up. He rolls over exhausted and reaches for the phone. "I'm sorry, young lady...but it's no use," he gasps. "It looks like I'm going to have to call the police after all."

Are You A Gaga Lout?

People complain about the young and their lack of manners, appalling language and general decorum, but what about some of the wrinklies? Oh, they may blame their boorishness on everything from the pills they're on to mild dementia, but the real reason they do it is because they know they can get away with it – and it's fun! So come on, own up – are you a gaga lout?

Do you use your walking stick not just as a mobility aid, but also as an offensive weapon? It's not for nothing that the humble and seemingly innocuous walking stick is known in some police circles as the "pensioners' baseball bat". And let's not get started on mobility carts, or "old bangers" as they are known.

When cold calling telephone salesmen ring do you turn up the ga-ga-ometer to 11 and engage them in a long and rambling conversation, at their expense of course, about your medical history, views on immigration and other sundry matters, before breaking into bouts of hysterical laughter?

Do you sit on city centre benches and swear at passers-by, knowing that the loopier you seem the less likely people are to come and sit next to you, and deprive you of somewhere to put your flask, sandwiches, newspaper and tartan blanket?

Do you make lewd remarks to younger people knowing that they'll simply regard you as a loveable old eccentric rather than the crusty old pervert you actually are?

Do you shoplift small items of groceries and then when caught say, "But I'm Napoleon, I own all ze shops in ze land and if you don't unhand me I will send you to the guillotine!"

Do you elbow your way to the front of the bus queue in the full knowledge that if anyone younger (and most people are) tries to stop you that you will then become a frail old pensioner again and they're the ones who'll be in trouble?

Do you pretend to be a bit deaf when people come to the door trying to sell cleaning materials, double-glazing or religion?

Or do you simply go into scary old person mode and frighten them off with such phrases as, "Ah, another victim! Would you like to come in and try some of my especially prepared sooooup?"

When children come trick or treating do you remove your false teeth, contort your features into a hideous gurn and open the front door holding a torch beneath your face?

Have you ever (now be absolutely honest here) feigned a fall in the street to get a ride home in an ambulance because you simply couldn't be bothered to walk?

Have you ever charged in mob-handed with a bunch of other coffin-dodgers to a Help The Aged shop and demanded all the money out of the till on the grounds that you want to cut out the middle man?

He / She Is So Old That...

He's so old that when he orders a three-minute egg, they ask for the money up front.

Milton Berle

Even his kids are drawing their pensions.

He remembers when Barbara Cartland didn't need make-up.

She can remember when Glenn Miller was considered a teenage fad.

If you ask him if he remembers the war, he asks which one.

She has to convert decimal prices to pounds, shillings and groats.

He compares the millennium celebrations with the previous lot.

The first time he celebrated Guy Fawkes Night it was the original one.

His first telephone book was just one foolscap sheet.

She can remember when the Queen Mum was a bit of all right.

When he took his driving test he had to pay a man to walk in front waving a red flag.

He can recall when a Czar was a Russian leader and not somebody who advised the government on drugs.

His earliest memories are all in black and white.

He can remember when the world heavyweight boxing champion was a white man.

She can remember when trains used to run on time.

He can remember when fast food meant Lent.

His first job was as a lamplighter.

He was a suspect in the Jack the Ripper murders.

He thought a pair of trainers was two sports coaches.

His bald head is coming up to its golden jubilee.

She still refers to the pictures as "the talkies".

They have to get the fire brigade to attend every time they light the candles on his birthday cake.

She can remember when Heinz only had one variety.

He could have been a waiter at the last supper.

He was the hot dog salesman at Custer's last stand.

When God said let there be light, he was the one who hit the switch.

In my lifetime I saw the Berlin Wall come and I saw it go. George Burns can say the same thing about the Ice Age.

Bob Hope

When he went to the Antiques Roadshow, someone appraised him.

When he walks past a graveyard, guys come running after him with shovels.

When he was a boy rainbows were in black and white.
He has an original autographed edition of the bible.

His birthday expired.

I told him to act his age and he dropped dead.

I'm so old they've cancelled my blood type.

Bob Hope

Old Bert says he's so old that when he was in school they didn't have history. Then it was called current affairs.

Her birth certificate is in Roman numerals.

In his school photo he was standing just in front of Moses.

He knew Burger King while he was still a prince.

She needs an archaeologist to do her make-up.

He's two years older than dirt.

When I was a boy the Dead Sea was only sick.

George Burns

She owes money to Caesar.

You Know You're Getting Old When...

Your children start saying, "Hey! That looks like a nice place, doesn't it?" when driving past nursing homes.

Your doctor doesn't bother giving you X-rays any more, he just holds you up against a sunny window.

Your ears are hairier than your head.

Your friends phone you up at nine o'clock at night and ask, "Did I get you out of bed?"

Your idea of a "night out" is spending an evening on the patio rocking chair.

Your insurance company has started sending you their free calendar... a month at a time.

Your knees buckle but your belt won't.

Your last visit to a specialist cost you more than you earned in your first four years at work.

Your memory is shorter and your complaining lasts longer.

Your mind starts to make contracts your body can't meet.

Your new reclining chair has more optional extras than your car.

Your photographic memory finally seems to have run out of film.

Your underwear starts creeping up on you… and you enjoy it.

Your wild oats turn to prunes and bran.

You're driving in your car, but can't remember where you're going – but it doesn't matter, you're not in a hurry.

You're 18 around the neck, 44 around the waist, and 105 around the golf course.

You're on a high-stakes TV game show and you decide to risk it all to go for the rocker.

You're on holiday and your energy runs out before your money does.

You're sitting on a park bench and have to ask a passing Boy Scout for help crossing your legs.

You're trying to straighten out the wrinkles in your socks, then discover you aren't wearing any.

Are You Trying Too Hard To Stay Young?

We all try to fight old age in our own way, don't we? We take up exercise, we try not to wear fuddy duddy clothes, we try as hard as possible not to use phrases like, "well, in my day...", we take up new hobbies and interests, do a bit of silver-surfing on the internet, absolutely refuse to buy *Saga* magazine and 101 other things, but sometimes we go too far. Extreme youthism is a dangerous game for an oldster, so have a look at the following list and see whether you are overdoing it a bit.

Do you find your walking stick a help or a hindrance when skateboarding?

Ladies – last time you put on make-up were you mistaken for Barbara Cartland?

When the teenagers next door have their music on a bit loud do you bang on the wall and shout "turn down the volume!" or bang on your drum kit and shout "pump up the volume!"

Men – are you torn between not wearing a trilby because it reminds you of what you wore in your youth or wearing one because Pete Doherty does?

Women – do you wear skimpy swimsuits that leave young men gasping – and running in the opposite direction?

Do you find that wearing a baseball cap back to front actually confuses you about what direction you should be going in when you walk away from the hall mirror?

When you attend raves in your hoodie do you find young people thinking they're hallucinating that you're a ghostly old monk?

Do you consider roller skates a fun mode of transport or an alternative mobility aid?

When you dance wildly at parties does a stranger attempt to pick you up – or just leave you lying on the floor?

Did you spend 45 minutes annoying the other people at your local internet cafe before you found out that you'd completely misunderstood what was meant by "internet chat room"?

When the local deli asks you if you want a "wrap" do you find yourself going into an impromptu impersonation of MC Hammer before being asked to leave by the management?

Do you need a specially adapted vacuum cleaner to administer your Botox injections?

Last Wishes

A very old man is lying on his deathbed. He summons his lawyer and tells him to make some last-minute changes to his will. "I wish to leave everything I own, all stocks, bonds, property, art and money to my nagging, spiteful, ungrateful, mean-spirited wife. However, there is one stipulation." "And that is?" asks the lawyer. "In order to inherit," says the old man, "she must marry within six months of my death." "That's a bit of an odd request," says the lawyer. "Why do you want to do that?" "Because," says the old man, "I want someone to be sorry I died."

Winston, an old Scotsman is dying and he calls for his best friend Rory to come to his bedside and listen to his dying wish. "Rory," whispers old Winston, his breath almost spent, "under my bed you'll find a bottle of the world's finest single malt. I've been saving it for this moment. When you come to my funeral would ye do me the great service of pouring the whiskey over my grave?" "Aye, of course I will, my friend," replies Rory and then adds, "But would you mind terribly if I pass it through my bladder first?"

A woman goes to the undertakers to see her late husband's body just before his burial. When she gets there she is shocked to find him dressed in a grey suit. "Oh no," she says. "I can't have him buried in a grey suit. He couldn't stand grey. He always said he wanted to be buried in a black suit." "I'm sorry, I can't do anything about it now, madam," says the undertaker. "It's too late. The funeral is going to begin in a few minutes." "But I insist!" shouts the woman, breaking into tears. "All right, madam," says the undertaker. "Calm down. I'll see what I can do." The undertaker pushes the trolley with the man's body out into the back room. A few moments later an assistant pushes the trolley back in with the woman's husband now dressed in a black suit. "My goodness that was quick!" says the undertaker under his breath. "How did you do it?" "Oh it wasn't too hard," says the assistant. "Luckily we had a bloke out there already dressed in a black suit so we just swapped the heads over."

An old lady in London decides to draw up her will and make her last requests. She tells her solicitor she is leaving her fortune to her daughters, but with two important conditions. Firstly, she says she wants to be cremated, and secondly, she wants her ashes scattered over the first floor of Harrod's department store. "Harrods!" says the solicitor. "Why Harrods?" "Well," says the old lady, "at least that way I'll be sure my daughters will visit my final resting place each week."

An old man lying on his deathbed summons his doctor, his lawyer and his priest. He hands out three separate envelopes to them. Each of the envelopes contains £30,000. "Gentlemen," he tells them solemnly, "they say you can't take it with you, but I am going to try. When they lower my coffin into my grave I want each of you to throw in these envelopes I have just given you." After the funeral the doctor confesses to the other two, "I've got to be straight with you. My health practice desperately needed some money to build a new clinic, so I kept £20,000 and just threw in £10,000." The priest also confesses, "The church is in desperate need of renovation. So I'm afraid I kept £10,000 and just threw in £20,000." The lawyer stands shaking his head in disgust. "I can't believe you two," he says. "Am I the only one of us who was decent enough to carry out the old man's dying wishes?" "So you threw in the entire £30,000!" say the doctor and the priest in astonishment. "Yes," says the lawyer. "Well… I threw in a cheque for the full amount."

Doris is dying and is already planning exactly how the funeral should be arranged, and calls in her husband. "Arthur," she says, "When you go to the church for my funeral I want you to promise that you'll sit next to my mother and keep her company." "Oh no," says Arthur, "Do I have to? You know I can't stand the woman, and she makes no secret of the fact that she can't stand me." "But Arthur," protested the woman, "it's my dying wish. Can't you make an effort just for me?" "Oh all right" says Arthur, "but I want you to know this is going to completely ruin the whole day for me."

The family of a rich old man gathers to hear his will being read. The solicitor solemnly opens the document and reads, "The last will and testament of John Smith. Being of sound mind, I therefore spent all my money."

You Know You're Getting Old When...

Licking the stamps to go on your letters to the hospital is a hard day's work.

Most of your co-workers were born the same year you got your last promotion.

Most of your day is spent making appointments with different doctors.

People tell you you're young-looking rather than telling you you're young.

Rocking all night means dozing off in your rocking chair.

Someone compliments you on your layered look – and you're wearing a bikini.

Taking out a year's subscription to a magazine is an act of positive thinking and real optimism.

The local "peeping tom" leaves a note saying: "Please pull the blinds down!"

The best part of your day is over when your alarm clock goes off.

The best way to make the wrinkles you see in the mirror disappear is simply to take off your glasses.

The car you bought brand new becomes a vintage model.

The clothes you put away until they come back in style... come back in style... for the second time.

The end of your tie doesn't come anywhere near the top of your trousers.

The girls at the office start confiding in you.

The little old lady you help across the street is your wife.

The names in your little black book are mostly doctors.

The only four-letter word you can think of to describe something you and your partner do in bed together is "read".

The only thing you find you ever exercise is caution.

The only thing you really want for your birthday is not to be reminded of your age.

The only time you kick-up your heels is when you fall down (and can't get up).

Wrinklies' End

Next time you hear anyone complaining about old age just ask them if they'd prefer the alternative. They'll probably say no – especially, of course, if the alternative is being bored to death with platitudes about old age. Death, they say is the last taboo. Well, it's the last everything really, isn't it? The good news is you only have to do it the once – unless you're a stand-up comedian with a rather poor act, when you can die every night or possibly die a thousand deaths in one solitary open mike spot. In fact, the real thing might actually be preferable to the sound of a couple of hundred unhappy punters screaming for your blood and chucking Belgian beer bottles. It's not for nothing that one of the most fearsome weapons in the world is known as a Heckler.

Two old men are talking. "I reckon death must be the best part of life," says one. "Why's that?" asks the other. "Because," says the first, "it always gets saved till last."

Dying is not popular; it has never caught on. That's understandable; it's bad for the complexion.

George Burns

Either he's dead or my watch has stopped.

Groucho Marx

It's not that I'm afraid to die, I just don't want to be there when it happens.

Woody Allen

Two recently bereaved women are chatting at a support group and one says, "Don't talk to me about solicitors, I've had so much trouble sorting out my late husband's will that I sometimes wish he hadn't died."

An old lady tells her friend, "My husband died the other day." "Oh dear," says her friend. "What of?" "The doctors aren't sure," says the old lady, "but they don't think it was anything serious."

Two old ladies bump into each other at the supermarket. "Hello, dear. How are you?" asks the first. "Oh I'm fine," says the second. "And what about your husband?" asks the first. "Oh, didn't you hear?"

says the second. "He died two weeks ago. He went out in the garden to dig up a cabbage for dinner, had a massive heart attack and fell over in the compost heap, stone dead." "Oh my goodness!" says the first old lady. "How absolutely terrible for you. What did you do?" "Well," says the second, "luckily I managed to find a tin of sweetcorn in the cupboard, so I had that instead."

A doctor had to inform an elderly lady that her husband had died as a result of a massive myocardial infarct. A short while later the doctor heard her reporting to the rest of her family that her husband had died of a "massive internal fart."

Two old men bump into each other in the park. One says to the other, "You've got to forgive me because my memory is getting terrible. Just remind me again will you, who was it died last week? Was it your wife or you?"

An old couple wake up one morning and the old man leans over to kiss his wife on the cheek. "No!" squeals his wife. "Don't touch me! I think I've died!" "What are you talking about, woman?" says the old man. "How can you have died when you're sitting up in bed with me." "I don't know," says the old woman, "but I think I've definitely died in my sleep." "Well, what makes you think that?" says the man. "Because," says the old woman, "I've just woken up and nothing's hurting."

I can't afford to die; I'd lose too much money.

George Burns

I don't mind dying, the trouble is you feel so bloody stiff the next day.

George Axlerod

I want to die peacefully, in my sleep, like my granddad. Not screaming and terrified, like his bus passengers.

Joe tells his friend Pete, "My granddad died last night." "Oh no," says Pete. "Yes," says Joe, "he was working late in the whisky distillery, he had to climb up to check in one of the vats, but being a bit doddery on his legs now he lost his balance and fell in." "Oh my goodness!" says Pete. "So what happened? Did he drown?" "Yes. After eight hours," says Joe. "Eight hours!" says Pete. "Why so long?" "Well it would have been quicker," says Joe, "but he had to get out three times to go to the toilet."

Roger and Catherine are talking one day and the subject turns to death. "What would you do if I died before you?" asks Roger. "Oh, I don't know really," says Catherine. "I suppose thinking about it, I'd have to sell this place, because it would be far too big for me, and then I'd get in touch with my best friend Julie and move in with her now her husband's gone. What about you?" "Hmm," says Roger, "probably exactly the same as you."

An old man asks his wife, "Darling, if I died, would you ever consider getting married again?" "I've no idea!" says his wife. "But maybe after a considerable period of grieving, I might consider it. After all, we all need companionship." "OK," says the old man, "but if I died and you got married again would your new husband live in this house?" "I've no idea!" says his wife. "But then again we've spent a lot of money getting this house the way we want it. I'm not going to get rid of it easily, so perhaps he would." "OK," says the old man, "and if I died and you got married again and your new husband came to live in this house, would he sleep in our bed?" "I've no idea!" says his wife. "But then again I suppose this bed is brand new and it cost us £2,000. It's going to last a long time, so maybe." "OK," says the old man, "and if I died and you got married again and he came to live in this house and slept in our bed, would you let him use my golf clubs?" "Oh no," says his wife. "He's left-handed!"

How young can you die of old age?

Steven Wright

There are worse things in life than death. Have you ever spent an evening with an insurance salesman?

Woody Allen

Fred tells Ethel, "Do you know, my granddad knew the exact date and the exact time that he would die." "That's uncanny," says Ethel. "Was he psychic then?" "No," says Fred. "The judge told him."

I know when I'm going to die... my birth certificate has an expiration date.

Steven Wright

Gertrude and Hilda are sitting in the bingo hall between games and looking out of the window. As they do so a funeral procession goes by and the name of the deceased, "Albert", is spelt out in flowers in the back of the hearse. Gertrude sniffs loudly and gets a hanky out of her handbag. Hilda says, "Oh you old softie!" "I can't help it," says Gertrude. "After all, he was a good husband to me."

Granddad was in hospital and one of his teenage grandchildren was looking after the cat while grandma was at work. One day the teenager went to visit her granddad in hospital and announced that the cat had died. "My poor old Polly?" said granddad, "You could have broken it to me gently. "How?" asked the teenager. "You could have said, Polly was playing on the roof, then she slipped and hurt herself, and you took her to the vet and he couldn't save her." "I see," said the teenager, "Sorry, Granddad." A week later the teenager went to visit granddad in hospital. "Hello," said Granddad, "How's Grandma?" "Well," said the teenager, "She was playing on the roof..."

Death is not the end. There remains the litigation over the estate.

Ambrose Bierce

If your time hasn't come, not even a doctor can kill you.

M A Perlstein

Funeral For A Wrinkly

Who was it who said, "Always go to other people's funerals or they won't come to yours" and was he speaking from experience? Still, it's the last chance you'll ever have of hearing lots of people saying nice things about you. Perhaps the only chance. And you in turn will have your last chance to inflict on them some dreadfully maudlin tune that may well have half of the congregation slitting their wrists and jumping in the coffin with you. Why should you be the only one who's suffering?

They say such nice things about people at their funerals that it makes me sad that I'm going to miss mine by just a few days.

Garrison Keillor

A funeral service is being held for a woman who has just passed away. At the end of the service, the pall bearers are carrying the coffin out when they accidentally bump into a wall, jarring the casket. They hear a faint moan! They open the lid of the coffin and are amazed to discover that the woman is still alive after all. She lives for another ten years before passing on. Once again, a funeral service is held and, at the end of it, the pall bearers pick up the coffin, and start carrying it out of the church. As they carry the coffin towards the door, the husband cries out: "This time will you watch out for that bloody wall!"

At an old man's funeral, the vicar talks at some length about the good life of the dearly departed, what a pillar of the community he has been, what a loving husband and kind father, and how he will be sadly missed by all his poor family. Listening to this, the old man's widow looks increasingly concerned. "Are you all right, Mum?" asks her son, fearing she is about to break down with emotion. "I'm fine," says the old lady, "but could you just go and have a quick look to make sure we've got the right person in the coffin. I'm not sure he can be talking about your father."

In the churchyard the undertaker is standing next to the grieving widow. The old woman is crying uncontrollably and so the undertaker tries to cheer her up by starting a conversation. "How old was your husband then?" he asks. "My Bert was 97," replies the widow. "Only a few months older than I am." "Oh dear. Is that so?" says the undertaker. "So really when you think about it, it's hardly worth you going home is it?"

A man is walking down a steep hill while at the top a funeral car has stopped at the church. As the back of the car is opened the coffin falls out and starts to slide down the hill, gathering speed as it does so.

The man hears the noise and turns round to see the coffin hurtling towards him, so he starts to run down the hill. By now the man and the coffin are rushing at breakneck speed, and the pharmacist comes out of the chemist's shop down the hill to see what the commotion is. As the man rushes past he shouts to the chemist, "Hey, can you give me something to stop this coffin!"

If you get fed up with elderly relatives coming up to you at weddings and saying, "You'll be next", try doing the same to them at funerals.

An elderly couple are discussing their funeral arrangements one day and the wife says to the husband, "So, Bert, when you die would you like to be buried or cremated?" "I don't know," replies her husband. "Surprise me!"

Did you hear about the local greengrocer's funeral the other week? Apparently there was a large turnip.

Wrinklies From Beyond The Grave

An old Jewish woman goes to a travel agent and asks for a holiday in Calcutta, because she wants to consult with the Indian mystics. "Oh, it won't be very suitable for a woman of your age," says the travel agent, "How about a nice cruise?" But the woman insists and takes the trip to Calcutta. When she gets there it's very hot, and there are flies buzzing round her as she comes out of the airport and boards a ramshackle old bus. She is on the bus for several uncomfortable hours and finally reaches a remote spot where there is a temple. There is a queue of people waiting to see the guru, so she waits and waits and waits until finally she is allowed in. "Now remember," says one of the men at the door of the temple, "You are only permitted to utter five words to the guru." The woman nods and goes in to where the guru sits in a dark corner. She approaches him and says, "Albie, come back home now!"

A widower who never paid any attention to his wife while she was alive now found himself missing her desperately. He went to a psychic to see if he could contact her. The psychic went into a trance. A strange breeze wafted through the darkened room and suddenly the man heard the unmistakable voice of his dearly departed wife. "Dearest!" he cried. "Is that you?" "Yes, my husband," she replied. "Are you happy?" "Yes, my husband." "Happier than you were with me?" "Oh yes, my husband, I am." "Wow," he said. "So Heaven must be an amazing place!" "I'm not in Heaven, dear," said his wife.

Jim's wife dies and he takes it very badly, breaking down during the funeral service and then being unable to face the guests at the wake. His best friend Tony goes up to his bedroom where he is lying on the bed weeping. "OK, mate, I know it's tough right now," says Tony, "but believe me, it'll get easier. You never know, in a year or two you may even meet someone else and have another relationship." "A year or two?" splutters Jim. "What about tonight?"

Everybody wants to go to Heaven, but nobody wants to die.

I want to die before my wife and the reason is this: if it's true that when you die your soul goes up to judgment, I don't want my wife up there ahead of me to tell them things.

Bill Cosby

A little old lady goes to a medium to help her contact her dead husband. "He's with me now, dear," says the medium, "Is there anything you want to ask him?" "Well," says the old lady, "just ask him if there's anything he needs." "He says he'd like a packet of cigarettes," says the medium. "OK," says the little old lady. "Did he say where I should send them to?" "No," replies the medium. "But he did say that where he is he won't be needing a lighter."

An old married couple have an accident in their car and go straight up to Heaven. When they get there they look round in amazement at the wonder and tranquillity of the place, and the overwhelming feeling of peace and contentment they feel. "Oh my!" says the wife. "It's so beautiful and peaceful, it's even better than I imagined." The husband hasn't said a word since they got there, so she turns to him and says, "What's the matter, Henry, don't you like it?"

"Like it?" replies the husband. "It's fantastic! And if it hadn't been for you and your flipping health foods I could've been up here years ago!"

A lawyer dies and goes up to Heaven and waits in front of the Pearly Gates. A few minutes later St Peter appears and says, "Ah! Mr Smith, it's such an honour to have you here at last. At 1028 you're the first person to have lived longer than Methuselah himself." "What are you talking about?" says the lawyer. "I died aged 65." "But you are John Smith, aren't you?" asks St Peter. "John Smith the lawyer of 32 Sebastopol Terrace, Hackney." "That's right," says the lawyer. "Oh I see where we've gone wrong," says St Peter. "We've worked it out from your billing hours."

A lawyer and the Pope died at the same time and both went to Heaven. They were met at the Pearly Gates by St Peter who conducted them to their rooms. The Pope's room was spartan, with a bare floor, an army bunk for a bed and a single bulb for light. They came to the lawyer's room. It was huge, with wall-to-wall carpeting, king-sized water bed, indirect lighting, colour TV, stereo, jacuzzi and fully stocked bar. The lawyer said, "There must be a mistake. This must be the Pope's room!" St Peter said, "There's no mistake. This is your room. We have lots of Popes, but you're our very first lawyer!"

A woman goes on holiday to South Africa. Her husband is on a business trip and is planning to meet her there the following day. When the woman reaches her hotel in Cape Town, she sends her husband an e-mail, but sends it to the wrong address. The next day the grieving widower of a recently deceased Sunday school teacher checks his e-mail, shouts out in horror and drops dead from a heart attack. Afterwards his cleaner finds a disturbing message on his computer screen: "Darling, Just got checked in. Everything ready for your arrival tomorrow. Your loving wife. P.S. Wow it's really hot down here."

After losing her husband a woman decides to go to a medium to try and contact him. After a while the medium says she thinks the husband is with them. "How are you?" the widow asks. "I'm fine," says the husband. "In fact, I'm great. I'm in a lovely green field surrounded by cows." "Oh," says the widow, rather surprised. "And some of them are very attractive," says the husband. "Really?" says the widow. "And are there angels there?" "No, just cows," says the husband. "I think I'm going to enjoy myself." "Well, that's good I suppose," says the widow. "But why do you keep going on about cows?" "Didn't I tell you?" says the husband. "I'm on a farm at Ilkley Moor – I've come back as a bull!"

St Peter is guarding the Pearly Gates when he hears a knock at the door. He goes to answer it, but there's nobody there. A few minutes later there's another knock. Again he goes to answer it, but once more there's nobody there. After another few minutes there's yet another knock at the door and this time there's an old man standing there. "What's your game?" asks St Peter. "Have you been playing 'knock down ginger' on my door?" "No," says the man. "The doctors were trying to resuscitate me."

They Shall Never Die...

Old academics never die, they just lose their faculties.

Old accountants never die, they just lose their balance.

Old actors never die, they just drop a part.

Old anthropologists never die, they just become history.

Old archers never die, they just bow and quiver.

Old architects never die, they just lose their structures.

Old astronauts never die, they just go to another world.

Old bankers never die, they just lose interest.

Old bankers never die, they just want to be a loan.

Old football players never die, they just go on dribbling.

Old beekeepers never die, they just buzz off.

Old bikers never die, but they're hard on tires.

Old biologists never die, they just ferment away.

Old blondes never fade, they just dye away.

Old book-keepers never die, they just lose their figures.

Old bookshop owners never die, they just go out of print.

Old bowlers never die, they just end up in the gutter.

Old bridge players never die, they just lose their finesse.

Old bridge players never die, they just sit around on their fat aces.

Old bureaucrats never die, they just waste away.

Old burglars never die, they just steal away.

Old businessmen never die, they just get consolidated.

Old canners never die, they are just preserved.

Old cars never die, they just get run into the ground.

Old cashiers never die, they just check out.

Old chauffeurs never die, they just lose their drive.

Old chemists never die, they just fail to react.

Old chemists never die, they just reach equilibrium.

Old cleaners never die, they just kick the bucket.

Old composers never die, they just decompose.

Old computer operators never die, they just lose their memory.

Old computer programmers never die, they just byte the dust.

Old cooks never die, they just get deranged.

Old couriers never die, they just keep on expressing it!

Old doctors never die, they just lose their patience.

Old drug addicts never die, they just get wasted.

Old electricians never die, they just lose contact.

Old farmers never die, they just go to seed.

Old mechanics never die, they just retire.

Old hippies never die, they just smell that way.

Old horticulturists never die, they just go to pot.

Old investors never die, they just roll over.

Old journalists never die, they just get de-pressed.

Old lawyers never die, they just lose their appeal.

Old limbo dancers never die, they just go under.

Old mathematicians never die, they just disintegrate.

Old milkmaids never die, they just lose their whey.

Old musicians never die, they just get played out.

Old number theorists never die, they just get past their prime.

Old numerical analysts never die, they just get disarrayed.

Old owls never die, they just don't give a hoot.

Old pacifists never die, they just go to peaces.

Old photographers never die, they just stop developing.

Old pilots never die, they just go to a higher plane.

Old policemen never die, they just cop out.

Old preachers never die, they just ramble on, and on, and on.

Old printers never die, they're just not the type.

Old programmers never die, they just branch to a new address.

Old sailors never die, they just get a little dingy.

Old schools never die, they just lose their principals.

Old sculptors never die, they just lose their marbles.

Old seers never die, they just lose their vision.

Old sewage workers never die, they just waste away.

Old skateboarders never die, they just lose their bearings.

Old soldiers never die. Young ones do.

Old steel-makers never die, they just lose their temper.

Old students never die, they just get degraded.

Old tanners never die, they just go into hiding.

Old teachers never die, they just gradually lose their class.

Old typists never die, they just lose their justification.

Old white-water rafters never die, they just get disgorged.

Old wrestlers never die, they just lose their grip.

There is no conclusive evidence about what happens to old sceptics, but their future looks doubtful.

The Wrinklies Will Not Be Forgotten

At my age I do what Mark Twain did. I get my daily paper, look at the obituaries page and if I'm not there I carry on as usual.

Patrick Moore

A rich old lady commissions an artist to paint her portrait. When he arrives she starts putting on some very expensive looking jewellery: a diamond necklace, diamond earrings and a diamond tiara. "Wow!" says the artist. "That's fantastic jewellery. It must be worth an absolute fortune, if you don't mind me saying." "Well, it is," replies the old lady, "but I've only rented it. I don't usually go in for this sort of thing." "Oh,

I see," says the artist, "you just want it to look good for the portrait?" "No," says the old lady, "but when I die my husband will probably remarry and I want the little gold-digger to go mad looking for the jewellery."

A man dies and his wife phones the local paper to arrange for his obituary to be printed. She is put through to the correct department and tells them she doesn't have much money, so she just wants the obituary to say, "Alf is dead." "That's quite short," says the man at the newspaper office, "but if you're worrying about the cost, don't forget you're entitled to have up to six words for the same price." "In that case," says the woman, "make it, 'Alf is dead: Toyota for sale.'"

A woman is at the solicitor's listening to the reading of her late husband's will. She is shocked and outraged to find that he has left all his money to another woman, so she stomps off to the graveyard, where the man from the undertaker's has just laid his headstone reading "Rest in Peace". Despite her protests the undertaker says it's too late to change the inscription. "All right then," she says. "After 'Rest in Peace' just add 'For the time being'."

Three old men are talking about what their grandchildren might be saying about them in 50 years' time. "I would like my grandchildren to say, 'He was successful in business,'" says the first old man. "Fifty years from now," says the second, "I want them to say,

'He was a loyal family man.'" Turning to the third old man, the first gent asks, "So what do you want them to say about you in 50 years?" "Me?" says the third old man. "I want them all to say, 'My! He looks good for his age!'"

A young man is building a brick wall outside his house one day when a man stops to congratulate him. "What a magnificent wall you've built, young man, I doubt whether even Cornelius Bagshot III could have built a wall as good as that." "Who?" says the young man. "Cornelius Bagshot III," says the passer-by. "He was an incredible man. He could do anything he set his mind to. An outstanding athlete, leading light of Mensa, a chess grandmaster, and a brilliant footballer, cricketer and mountain climber. And he was an incredible lover as well by all accounts. He knew exactly what women wanted in the bedroom department, if you know what I mean. He was certainly an incredible, brilliant man, the like of whom we will not see again." "So was he a friend of yours then, this Cornelius Bagshot III?" asks the young man. "No. I never met him," says the passer-by. "I just married his widow."

An old spinster dies a virgin and has asked that the following inscription be put on her headstone, "Born a virgin, lived a virgin, died a virgin." Being a bit short of time the undertaker shortens this to: "Returned, unopened."

The Mathematics Of Ageing

Do you realize that the only time in our lives when we like to get old is when we're kids? If you're less than ten years old, you're so excited about ageing that you think in fractions. "How old are you?" "I'm four and a half!" You're never thirty-six and a half. You're four and a half, going on five! That's the key. You get into your teens, now they can't hold you back. You jump to the next number, or even a few ahead. "How old are you?" "I'm gonna be sixteen!" You could be thirteen, but hey, you're gonna be sixteen! And then the greatest day of your life... You become twenty-one. Even the words sound like a ceremony. YOU BECOME twenty-one. YESSSS!!! But then you turn thirty. Oooohh, what happened there? Makes you sound like bad milk! He TURNED; we had to throw him out. There's no fun now, you're just a sour-dumpling. What's wrong? What's changed? You BECOME twenty-one, you TURN thirty, then you're PUSHING forty. Whoa! Put on the brakes, it's all slipping away. Before you know it, you REACH fifty and your dreams are gone. But wait!!! You MAKE it to sixty. You didn't think you would! So you BECOME twenty-one, TURN THIRTY, PUSH FORTY, REACH FIFTY and MAKE it to SIXTY. You've built up so much speed that you HIT seventy! After that it's a day-by-day thing; you HIT Wednesday! You get into your eighties and every day is a complete cycle; you HIT lunch; you TURN 4:30pm; you REACH bedtime. And it doesn't end there. Into the nineties, you start going backward: "I was JUST ninety-two." Then a strange thing happens. If you make it over one hundred, you become a little kid again. "I'm one hundred and a half!"

George Carlin

She says she's looking forward to her 39th birthday but you can't help thinking she must be looking in the wrong direction.

When I turned two I was really anxious, because I'd doubled my age in a year. I thought, if this keeps up, by the time I'm six, I'll be ninety.

Steven Wright

When you're three years old, success is not peeing in your pants. When you're eleven, success is having friends. When you're seventeen, success is having a driving licence. When you're twenty, success is having sex. When you're thirty, success is having cash. When you're fifty, success is having money. When you're sixty, success is having sex. When you're seventy, success is having a driving licence. When you're seventy-five, success is having friends. When you're eighty, success is not peeing in your pants.

Growing Old Carefully

Two old ladies are having a natter about their favourite subject, their various medical conditions. The first tells the second, "The doctor says I need another operation but I can't afford to get it done privately and there's a 12-month waiting list on the NHS." "That's a disgrace," says her friend. "Still never mind. We'll just have to talk about your old operation for another year."

A 90-year-old man goes to his doctor and says, "Oh doctor, I'm having terrible trouble with my right knee. It's awfully stiff and painful." The doctor has a look and says, "I'm afraid there's not much I can do. You have to remember you've had that knee for 90 years now, so you can't expect too much." "What are you talking about?" says the old man. "I've had my left knee for exactly the same length of time and there's nothing wrong with that one at all."

A little old woman lady phones the hospital and says, "Is that the City Hospital? Could you put me through to someone who can give me some information about one of your patients?" "Hold on, please," says the voice at the other end of the line and puts the old lady through. "Hello, can I help you?" says another voice. "Oh yes," says the old lady. "I want to find out how one of your patients is getting on. It's Mrs Elsie Harris and I believe she's in room 302 in the Davenport Ward." "Let me see," says the voice. "Ah yes! Mrs Harris in room 302 in the Davenport Ward. Yes, Mrs Harris is doing very well. She's making a full recovery from her operation, she's had two full meals and her doctor says if she continues improving at this rate, she can go home on Tuesday at 12 o'clock." "That's wonderful news," says the old lady. "Absolutely wonderful!" "From your enthusiasm," says the voice on the phone, "I take it you must be a close relative?" "No," says the old lady, "I am Mrs Harris in room 302 on Davenport Ward. I can't get anyone round here to tell me a flipping thing!"

A man walked into a doctor's office and the receptionist asked him what the problem was. He replied, "I've got shingles." She said, "Fill out this form and supply your name and address, medical insurance number. When you're done, please take a seat." Fifteen minutes later a nurse's aide came out and asked him what he had. He said, "I've got shingles." So she took down his height, weight and complete medical history, then said, "Change into this gown and wait in the examining room." Thirty minutes later a nurse came in and asked him what he had. He said, "I've got shingles." So she gave him a blood test, a blood pressure test, an electrocardiogram, and told him to wait for the doctor. An hour later the doctor came in and asked him what he had. He said, "Shingles." The doctor gave him a full-cavity examination, and then said, "I just checked you out thoroughly, and I can't find any sign of shingles anywhere." "No," the man replied. "That's because they're outside in the truck. Where do you want them?"

An old man goes to the doctor. "Doctor," he says, pointing to different parts of his body, "when I touch my arm it hurts. When I touch my neck it hurts. And when I touch my stomach it hurts. Do I have some rare disease?" "No," says the doctor, "you have a sore finger."

A 90-year-old man is snoozing in the chair one day when a life insurance salesman knocks at the door. He gives him the hard sell, but the old man is a bit wary about the cost of the insurance which at his age isn't cheap. After about 45 minutes of haggling, the salesman finally says, "Look, I'll tell you what, you have a think about it, sleep on it tonight, and if you wake up in the morning give me a ring, OK?"

Boys And Girls

An elderly couple had dinner at another couple's house, and after eating, the wives left the table and went into the kitchen. The two gentlemen were talking, and one said, "Last night we went out to a new restaurant and it was really great. I would recommend it very highly." The other man said, "What's the restaurant called?" The first man thought and thought then finally said, "What is the name of that flower you give to someone you love? You know... The one that's red and has thorns." "Do you mean a rose?" "Yes, that's the one," replied the man. He then turned toward the kitchen and yelled, "Rose, what's the name of that restaurant we went to last night?"

An elderly couple stop off at a restaurant for lunch. After finishing their meal, they go back to their car and drive away. Unfortunately the elderly lady has forgotten to pick up her glasses from the table and doesn't miss them until they have been driving for half an hour. Her husband fusses and complains constantly as he drives her back. "You're virtually senile," he tells her. "If your memory gets any worse you know what I'll do: I'll put you in a home!" Finally they arrive back, the elderly lady climbs out of the car and walks across to the restaurant. Just as she reaches the door, she hears her husband call out to her, "And another thing: while you're in there, get my hat for me!"

By Any Other Name...

An old actor falls on hard times because he has found it increasingly difficult to remember his lines. After many years he finds a theatre where they are prepared to give him a chance to shine again. The director says, "This is the most important part, and it has only one line. You walk on to the stage at the opening carrying a rose. You hold the rose to your nose with just one finger and thumb, sniff the rose deeply and then say, 'Ah, the sweet aroma of my mistress.'" The actor is thrilled. All day long before the performance, he's practising his line over and over again. Finally, the time comes. The curtain goes up, the actor walks onto the stage, and with great passion delivers the line, "Ah, the sweet aroma of my mistress." The theatre erupts. The audience is screaming with laughter, but the director is steaming! "You fool!" he cries. "You've ruined me!" Bewildered, the old actor asks, "What happened, did I forget my line?" "No!" screams the director. "You forgot the rose!"

An old couple are arguing in bed one night about which of them has become more forgetful. In the end, the old woman tells her husband, "Oh, never mind. Just go and get me a cup of tea, will you? You won't manage to forget that on your way down the stairs, will you?" "Of course not," says the old man. "And don't forget to put in some sugar this time," says his wife. "Will you stop going on at me!" says the old man. "I'm sure I didn't forget to put the sugar in last time." "Yes, you did," says the old woman. "And you forgot to put in the milk." "Will you just shut up!" says the old man. "There's nothing wrong with my memory. Now just let me go and get your tea." He plods off down the stairs but a few minutes later he's back again. "I told you," says his wife, very slowly and sternly, "I want a cup of tea with milk and one sugar." "Yes, I know that," says the old man, "but could you just remind me again: how do I get to the kitchen?"

Never Too Old For A Round

Old Jack gets in from a game of golf. "How was it, dear?" asks his wife, Beryl. "Well, I was hitting pretty well, but my eyesight's so bad now I couldn't see where the ball went," he answers. "What can you expect," says Beryl. "You're seventy-five years old!" "I know!" says Jack. "Why don't you take my brother Arthur along?" asks Beryl. "But he's eight-five and he doesn't even play golf," says Jack. "Never mind," says Beryl, "he's got perfect eyesight so he'll be able to watch the ball for you." The next day Jack tees off with Arthur looking on. He takes a swing and the ball disappears down the middle of the fairway. "Did you see where it went?" asks Jack. "I certainly did," replies Arthur. "Excellent," says Jack. "So where is it?" "Er...." says Arthur peering off into the distance. "No, sorry: I've forgotten."

Quite A Mouthful

Yes, my teeth are my own! I can show you the receipt if you want.

Two old men go out fishing one day. The sea is quite rough and as a result one manages to lose his dentures over the side of the boat. He was so incensed that his friend decides to play a joke on him. He surreptitiously slips out his own teeth and fixes them onto the end of his fishing line. Then when he hauls the line in with the teeth on the end, he calls out to his friend, "Hey, look what I've caught! It looks like your missing gnashers!" Before he can be stopped his friend unhooks the dentures, tries pushing them into his mouth and then hurls them into the sea with a disgusted cry, "You idiot! Those aren't mine – they don't fit!"

A bus driver is driving along one day when he notices in his mirror that his passengers are all in uproar. He stops the bus and goes to investigate. He discovers an elderly man crawling up and down the bus, looking for something on the floor. "What on earth do you think you're doing?" asks the bus driver. "You're being a nuisance to all the other people on the bus." "I can't help that," says the old man, "I'm looking for my chewing gum." "What do you mean, you're looking for your chewing gum?" says the driver. "You're making this amount of fuss over some old chewing gum that's been on the floor of the bus, which you wouldn't be able to use again anyway." "That doesn't matter," says the old man, "but I've still got to find my chewing gum." "Well, what the hell's so special about this chewing gum?" asks the driver. "My teeth are still in it," says the old man.

An old lady goes to her dentist to have her dentures adjusted for the umpteenth time. Every time she comes back she tells the dentist the same thing, "These dentures still don't fit." "What are you talking about?" says the dentist. "We've adjusted them for you over and over again. How can they possibly still not fit?" "You don't believe they still don't fit, then I'll prove it to you!" says the old woman. "I've brought the tumbler from the side of my bed with me..."

Any Old Number?

Statistically speaking, by the time you get to the age of seventy there are five women to every one man. It's rather cruel of God to give you that kind of odds at that stage in your life.

A young English woman visits America on holiday and goes sightseeing at an Indian reservation. She passes an old Indian and as she walks by, he raises his hand and says, "chance". The woman is puzzled, but walks on. Later she walks back and the old Indian raises his hand again and says, "chance". The woman is intrigued so tries walking past for a third time a bit later. As she does so the old man raises his hand and says "chance" again. She says, "Hello, I hope you don't mind me saying, but I'm from England and I always thought that the Native American greeting was 'how', not 'chance.'" "Lady," says the old Indian, with a twinkle in his eye, "when you get to my age you know how, but the best you can hope for is a chance."

Another of nature's cruel jokes – the menopause (menopause – you just knew men would have something to do with it, didn't you?). A lot of men don't even realize their wives are going through the change of life. Yes, they see the mood swings, the odd behaviour, etc, but how are they supposed to know it's not just the usual mood swings and roundabouts? Women of course know all about it, with the hot flushes and everything, but at least it's the end of that dreadful monthly ritual – and no, we're not talking about sex with their husbands!

Badly Bitten

Two ageing ladies are long-time rivals in their social circle. One year they bump into each other at a Christmas party at their country club. "Why, my dear," says the first, noticing the other's necklace. "Don't tell me those are real pearls?" "Yes, they are," says the second. "You may say that," says the first woman with a thin smile, "but of course the only way I could tell for certain would be to bite them." "Well, I'd be happy for you to do that," says the second woman. "The only trouble is, you'd need real teeth."

Hip, Hip, Hooray!

An old man goes into hospital to have a hip replacement. The hospital puts in a new plastic one with a sensitive spring-based action. When he gets home his grandchildren are delighted to discover every time they push granddad's head down, he takes a penalty.

You don't know what real embarrassment is like until your hip sets off a metal detector.

Positively Disappointed

A woman accompanied her husband to the doctor's. After his check-up, the doctor called the wife into his office alone. He said, "Your husband is suffering from a very severe disease, combined with horrible stress. If you don't do the following he will surely die. Each morning, make him a healthy breakfast. Try to be pleasant in general, and make sure he stays in a good mood. For lunch, make him a nutritious meal. For dinner, prepare something nice and healthy again. Don't burden him with chores, as he probably had a hard day. Don't discuss your problems with him, it will only make his stress worse. And most importantly, make love with your husband several times a week and satisfy his every whim. If you can do this for the next one to two months, I think your husband will regain his health completely." On the way home, the husband asked his wife, "What did the doctor say?" "You're going to die," she replied.

Bin There, Dun That...

A bin man is on his rounds, collecting the rubbish on his bin lorry. As usual, most of the bins have been left ready on the kerb but one old lady has forgotten to put hers out. Hearing the lorry pass by, she runs out in her dressing gown and curlers, and calls out, "Am I too late for the collection?" "Of course not, love," says the bin man, emptying another load into the back of the truck. "Come on, hop in!"

Junk is something you've kept for years and throw away three weeks before you need it.

Getting Catty

A little old lady comes hobbling into an adult goods store looking as though she's suffering some kind of fit. She makes it to the counter and grabs it for support. "D-d--d-d-do y-y-you s-s-s-tock v-v-v-ibrators?" she asks the man on the counter. "Yes," he replies, "we stock vibrators." "D-d-d-do y-y-y-you h-h-h-ave one that's p-p-pink, t-t-tt-twelve inches l-l-l-long and t-t-t-two and a h-h-h-half inches th-th-th-thick?" "Yes," says the man on the counter. "We have that one in stock. Shall I get one for you?" "N-n-n-no," says the old woman, "I d-d-d-don't want to b-b-b-buy one. I w-w-w-want you to t-t-t-tell me h-h-h-how t-t-t-to t-t-t-turn the f-f-f-flipping thing off!"

An old woman comes homes from afternoon bingo one day and finds there's nothing in the fridge for her husband's dinner. It's too late to get any shopping, so she takes a tin of cat food from the cupboard, chops up an onion, adds a few spices and makes the whole lot into a meaty stew. When her husband comes home she gives it to him, and to her amazement he scoffs the lot and says it's delicious. Next day at bingo, she tells her friends what has happened and says she'll try it again as he enjoyed it so much. A couple of weeks later her friends are horrified to find that she is still feeding her husband with cat food. "You'll kill him," they warn her, and sure enough a week later he is dead. Her friends tell her that she should have listened to their warnings. "It wasn't the cat food that killed him," says the woman indignantly, "If you must know, he fell off the fence." "What was he doing up there?" asked one of her friends. "Trying to lick his backside," said the woman.

How To Calculate Your Correct Wrinkly Age – Word Association Test

So what's your wrinkly age? A bit like counting the rings in trees and carbon dating, and other advances in modern technology, we can now work out how old you are and when you were born by simply using bit of mental arithmetic and word association.

So try this simple quiz and find out – *just how wrinkly are you?*

When the name Brigitte Bardot is mentioned, do you think of:

A) A sex symbol
B) An animal rights campaigner
C) Nothing, because you don't have the foggiest idea who she is

When the word "holiday" is mentioned, do you think of:

A) A lot of faffing around, all for the sake of a change of scenery
B) A nice break from the normal routine
C) Two weeks of sun, booze and sex

When the words "rock music" are mentioned, do you think of:

A) A godawful racket perpetrated by gormless long-haired morons
B) A bit of nostalgia for your long-lost youth
C) The sort of stuff your mum and dad used to listen to before ringtones were invented

When the word "phone" is used, does it conjure up images of:

A) Black bakelite, switchboard operators, the talking clock and red telephone boxes
B) Cold-calling salesman, teenage children chatting for hours and huge bills
C) A mobile entertainment centre, the loss of which would be the equivalent to the loss of a vital organ

When the words "the doctor" are mentioned, do you immediately think:

A) The man who seemingly holds the balance of your life in his frighteningly young hands
B) The smug overpaid bloke whose answer to every ailment is a prescription for antibiotics
C) David Tennant

When the word "pot" is uttered, do you think of:
A) The emergency convenience under your bed
B) Your rotund, middle-aged stomach
C) What your parents used to smoke at university

Asked to name a famous artist, would you be more likely to say:
A) Rembrandt
B) That Damien Hurst fella
C) Banksy

Asked to think of a famous English victory, would you be more likely to say:
A) World War Two
B) The 1966 World Cup
C) It sounds a bit racist, dunnit?

Asked to name a famous duo, would you be more likely to say:
A) Laurel and Hardy
B) Lennon and McCartney
C) Drunk and disorderly

ANSWERS:

Mostly A's
Hmm, you're quite old, aren't you? Either that or you have a few attitude issues to sort out and have been reading too many nostalgia books.
Mostly B's
You're hovering on the precarious verge of wrinkliedom and one large utility bill or yet another reality TV series could push you over the edge – watch out!

Mostly C's
You young whippersnapper! What on earth are you doing reading this book? Shouldn't you be reading some booky wook by Katie Price or something?

Under The Knife

These days there's not so much stigma attached to having cosmetic surgery though there's a hell of a lot attached to looking old. In fact it's virtually illegal in some quarters. How many supermodels can you name over forty? How many can you name over thirty come to that? And no, we're not talking about their IQ. How many Hollywood actresses get to the age of fifty without a spot of nip and tuck? And have you ever seen a pole dancer dancing round her walking stick – even if half the audience have brought theirs? Exactly. So more and more people are resorting to the surgeon's knife to enhance their sagging features. But it's not cheap, so here are a few handy hints on how to look heavenly without spending the earth.

The beginnings of a fat tummy? Join a weight-watchers club and do nothing. Simply by walking through the door and mixing with the lumps of lard on display you will immediately look and feel thinner.

Bags under the eyes? You may remember a punk singer by the name of Siouxsie Sioux, or if you were too old even then, how about Dusty Springfield? Each of them seemed to finish off a tub of mascara and eye shadow every morning. They had so much make-up round their eyes that they managed to make pandas look understated. But the point is that no one knew whether they had bags under their eyes beneath that lot. In fact you weren't even sure whether they had eyes beneath that lot. So, keep 'em guessing with the black stuff!

Lines on face? Everyone these days has tattoos. They're not just for the likes of sailors and builders anymore. Many people have them on their faces too, so get your friendly neighbourhood tattooist to expertly link the lines with tattoo ink and create a fabulous design – how about one of those low-depression weather maps with a couple of little clouds and a sun thrown in, or an aerial view of the windswept sands of the Sahara? You might even set a new trend!

Unsightly nose? Become a clown. Does anyone laugh at a clown because he has a bulbous red nose? Does anyone laugh at a clown full stop? But whatever the shape of the offending proboscis it will be skilfully masked by the addition of Coco's conk. All together now, "I wish it could be Red Nose Day every day-i-yay!"

Flabby bottom? Even if you could afford liposuction, would you really want to witness your excess fat being sucked up the end of a glorified hoover? No, neither would we, thank you very much. The trick is to become a mechanic. No mechanic alive has ever found a set of overalls that will fit, so having a couple of spare yards of grease-stained denim flapping round your backside will not look odd in the slightest. And you won't have to pay to have your car serviced any more. Double bubble!

Drive Me Round The Bend!

A senior citizen was out driving his brand new BMW convertible down the motorway. He put his foot down and went up to 90 miles per hour, enjoying the wind blowing through what little hair he had left. "Amazing!" he thought as he flew down the motorway, but then he noticed in his rear-view mirror, the flashing blue light of a police car as it sped up to catch him. "I can get away from him – no problem!" thought the old man, speeding up to a 110mph, then 120mph and then 130mph. Suddenly, he thought, "What on earth am I doing? I'm too old for this nonsense!" So he pulled over to the side of the road and waited for the police car to catch up with him. Pulling in behind him, the police officer walked up to his window, looked at his watch and said, "Sir, my shift ends in 15 minutes. Today is Friday and I'm taking off for the weekend. If you can give me a reason why you were speeding that I've never heard before, I'll let you go." The man looked very seriously at the policeman, and replied, "Years ago, my wife ran off with a policeman. I thought you were bringing her back." There was a short pause before the policeman said, "Have a good day, sir."

A young man in a Ferrari stops at a red light and notices an ancient old man on an even more ancient old moped pull up next to him. The old man looks over at the Ferrari and says, "Nice car. Mind if I take a look inside?" "No problem," replies the owner. So the old man pokes his head in the window and looks around. Then, sitting back on his moped, the old man says, "That's a pretty nice car, all right!" Just then the light changes so the guy decides to show the old man just what his car can do. He floors it, and within a few seconds his speedometer has reached over 150mph. Suddenly, he notices a dot in his rear-view mirror. It seems to be getting closer! He slows down to see what it could be and suddenly, whoosh! Something whips by him, going much faster than he is! "What on earth could be going faster than my Ferrari?" the young man asks himself. Then, ahead of him, he sees a dot coming toward him. Whoosh! It goes by again, heading in the opposite direction! And it looked like the old man on the moped! "It can't be!" thinks the young guy. But when he looks in his rear-view mirror he sees it approaching again at incredible speed and with another whoosh it ploughs straight into the back of his car. The young man jumps out and sees that it is the old man on a now badly mangled moped. He runs round to the old fellow and says, "Is there anything I can do for you?" "Yes, please," whispers the old man. "Could you unhook... my braces ...from your side-view mirror..."

There is a long tailback on the motorway and a police car passing on the other side notices it's caused by a car doing 20 miles an hour. The two policemen eventually stop the offending vehicle and inside they discover two little old ladies, one driving and one sitting in the passenger seat, looking shaken and white as a sheet. "Now, madam," says one of the policemen to the driver, "why were you going so slowly?" "I always go at the speed that it says on the sign," explained the old woman. "And what sign was that, madam?" asks the second policeman. "It said M20," explained the little old lady. "So I did 20 miles an hour the same way I did 31 miles an hour on the A31, then 40 miles an hour on the A40, and..." "And what's wrong with your friend?" the policeman asks, referring to the passenger who is still staring blankly into space, clutching onto the seat for dear life. "Oh, you won't get any sense out of her," says the driver, "she's been like that ever since we came off the A159."

Bon Appétit

A little old couple slowly hobble into a fast food restaurant one cold winter's evening. The old lady takes a seat, while the little old man goes to the counter and orders a meal. The old man takes his food back to the table, sits down, unwraps his burger, cuts it in half and places one half in front of his wife. He then carefully divides the French fries into two piles and places one in front of his wife. The old man then takes a sip of the drink and begins to eat. The old couple and their meagre meal attract pitying looks from other diners and a young man goes to ask them if they would like another burger and fries, so they don't have to share. "No thanks, sonny," says the old man. "We're used to sharing. We share everything." The young man then notices that the little old lady still hasn't touched her food and is just sitting there watching her husband eat occasionally and sip some of the drink. Again the young man asks if he can buy them another meal. "No thank you, young man," says the old lady. "We're used to sharing. We share everything." "But you're not eating anything," says the young man. "Don't you like it? Shall I get you something else?" "No," replies the old lady. "This will be fine. In fact I can't wait to get stuck in." "Then what are you waiting for?" asksthe young man. "I'm waiting," says the old woman with a big toothless smile, "for him to finish with the dentures."

An old man goes into a restaurant one day. He looks at the menu and orders, "just a bowl of soup and some bread." The old fellow eats his soup and bread but when the restaurant manager asks him if he enjoyed his meal, he says, "Yes. It was quite passable but you're a bit mean with the bread aren't you? I only got two pieces." The next day, the old man turns up at the restaurant again and orders exactly the same meal. This time the manager gives him four pieces of bread but still when he asks him if he enjoyed the meal, the old man replies, "Yes. It was OK, but I just can't understand why you're so mean with the bread." When the old fellow returns again the next day, the manager is determined to give him enough bread. This time he gives him eight pieces with his soup but still the old man tells him, "It was quite passable but I still could have done with more bread." The restaurant manager is now completely exasperated by the fussy old man's behaviour but he refuses to be beaten. So when the old man returns the next day and orders his soup and bread, the manager produces a huge, six-foot French loaf that he's had the bakery next door prepare specially. The manager serves the old man his soup, produces a chainsaw to slice the huge French loaf and heaves the bread up onto the man's table. Incredibly the old man manages to eat not only his soup but the large loaf of bread as well. As he goes to pay, the manager asks him, "So? How was your meal today?" "It was passable." says the old man. "But I just can't believe you're so mean with the bread." "What the hell are you talking about?" squeals the manager. "Well," says the old man, "I notice you've gone back to serving only two pieces now."

Then And Now

Then: Dreaming about one day having a BMW.
Now: Dreaming about one day having a BM.

Then: Killer weed.
Now: Weed killer.

Then: Taking acid.
Now: Taking antacid.

Then: The perfect high.
Now: The perfect high-yield mutual fund.

Then: Listening to Chris Rea.
Now: Listening to diarrahea.

Then: Single Malt.
Now: Hair moult.

Then: A lot of men
Now: Allotment

Then: 9 to 5
Now: 9 to 9.30am

Then: Waiting for Santa to come.
Now: You are Santa.

Then: LSD
Now: LBW

So Near To Thee...

Another old man is on his deathbed and his wife too is talking to him in his last hours. "Tell me," says the husband, "I've never asked this before because it's so awkward, but I can't go to my grave without knowing." "What is it?" asks his concerned wife. "Three of our sons are tall with straight red hair," says the husband, "but little Adam is short with curly blond hair. Tell me, is he really my child?" "Of course he is, darling," says the wife, and the husband closes his eyes, turns over and dies peacefully. "Thank goodness he didn't ask about the other three," says the wife.

As people come to the end of their life they often feel compelled to finally tell the truth and go to meet their maker with a clear conscience. Which is all very well unless the truth happens to be, "Thanks for nursing me all these years through my terrible illness, but I have to tell you we're not actually related. I came to read the gas meter in 1964, had a cup of tea with your mum, one thing led to another, and I never got round to leaving, so I'm leaving all my money to the boilermaker's union and..."

An old man is lying on his deathbed with his wife sitting near him. He says, "Dear wife, I must confess certain things to you before I die." She says, "Hush now, husband, you're fading fast." He says, "But this is really important, I must tell you so I can die with a clear conscience! I slept with your best friend, your sister, and your mother!" She says, "I know. Of course I know all about it." "You do?" says the old man. "Of course," says his wife. "Why do you think I poisoned you?"

Talk Is Cheap

A new young priest is nervous about hearing confessions so he asks his older more experienced colleague to sit in on his sessions. The new priest hears a few confessions but then the old priest asks him to step out of the confessional for a moment. "OK," says the old priest, "when you hear confessions, try crossing your arms over your chest and rubbing your chin with one hand. It'll make it look like you're deep in thought." The new priest tries this. Then the old priest suggests, "Also, try saying things like, 'I see, yes, go on,' and 'I understand', or 'How did you feel about that?'" The new priest takes these suggestions on board as well. "And finally," says the old priest, "when you're hearing people confess their private, most intimate sins, try not to keep slapping your knee and saying, 'Wow! Cool, man! So what happened next?'"

Four elderly ladies are sitting playing bridge. The first lady says, "Girls, I've known you all many years and there's something I've got to get off my chest. I'm a kleptomaniac. But don't worry, I've never stolen from any of you and I never will." The second lady pipes up, "Well, since we're confessing all, I must tell you I'm a nymphomaniac. But don't worry, I've never tried to seduce your husbands and I never will." "Well," says the third lady. "I've something to confess too. I'm a lesbian. But don't worry, you're not my type." The fourth lady stands up. "I must confess," she says, "I'm an incurable gossip, and I've just got some phone calls to make."

An elderly Italian man goes to confession. "Father," he says to the priest, "I need to unburden my guilty conscience." "Very well," says the priest, "what's the problem?" "Well," says the old man, "during the war, a beautiful Jewish woman knocked on my door and asked me to hide her from the Germans. I hid her in my attic, and they never found her." "Why would you feel guilty about such a thing?" says the priest. "That was a wonderful thing you did." "But, father," says the old man, "I was weak and I told her that she must repay me for this kindness by performing sexual favours, which she did." "I see," says the priest. "You shouldn't have taken advantage of the poor woman. But nevertheless you did a good deed in saving her life. Say five Hail Marys." "Thank you, father. That's a tremendous weight off my mind," says the old man. "But there's just one other thing..." "What's that?" asks the priest. "Do I need to tell her the war is over?" asks the old man.

An old man walks into a church to make his confession. "Forgive me father, for I have sinned," says the old man. "I am 80 years old and I was walking home from the pensioners' dinner club the other day when a couple of 20-year-old girls stopped their car and said they needed directions. We got into a discussion and they offered to drive me home and on the way, one of them asked me the last time I'd had sex and I told them it had been years, and she said, would I like to have some fun and before I knew it, we were all in my bed performing the most erotic shocking acts I've ever known." The priest sits tutting through all this. Finally he asks, "OK, so how long is it since your last confession?" "Never," says the old man. "I'm Jewish." "What do you mean?" says the priest. "If you're Jewish, why are you telling me all this?" "I'm not just telling you," says the old man, "I'm telling everyone."

Dazed And Confused

An eminent and rather pompous QC is out shooting in the country. He brings down his first pheasant and it lands in the next field. He spots an old farmer nearby and calls out, "Hey you! Pass me that bird, would you?" The old farmer says, "No. This be moi field, so this be moi bird." "Now come on!" says the QC. "Be a good chap and pass it over, will you?" "Round these here parts," says the farmer, "we settles our disputes with the 'three whacks' rule." "What's that?" asks the QC. "Well, oi whacks you three toimes with moi stick," says the farmer, "and you whacks me three toimes with your stick, and whomsoever whacks the hardest is declared the winner." "Oh, all right then," says the QC, and the farmer climbs over the stile and gives the QC three almighty whacks with his stick, knocking him to the ground. The QC stands up, dusts himself off and says breathlessly, as he brandishes his stick, "OK, chum. Now it's my turn." "No, you're all roight," says the farmer, "you can keep the rotten bird."

A young man is walking round a supermarket one day when he notices an old lady following him around. He ignores her at first but when he gets to the checkout, he finds her in the queue in front of him. "Pardon me," she says. "I'm sorry if I've been staring, but you look so much like my son who died recently." "I'm sorry to hear that," says the young man. "Is there anything I can do for you?" "Well," says the old lady, "this may sound silly to you but if you could just call me mother, it would make me feel so happy. Just say, 'Goodbye, mother!' as I'm walking out of the shop." "Of course," says the young man, "it's the very least I can do." And so just as the old lady is collecting her shopping bags from the end of the checkout, he says, "Goodbye, mother!" before she walks out of the shop. When he comes to pay, he finds his bill is £100 more than he expected. "It can't be that much," he says. "I only bought a couple of things." "I know that," says the cashier, "but your mother said you would pay for her shopping as well."

An old man meets up with one of his friends from his younger days who had always suffered from a terrible stammer. The old man is astonished to see his stuttering friend now dressed in an expensive suit and driving a Rolls-Royce. "You seem to have done well in life," says the old man. "What line of business did you end up in?" "I s-s-s-sold Bibles d-d-d-door to d-d-d-door," says his friend. "You managed to make good money selling Bibles door to door?" says the old man. "How on earth did you do that?" "W-w-well," says his friend. "I j-j-just kn-kn-kn-knocked on p-p-p-p-p-p-p-peoples' d-d-d-d-doors, and said, 'H-h-h-hello. Do you w-w-want to b-b-b-buy a B-B-B-Bible? If you don't w-w-want to b-b-b-buy a B-B-B-Bible, I can always j-j-j-just r-r-r-read it to you!"

Jason is walking across the common one day when he sees a little old man sitting on a bench nowhere near any water, dangling a fishing rod over the grass. Intrigued, he goes up to the old man and asks him what he's doing. "Fishing," says the old man. Deciding to humour him, Jason asks, "And what were you hoping to catch today?" "Just something for my lunch," says the old man. Jason feels sorry for the poor deluded old codger and says, "Come on! Come with me and I'll buy you a nice lunch." So he takes him to a restaurant and they enjoy a large mixed grill, a beautiful pudding, a bottle of wine and coffees. As he pays the bill and leaves the restaurant, Jason says to the old man, "That was better than anything you'd find out there on the common, wasn't it? I mean, do you ever catch much out there?" "To be honest," says the old man, "you're the third one today."

The hardest years in life are those between ten and seventy.

Helen Hayes

Green Fingers

When you're young you play in the garden, when you're a bit older you lie in the garden, and when you're properly grown up and middle-aged you suddenly find you can grow stuff out there too! Also, it gives you the fabulous opportunity of having something new to moan about. "If that cat from next door poops on my tomato plants again I'll get my air rifle out of the loft!", "Ooh, I think I've pulled something planting those hollyhocks," "If it wasn't for this bloomin' climate change I'd have won the prize pumpkin category hands down." And so on. See? You wouldn't have half the fun of middle-age if it wasn't for a spot of gardening.

A vicar is walking through his parish one day and stops to admire an area that an elderly parishioner has turned from a piece of wasteland into a beautiful garden. "Ah," says the vicar, "It's so inspiring what man can achieve with the help of the Almighty." "Yes," replies the old man. "But you should have seen the mess it was in when He had it all to Himself."
Did you hear about the keen gardener who managed to give himself a double hernia last week lifting his huge prize marrows? He's turned his attentions to pumpkins and has developed two new strains.

Two old men are down at the allotments comparing notes when one says, "What do you put on your rhubarb then, Arthur?" "Fresh horse manure," replies Arthur, "you can't beat it." "Oh yes," replies his friend, "to be honest with you, I prefer custard."

An old Muslim man living in London plants some potatoes in his back garden. However, when the time comes to dig them up, he finds the work is too hard for him. He emails his son in Pakistan and asks for his advice. "Don't worry, Dad," replies the son. "I'll take care of it." Two hours later there's a squeal of brakes outside the old man's house and a squad of armed police officers run in and start digging up the potato patch. When they've dug it all up, they give the old man a look and drive off. The old man is intrigued until he notices a new message in his inbox saying, "I've buried the stuff in the potato patch. You know what to do."

Did you hear about the elderly man who got stuck out in his allotment during the recent snowy weather? When they eventually dug him out they found him frozen to the marrow.

A man and his wife are looking out of the back window at their vegetable patch in the back garden. The wife turns to the husband and says, "You know, Bert, sooner or later you're going to have to make a proper scarecrow for this place." "Why?" asks her husband. "Because," she says, "your mother's arms must be getting awfully tired by now."

Two elderly women gardeners enter their carrots in the village vegetable show. One is declared the winner and starts crowing about her success. "Well, I'm not surprised I won, to be honest," she says. "Your carrots were a bit on the small side quite frankly." "That's true," says the other woman. "Mind you, I did grow them to fit my mouth, not yours."

The Generation Game

Why do grandchildren get on so well with their grandparents? They both have a common enemy.

Grandchildren are God's reward for not killing your children.

It's not the arrival of grandchildren that suddenly makes a man feel old. It's the sudden realization that he's married to a grandmother.

A little boy goes to his best friend's house in the morning so they can walk along to school together. When his friend comes out he sees him saying goodbye to an old lady. "Who was that old lady in your house?" asks the little boy. "That's my grandmother," says his friend. "She's come to stay with us for a few weeks." "Where does she usually live?" asks the little boy. "At the big train station in the city," says his friend. The little boy is astonished. "She lives in the big train station in the city!" he says. "Yes," says his friend. "Whenever we want her, we just go along there and get her."

Little Billy is very happy to see his grandmother come to visit again. He runs up, gives her a hug and tells her, "I'm so happy to see you, Grandma. Now Daddy will have to do that trick he's been promising to do." "What trick is that, dear?" asks his grandmother. "Well," says little Billy, "Daddy told us he would climb up the flipping wall if you came to visit us again."

An elderly man shuffles into a toy shop and points out an expensive model train set in the window. "Oh yes," says the shop assistant, "I'm sure your grandson will love playing with this, sir." "Oh yes, that's a point," says the old man. "You'd better give me two."

Every Saturday morning granddad had to baby-sit his three little grandsons. The boys always wanted to play "war", and granddad always got coaxed into playing along. His daughter came to pick up the children one Saturday and saw granddad get shot by one of the boys using a toy gun. Granddad slumped to the floor and lay there motionless. The daughter rushed over to see if he was all right. Granddad opened one eye and whispered, "Shh, I always do this. It's the only chance I get to have a bit of a rest."

A grandmother buys a toy water cannon for her three-year-old grandson. When the little boy opens his present his dad says to the grandmother, "I'm really surprised you'd buy him something like that. Don't you remember how I used to drive you mad, firing my water cannon at you when I was little?" "Yes," says the grandmother with a wicked smile. "I remember very well indeed."

A little boy runs up to his granddad and asks him, "Granddad, do you think you could do a frog impression for Mummy and Daddy?" "Why do they want me to do that?" asks Granddad. "I don't know," says the little boy, "but they were just saying we're all going to go on holiday to Disneyland as soon as you croak."

A grandmother was helping to teach her young granddaughter the names of different colours. So everywhere they went she would point something out, ask the little girl what colour it was and the little girl would answer. After a little while of doing this the little girl was beginning to get them right each time but still the grandmother carried on asking her the colours of different things until the little girl finally turned to her and said, "Grandma, I really think you should try and work some of these out for yourself!"

One Christmas a mother decides that she can't be bothered badgering her children to write thank-you notes for their presents. The result is that their old granddad doesn't receive any thank-you notes for any of the generous cheques he has sent. The next year things are slightly different and granddad receives a visit from all of his grandchildren, who come to thank him in person for their cheques. "That's nice to see, isn't it?" says their mother. "At last it seems they've learnt their manners." "It could be that," says granddad. "On the other hand, it could be the fact that this year I didn't sign the cheques before I sent them."

A little boy goes to his daddy and asks, "Daddy, why does Grandma read the Bible all the time?" "Because, son," says Dad, "your grandmother's currently cramming for her finals."

A teenage granddaughter comes downstairs for her date wearing a see-through blouse and no bra. Her grandmother has a fit when she sees this and tells her not to go out like that. The teenager tells her, "Don't tell me what to do. Things have changed since your day. You've got to let your rosebuds show!" The next day the teenager comes downstairs and the grandmother is sitting there with no top on. The teenager wants to die with embarrassment. She explains to her grandmother that she has friends coming over and dressing like that is simply inappropriate. The grandmother says, "Look, dearie. If you can show off your rosebuds, then surely I can display my hanging baskets."

Little Samantha's grandmother comes round for tea one day. All through the meal Samantha stares at her without saying a word. "Samantha!" says her mother, rather embarrassed. "It's very rude to stare. Aren't you going to say anything to your granny?" "Granny,"

Samantha finally says, "how come your skin doesn't fit your face?"

A little boy is staying with his grandparents for a few days. While he's there he makes friends with the family next door, who have children his age. After an afternoon playing with them he comes back and asks his grandmother, "Grandma, what do you call that thing when two people sleep together and one of them goes on top of the other?" "Oh my goodness," says the grandmother. She is rather taken aback, but decides to tell him the truth. "It's called sexual intercourse, dear." The little boy says, "OK" and runs back to the house next door. A few minutes later he comes back again and tells her, "Grandma, you were wrong. It is not called sexual intercourse. It's called bunk beds. Oh, and Timmy's mum would like a word with you!"

Love And Marriage

People usually get married young and grow old together. It's a good system because ageing is such a gradual process that neither partner realizes until it's too late that they've married a wrinkly. Plus the wedding pictures look so much better with a fresh-faced young couple rather than a pair of old crones who need bridesmaids and a best man just to help them up the church steps.

Did you hear about the man of 86 who married a woman of 79? They spent their honeymoon getting out of the car.

An 80-year-old man is going through passport control at the airport when he is pulled over by a customs official for a random search. "Excuse me, sir," says the official, "do you mind telling me how old you are?" "I'm 40," says the man. "But," says the official, "according to the date on your passport, sir, you're 80 years old." "Yes," says the old man, "but I was married for 40 years of that and you don't call that living, do you?"

A middle-aged couple are walking along the beach one day when the wife points out a little old man and a little old lady walking together. "Look at those two," she says. "They look like a really happily married couple." "Maybe," says the husband. "But on the other hand they might be pointing at us and saying exactly the same thing."

An old couple are arguing one day. "I don't know why I married you!" says the old woman. "Six other men proposed to me, you know." "Six other men!" says her husband. "You should have just married the first idiot who asked you." "I did!" says the wife. "The other six proposed afterwards."

A middle-aged woman tells her husband, "Let's go out and have some fun tonight." "Good idea!" says her husband. "But if you get home before I do, leave the hall light on."

An ageing couple are arguing. "Before we got married," yells the husband, "you told me you were oversexed." "No, I didn't!" shouts the wife. "I said I was over sex."

A woman tells her friend, "Last week my husband turned sixty." "So what are you going to do?" asks her friend. "I'm going to see if I can swap him for three twenties," says the woman.

An old man and his wife are having one of their many arguments. The husband says, "You remember when we got married, you promised to love, honour and obey me!" "I know," replies the wife. "But I didn't want to start an argument in front of all my friends and family, did I?"

Marriage is a gamble, let's bc honest.

Yoko Ono

A reporter goes to visit an ageing Native American and his wife. The reporter asks the old man the name of his wife. "My wife's name," he says, "is Three Horses." "That's a good Native American name, isn't it?" says the reporter. "Presumably when she was born her father saw three horses." "No," says the old man, "it's because all she does is Nag, Nag, Nag. Nag. Nag."

A husband and wife are at a party chatting with some friends when the subject of marriage counselling comes up. "Oh, we'll never need that. My husband and I have a great relationship," says the wife. "My husband worked in communications all his life and I worked in the theatre. So he communicates really well and I just act like I'm listening."

An ageing woman asks her husband, "Will you still love me when I'm old and ugly?" He replies without thinking, "Of course I do."

I'd rather have two girls at 21 each, than one girl at 42.

W. C. Fields

An old couple are on the underground during the rush hour with everyone squeezed into the carriage when a beautiful and voluptuous young woman gets on and stands directly in front of the husband. When she gets out at the next stop she has her bottom pinched and turns round to see the old man smiling at her. "You disgusting old man!" she screams. "How dare you pinch my bottom? You ought to be ashamed of yourself at your age!" The old man looks to his wife for support. "I didn't do it!" he protests. "Honestly, I didn't touch her." "I know," says the wife, "I did!"

An elderly couple stood before a judge following a lengthy divorce hearing. The judge addressed the woman who was 75, "So, after 50 years of marriage, love, tears, babies, grandchildren, birthdays, sicknesses and joys, why do you want to divorce your husband now?" The old woman looked first at her husband, then at the judge and slowly replied, "Because... ENOUGH IS ENOUGH!"

An old man is reading a newspaper article about a scientific study into how much men and women speak during the day. "Look at this!" says the old man triumphantly to his wife. "Apparently the average woman says 30,000 words a day while the average man only says about 15,000." "Well you know why that is, don't you?" says his wife. "That's because the average woman has to repeat everything she says to the average man." The old man has carried on reading but after a moment looks up and says, "Sorry. What?"

A little old man and a little old lady are celebrating having been happily married for 60 years. A newspaper reporter goes to ask them about their secret after such a long time together without ever having a cross word. "Well," says the little old husband, "it all dates back to our honeymoon in the USA 60 years ago. While we were there we visited the Grand Canyon, in Arizona, and took a trip right down to the bottom on horseback. We hadn't gone too far when my wife's horse stumbled and she almost fell off. My wife looked down at the horse and quietly said, 'That's once.' We proceeded a little further and her horse stumbled again. Again my wife quietly said, 'That's twice.' We hadn't gone a half-mile further when the horse stumbled for the third time. My wife then very quietly and calmly took out a revolver from her bag and shot the horse dead. I looked at her and yelled, 'WHAT THE HELL DO YOU THINK

YOU'RE DOING, WOMAN! WHAT'S THE FLIPPING MATTER WITH YOU! YOU'VE JUST SHOT THE POOR HORSE!!!!' And my wife looked at me and very quietly and calmly said, 'That's once.' ...And from that moment on, we've lived happily every after."

An old man is invited over for dinner with a similarly aged couple. While he is there he is impressed by the way the husband precedes everything he says to his wife with endearing terms. Despite his age he constantly calls his wife "dear", "darling", "my love", "sweetness" or "beautiful". When the wife is out of the room for a few minutes, the elderly man says to the husband, "I think this is wonderful. You've been married for seventy years and yet you're still very much in love." "Why do you say that?" asks the husband. "Well," says the visitor, "because of all the pet names you keep calling your wife." The old man checks the door and then says in a whisper, "To be honest with you, I forgot what her name is about ten years ago."

At the age of 60, after nearly 40 years of marriage Sid suddenly says to his wife Margaret, "I think we should divorce." "Divorce?" says Margaret. "But we've been through everything together. We're a team. Remember when you had that car accident and I nursed you back to health; when you had your drink problem and I helped you get through it; then you had those business problems and I helped support you through your bankruptcy; and then last year when the house began to subside and we had to move. Not to mention all those minor illnesses I've nursed you through." "I know," says Graham, "that's just what I mean. I've finally realized you're a jinx!"

Two middle-aged women are talking about their marriages. "I wonder," says the first, "if my husband will still love me when my hair is grey." "Why the hell not?" says her friend. "After all, he's loved you through three shades already."

An old married couple are lying in bed one night when suddenly, out of the blue, the wife whacks her husband on the head with a rolled-up newspaper. "Ow!" says the old man. "What on earth was that for?" "It's for the past 45 years of rotten sex," says the old woman. After a moment, the husband picks up the newspaper and whacks her with it. "Ow! And what was that for?" she asks. "For knowing the difference!" says the old man.

A middle-aged woman wakes up in the night and discovers that her husband is not in bed with her. She puts on her dressing gown and goes downstairs to look for him. Downstairs she sees the kitchen light on and finds him sitting there at the table, sobbing over a mug of tea. "Oh dear," says the woman. "What's the matter? What are you doing down here at this time of night?" The husband looks up from his mug of tea and asks solemnly, "Do you remember 30 years ago when we were going out together when you were only 16?" The wife is moved to tears at the thought that her husband has been so affected by the thought of their courting years. "Yes, I do," she says. The husband pauses for a moment before carrying on with a quiver in his voice, "Do you remember when your dad caught us making love in the back seat of my Ford Escort?" "Oh yes, I remember," says the wife, sitting down in the chair beside him and taking his hand. "And do you remember," says the husband, "when he pulled out that gun, held it to my head and said, 'Either you marry my daughter, or I'll make sure you go to prison for 30 years for this?'" "Oh yes," says the wife. "I remember that too. So why are you crying?" "Because," says the husband, "today's the day I would have got out."

An old man and woman were married for many years, even though they clearly both hated each other's guts. Whenever they had an argument the neighbours could hear them yelling and screaming at each other all through the night. The old man would shout, "When I die, I'll dig my way up and out of the grave. Then I'll come back and haunt you for the rest of your life!" The neighbours were certainly frightened by this threat and when the old man eventually died and was buried they were surprised to see his wife celebrating and having a gay old time in the local pub afterwards. "Aren't you worried," asked the neighbours, "that your husband will do what he said and dig his way up and out of the grave, and come back to haunt you for the rest of your life?" "No," says the old woman, "I'm not worried. He can dig as much as he likes. I had them bury him lying face down."

An 85-year-old man goes to have his annual check up. The doctor asks him how he's feeling. "Never better!" boasts the old man. "I've got an 18-year-old bride who's pregnant with my child! What do you think about that?" The doctor considers this for a moment, then says, "Let me tell you a story. I knew a guy who was an avid hunter. He never missed a season. But one day went out in a bit of a hurry and he accidentally grabbed his umbrella instead of his gun. When he got to the woods, he suddenly saw a grizzly bear in front of him! He raised up his umbrella, pointed it at the bear's head, squeezed the handle and do you know what happened next?" "No," said the old man. "The bear dropped dead right in front of him, shot straight through the head!" "Ah well," says the old man, "it's obvious what happened there. Someone else must have shot that bear." "Exactly," says the doctor. "Now, getting back to this child your wife is having…"

Sid and Ethel are celebrating their fiftieth wedding anniversary. Sid says to her, "Ethel, I was wondering… have you ever been unfaithful to me?" Ethel replies, "Oh Sid, why would you ask such a question now?" "I need to know," says Sid. "Well, all right," says Ethel. "Yes, there were three times..." "Three? Well, when were they?" he asks. "Well, Sid, remember when you were thirty-five years old," says Ethel, "and you really wanted to start the business on your own and no bank would give you a loan? Remember, then one day the bank manager himself came over to the house and signed the loan papers, no questions asked?" "Oh, Ethel," says her husband, "you did that for me! I respect you more than ever. So, when was number two?" "Well, Sid, remember when you had that last heart attack," says Ethel, "and you needed that very tricky operation, and no surgeon would touch you? Then remember how Dr Wilson came all the way up here, to do the surgery himself?" "I can't believe it," says Sid. "You saved my life! I couldn't have a more wonderful wife. So, when was number three?" "Well, Sid," she says, "remember that time a few years ago, when you really wanted to be president of the golf club and you were seventeen votes short...?"

An elderly man has just got married to a young woman many years his junior. The couple have decided they want to have children together but find they have difficulty conceiving. In the end the old man decides to go to the doctor to have a fertility test. The doctor tells him to take a specimen cup home, fill it and bring it back the next day. The next day the elderly man appears back at the surgery with his specimen cup still empty. "What happened?" asks the doctor. "Well," says the old man, "first, I tried with my right hand, but nothing. So then I tried with my left hand... still nothing. My wife had a go with her right hand... nothing. She tried with her left hand... nothing. She even tried with her mouth... nothing. Then we had to call my next-door neighbour in...

still nothing." The doctor is now completely stunned. "You mean," he says, "you got your neighbour in to help." "Yes, we did," says the old man, "and do you know what? Not a single one of us could get the lid off this damn cup!"

In Sickness And In Health...

An old man marries a young woman several decades his junior. Although they're in love and although the old fellow tries his best, the young wife is not satisfied with their lovemaking. In the end the old man goes to a psychiatrist for advice. The psychiatrist says, "Why not try this. Hire a strapping young man. While you're making love, have him wave a towel over your bodies." "A towel?" asks the old man. "Yes," replies the doctor. "Your wife will be able to fantasize about the young man and waving the towel will cool you down while giving the young man something to do." The old man is desperate, so he does what the psychiatrist suggests and hires a strapping young male escort, who he orders to stand waving a towel over himself and his wife during their next attempt at lovemaking. Unfortunately the wife still doesn't seem satisfied. "I've got an idea," she says to her husband. "Why don't you and the male escort swap places for a little while?" Willing to try anything, the husband and the strapping young stallion switch positions. Within a few minutes the wife is finally satisfied. "Ah ha!" says the elderly husband in triumph to the male escort. "You see! That's how you wave a towel!"

An 85-year-old man marries a beautiful and vivacious 20-year-old. Because her new husband is so old and she is worried he may over-exert himself, the woman decides that on their wedding night they should have separate bedrooms. After the festivities she prepares herself for bed and for the expected knock on the door. Sure enough, the knock comes and there is the old man all ready for action. The marriage is successfully consummated and the old man goes back to his own room and she lies down to go to sleep for the night. After a few minutes there's a knock on the door and there's the old man ready for action once more. The woman is somewhat surprised but goes along with it all once more, after which the octogenarian again bids her good night and goes back to his own room. Now the woman is really ready for a good night's sleep. She's just dropping off when unbelievably there's another knock on the door and there is her aged husband ready for action yet again. Not wanting to disappoint him, she once again succumbs to his desires. Afterwards as he is taking his leave and preparing to go back to his own room for the third time that night, she says to him, "I must say I'm really impressed that a man of your age has enough energy to do that three times in one night. I've known men less than half your age who couldn't do that. You really are a great lover." At which point her 85-year-old husband looks at her and asks, "What? Was I already here?"

The old farmer married an 18-year-old girl but after a month of wedded bliss he had to visit his doctor for some advice. "It's so tiring, doctor," he said, "I'm still working the farm, and when I'm out in the field and get the urge I have to run back to the house, jump into bed, and afterwards, I have to walk back to the job again. It's wearing me out." "Well, no wonder," said the doctor. "You're 82 and she's only 18. She should be running to you." The doctor's solution to the problem was to suggest that the farmer take a shotgun out into the field, and every time he got the urge he could fire a shot to signal that his young wife should come running. A month later the doctor bumped into the old man down the high street and out of curiosity asked him how the shotgun scheme was working. "Oh, it worked very well for the first couple of weeks," said the old farmer, "but then the duck season started and I haven't seen her since."

You Know You're Getting Old When...

You can go bowling without drinking.

You can hide a spare house key in a wrinkle.

You can no longer remember your true hair colour (unless grey is the answer you're looking for).

You can remember seeing adverts for brands of cigarettes which were recommended by doctors.

You can remember when you didn't have to call the bank before you called the plumber.

You can sing and brush your teeth at the same time.

You can't tell the difference between a heart attack and an orgasm.

You can't understand all the high-tech new-fangled gadgets they have nowadays... like flush toilets.

You chat to your friends about "good grass", but you're talking about your lawns.

You confuse having a clear conscience with having a bad memory.

You daughter says she got pierced and you look at her ears.

You dim the lights for economy, not romance.

You discover that all your favourite films have been re-released in colour.

You discover the words, "whippersnapper", "scallywag" and "by crikey" creeping into your vocabulary.

You don't care where your wife goes, just so long as you don't have to go there with her.

You don't get satellite TV for the porn, you get it for the weather channel.

You feel you can get away with a combination of black socks and sandals.

You finally reach the top of the ladder, and you find it's leaning against the wrong wall.

You find you can live without sex, but not without your glasses.

You own 10 pairs of reading glasses. One for each room of the house.

You own a TV as big as the sofa.

Your password for everything is 'password', so you can never forget it.

Wise Old Words

An ageing priest's parishioners organize a retirement dinner for him after his many years of service. The local Member of Parliament is to give a short speech before making the evening's formal presentation but unfortunately he gets held up on the way. In the MP's absence the priest decides to say a few words. "I got my first impression of this parish," he tells his parishioners, "from the very first confession I heard when I arrived here and I thought the bishop had sent me to a terrible place. The first person who came into my confessional told me he had stolen a television set and, when stopped by the police, had almost murdered the officer. He had stolen money from his parents, embezzled from his place of business, had an affair with his boss's wife and taken illegal drugs. I was horrified but as the days went on, I knew that not all my congregation were like this miscreant and that I had, indeed, come to a fine parish, full of good and loving people." Just as the priest finishes speaking the MP walks in and apologizes for being late. He immediately steps up to make his speech and begins by saying, "I'll never forget the first day our parish priest arrived. In fact, I had the honour of being the first person here to go to him for confession."

A young lawyer is trying a complicated fraud case and is constantly frustrated by the judge's interjections and directions for the jury to ignore certain evidence the ambitious legal eagle is putting forward. Suddenly the young lawyer turns to the judge and says, "Your honour, what would you do if I called you a stupid old twit who's way past his sell-by date?" "Why, young man," says the judge, "I'd seek to have you suspended as being in contempt of this court and I'd do my utmost to see that you never practised law again." "And what if I only thought that you were a stupid old twit who was way past his sell-by date?" asks the lawyer. "If you only thought it, young man," says the judge, "then unfortunately there would be nothing I could feasibly do about it." "OK!" says the lawyer. "In that case... I think you're a stupid old twit who's way past his sell-by date."

Old Sid is sitting at his usual table in the pub taking his time over half a pint of stout. He goes to the bar halfway through the evening to order another when a well-dressed man gets the landlord's attention first. "I'll have two crates of lager, please," says the man. "And a crate of cider, and a crate of bottled beer, a dozen bottles of red wine and a dozen bottles of white..." Old Sid rattles his change around to catch the landlord's attention but the man continues, "...A bottle of whisky, a bottle of vodka and a bottle of gin please..." Sid bangs on the counter but the landlord ignores him while he continues to take the other man's order. "...a dozen bottles of tonic, a dozen bitter lemon and a couple of dozen bottles of mineral water..." Sid bangs on the bar again, but the man carries on, "...Oh, and 15 packets of peanuts, and a couple of dozen assorted packets of crisps. And what the heck, I'll have a couple of bottles of champagne as well." By this time Sid is seething, and when the man has gone he orders his half pint of stout. "I tell you what," says Sid, "You're going to go out of business the way you're carrying on." "Why do you say that?" asks the landlord. "Because," says Sid, "I'm here every bloomin' night while that flash git only comes in once a week."

After working on the railways for 50 years, old Bill is finally retiring. The train company he works for asks him what he would like for his retirement present and Bill says he'd like his very own rail carriage, which he can keep in the back garden. The carriage would serve as his very own private hideaway, in which he could sit and think back on all the years he worked on the railways. So, to honour their most loyal employee, the train company gives Bill his very own luxury carriage and positions it just as he wants in his back garden. A year later, Bill's former boss calls by to see how he's getting on. Bill's wife answers the door and takes him through to the back garden. There, the boss is rather surprised to find Bill sitting in a seat next to his carriage smoking his pipe despite the fact that it's pouring with rain. "What are you doing?" asks the boss. "Why are you sitting out here in the rain when you could sit inside that beautiful luxury carriage we gave you?" "I've got no choice," says old Bill. "You gave me a non-smoker."

Not A Prayer

Some parents are so desperate to get their children into the right schools that they actually lie about their religion to get the place they want. Similarly, some people start going to church more when they're older to make sure they get into Heaven. When someone was surprised to find W.C. Fields reading the Bible and asked him what he was doing, he replied, "Looking for loopholes." So, religion for some people seems to be a means to an end and for others it's the meaning to The End. But in the meantime while we're down here on Earth, trying to find the punch line to the great cosmic joke, let's not forget that some of the best jokes ever uttered were about religion.

The Devil walks into a crowded bar. When the people see who it is, they all run out except for one old man. So the Devil walks up to him and says, "Do you know who I am?" The old man slowly sips his beer and answers, "Yes, I do." The Devil says, "Well then, why aren't you afraid of me?" The old man looks the Devil over and says, "Why the hell should I be scared? I've been married to your sister for 38 years."

An old Jewish man is very ill and in his final hours he asks for a Catholic priest to be called to his bedside. His family are very confused by this but they call for the priest anyway. "Now my son," said the priest, "I have been told you are Jewish, so why have you called for me?" "I want to convert," says the man. "But why, at this late stage in your life?" asks the priest. The old man replies, "If someone's going to die, I think it's better that it's one of your lot than one of ours."

The old person's prayer: God, grant me the senility to forget the people I never liked anyway, the good fortune to run into the ones I do, and the eyesight to tell the difference.

The air conditioning in a Catholic church breaks down, so they have to hire a man to crawl around in the ducts and fix whatever has broken. As the man peeks down through one of the vents in the sanctuary, he sees the elderly Mrs Murphy kneeling and saying her prayers in front of a statue of the Virgin Mary. The repairman decides to have some fun with the old lady and calls down to her, "Old lady! Old lady! This is Jesus! I tell thee thy prayers will be answered!" The little old lady doesn't even blink so the repairman presumes she can't have heard him. "This is Jesus here," he says, a little more loudly. "The Son of God! I tell thee thy prayers will be answered!" But again the little old lady doesn't answer. So the repairman tries one last time and yells at the top of his voice, "HELLO THERE, OLD LADY! THIS IS JESUS CHRIST, THE SON OF GOD! YOUR PRAYERS WILL BE ANSWERED!" At which point the little old lady looks up and says very crossly, "WILL YOU JUST SHUT UP! I'M TRYING TO TALK TO YOUR MOTHER HERE!"

A pious old man reaches the age of 100 and suddenly stops going to church. The priest is alarmed that the old fellow has suddenly decided not to come to the services any more so he goes to visit him at home. He finds the old man in perfect health and completely mobile. So the priest asks, "Why is it we never see you in church any more?" "Well, I'll tell you, father," says the old man. "I got to be 80 and I thought God would take me any day. Then I got to be 85, then 90, then 95. Now I'm 100 years old and I reckon God must have forgotten me. So I'd better not go and remind him I'm still here."

A little old lady who is a devout Christian lives next door to a young man who is an equally devout atheist. Every morning the lady comes out onto her front step and exclaims, "Praise the Lord for the new morning!" Every morning the atheist next door shouts back to her, "Shut up, you old fool! There is no God!" Every morning the same exchange happens. As time goes on, the lady runs into financial difficulties and has trouble buying food. One morning she goes out onto her front step and prays aloud to God for help with her groceries, before finishing with her usual, "Praise the Lord!" The next morning she opens her door and is astounded to find a bag full of groceries sitting there, waiting for her. Her response is of course, "Praise the Lord for he has provided me with groceries!" At this moment the atheist jumps up from behind her garden wall and says, "Ha, I got you! It was me that bought you those groceries. You see, there is no God!" The little old lady looks at him for a moment and then cries, "Praise the Lord, not only did you get me my groceries, oh Lord, you got Satan to pay for them!"

An old man was sitting on his porch one day watching the rain come down. Soon the water was lapping over the porch and into the old man's house and still he sat there watching it. A rescue boat came by and the people on board told him, "You can't stay there. You'll have to come with us." "No, don't worry," the old man told them, "God will save me." The boat moved on and the rain kept coming down until it was lapping up the old man's stairs. Another rescue boat appeared and the people on board again told the old man he had to come with them. "No, don't worry," said the old man again. "God will save me." So the boat left and the rain carried on coming down until the old man was left sitting on his roof, surrounded by water. This time a rescue helicopter appeared and told the old man to climb aboard but again he said, "No, don't worry. God will save me." So the helicopter flew off and the water kept rising until the old man was swept away and drowned. When he arrives in Heaven, the old man tells God, "I placed my faith in you but you did nothing to save me." "What do you mean, I did nothing?" says God, "I sent you two boats and a bloody helicopter!"

One day a post-office sorting worker finds a letter that has arrived addressed to God. He opens it and reads: "Dear God, I hope you can help me. Last Thursday I was mugged and had my purse stolen. In it was £50 which I had been saving for a toy for my great-grandson's birthday. It has really upset me that I won't be able to buy it. I am crying as I write this letter. Please help if you can. Yours faithfully, Ethel Higginbotham, aged 83." The letter is shown round the staff in the sorting office and the workers are all touched by the sad story. Being generous souls they decide to have a whip round for the old lady and they raise £46. They put the money in an envelope and send it back to Ethel. One week later another letter turns up addressed to God. The staff gather round eagerly as the letter is opened: "Dear God," says the letter, "I can't thank you enough. I bought my grandson his present and his little face lit up and we had a wonderful day – thank you, Lord. Yours faithfully, Ethel. P.S. When I opened your letter I noticed it was £4 short. I expect it was those thieving bastards at the Post Office!"

Old Matilda was well known at her local church as the town gossip and self-appointed monitor of morals in her neighbourhood, forever sticking her nose into other people's business. Many of the other members of the church congregation did not approve of her activities, but feared her enough to maintain their silence. She made a mistake, however, when she accused Bert, another elderly churchgoer, of being an alcoholic after she saw his bright orange P Reg Skoda parked in front of the local pub one afternoon. She told Bert and everyone else within earshot that anyone seeing his car there would immediately recognize it and know just what he was doing. Bert, a man of few words, stared at her for a moment and then just turned and walked away. He didn't explain, defend or deny; he said nothing. Later that evening however, Bert quietly parked his bright orange P Reg Skoda in front of Mildred's house and then walked home, leaving the car there all night.

An old lady is talking to her parish priest. The priest tells her that at her time of life, she should be giving some thought to what he calls "the hereafter". "Oh I already think about that all the time," she tells him. "You do?" says the priest, surprised. "Oh yes," she says, "whenever I go into a room or open a drawer or wardrobe I always have to think to myself, 'Now then, what was it I'm here after?'"

Never Too Late To Woo

An old man and an old lady have been good friends for many years. Finally one day the old man decides he will ask the old lady out for dinner one night and request her hand in marriage. "Oh yes," says the old lady, as she tucks into her dessert. Later, the pair go home to their respective houses. When the old man wakes up the next morning the events of the previous evening are a little hazy and he is unable to remember whether his lady friend said yes or no to the offer of marriage. After fretting about this all morning, he decides he will have to phone and ask her. "This is rather embarrassing," he says. "Last night I asked you to marry me but now I'm afraid I can't remember what you said." "Oh, I said yes," says the old lady, "but I'm glad you called because, to be honest with you, I woke up this morning and couldn't remember who it was who had asked me."

An elderly couple are watching an evangelist on television one night. The preacher faces the camera and announces, "My friends, I'd like to share my healing powers with everyone watching this programme. Place one hand on top of your television set and the other hand on the part of your body which ails you and lo, I will heal thee!" The old woman has been having terrible stomach problems, so she places one hand on the television, and her other hand on her stomach. Meanwhile, her husband approaches the television, placing one hand on top of the TV and his other hand on his groin. With a frown his wife tells him, "Ernest, the man is healing the sick, not raising the bloody dead!"

The Dating Game

A doctor gets a visit from an old man. "I seem to have a terrible problem whenever I have sex, doctor," he says. "The last time I had sex with my wife I felt terribly hot and sweaty, but the time before that it was completely the opposite. I felt terribly cold and shivery." "Oh dear," says the doctor. "This sounds as though you may have a serious condition. I'd better have a word with your wife." So the doctor goes to see the old man's wife and tells her all about the symptoms her husband has been suffering. "Oh, the stupid old fool!" says the old lady. "Do you know what might be causing the problem then?" asks the doctor. "I certainly do," says the old woman. "We only have sex twice a year. Last time it was in the middle of July and the time before that it was the middle of winter."

A couple in their seventies go to a private doctor's surgery. "OK," says the doctor. "What can I do for you?" The old man says, "Will you watch us have sexual intercourse?" The doctor is rather puzzled, but agrees. When the couple have finished, the doctor says, "Well, I can't see any particular problem there. And of course as this is a private practice I'm going to have to charge you £25 for the consultation." The couple pay up, but a week later they're back asking for the doctor to watch them having sex once again. Again he can't see any particular problem and charges them £25. When they turn up for the third week in a row, the doctor asks them, "Just what exactly are you trying to find out?" "We're not trying to find out anything," says the old man. "She is married to someone else so we can't go to her house. I'm married so we can't go to my house. The only hotel round here charges £75. Here, it only costs £25 which, because I'm a pensioner, I can claim back from the NHS."

Two ageing widows are talking to one another. The first says, "That nice George Johnson asked me out for a date. I know you went out with him last week, and I wanted to talk with you about him before I give him my answer." "Well," says the second, "I'll tell you about him. He showed up at my house right on time at seven o'clock. He was dressed very smartly in his suit and tie and he brought me a lovely bunch of flowers! Then he took me downstairs and showed me into a beautiful Rolls-Royce complete with uniformed chauffeur. Then he took me out for a wonderful dinner at the finest restaurant in town. We had lobster, champagne, dessert and a bottle of vintage wine. Afterwards we went to the theatre and enjoyed the show immensely but then on the way back home, I could hardly believe it. He turned into an ANIMAL. He went completely berserk and started tearing off my expensive new dress in his desperate desire to get his hands on my body and ravish me." "Oh my goodness," says the old lady's friend. "So you're telling me you don't think I should go out with him?" "No," says the first old lady, "I'm telling you that when you go out with him, remember to wear an old dress."

A coach driver is taking a group of old people on a day trip. An old lady appears from the back of the bus and tells him that she has just been molested. "Don't be ridiculous," says the coach driver. "Who would have molested you on this trip?" A few miles further on, another old lady totters to the front of the bus and tells him she has also been molested. "What's the matter with you?" says the driver. "You must all be senile." But after a third old lady comes forward to say that she too has just been molested, the driver thinks he had better stop and investigate. At the back of the bus he finds an old man crawling round on his hands and knees under the seats. "What do you think you're doing?" asks the driver. "I've dropped my toupee," says the old man. "Three times now I thought I'd found it, but when I tried to grab it, it ran off."

A little old lady is in court describing what happened during a particularly shocking recent crime in a local park. "Please tell the court," says the lawyer, "what happened when the young man sat down next to you on the park bench." "He started rubbing my thigh," says the little old lady. "And were the police called at this point?" asks the lawyer. "No," replies the old lady. "Please tell the court what happened next," asks the lawyer. "Then he started to fondle my bosoms," says the little old lady. "I see," says the lawyer, "and was this when the police became involved?" "No," says the little old lady. "Then please tell the court what happened after that," asks the lawyer. "That's when he started kissing me and suggested we go into the bushes for a bit of you know what," says the little old lady. "I see," says the lawyer. "And is that when the police were called to the scene?" "No," replies the old lady. "In that case, madam," says the lawyer. "Please could you tell the court at exactly what stage the police were called to the scene." And the old lady replies, "When he shouted 'April fool!' and I got out my gun and shot the teasing bastard!"

An old couple have been married for 50 years. One morning they are sitting at the breakfast table when the old gentleman says, "Just think, my darling, we've been married for 50 years. Remember all the passion we used to have for each other. When we were first married we used to wander round the house naked as nature intended." "Well, why shouldn't we do the same now?" asks his wife and strips off her clothes right there at the breakfast table. "What are you doing, woman?" says the old man. "What if someone comes to the door?" "Come on!" says the old woman, leaning across the table. "Where's your passion gone? Doesn't the sight of me naked stir anything in you?

You know I've got a warm feeling in my breasts for you right now." "I'm not surprised," says her husband, "you've just dipped one of them in your coffee and the other in your porridge."

An old lady is upset because her ageing husband is no longer able to satisfy her physical needs. She visits the doctor to ask for advice. The doctor gives her a prescription for Viagra and tells him to put three drops in his milk before he goes to bed. A couple of weeks later, the woman returns. The doctor asks if the Viagra was effective. "I'm afraid not," says the old lady. "I put 30 drops in his milk by accident. Now my husband has died and I've had to come to you for the antidote." "Why do you need an antidote if he's already dead?" asks the doctor. "Because," says the old lady, "how else am I going to be able to get the lid down on his coffin?"

An 80-year-old man goes to the doctor for a check-up. The doctor is amazed at what good shape the guy is in and tells him, "You're doing incredibly well for a man of your age. Tell me, how old was your dad when he died?" "Who said my dad's dead?" says the old man. The doctor is amazed. "You mean you're 80 years old and your dad's still alive? How old is he?" "He's 100 years old," says the old man. "How extraordinary," says the doctor, "How about your dad's dad? How old was he when he died?" "Who said my granddad's dead?" says the old man. The doctor is stunned. "You mean you're 80 years old," he says, "and your grandfather's still living? How old is he?" "He's 118," says the old man. "In fact he got married just the other week." "Married!" exclaims the doctor. "Why would a 118-year-old man want to get married?" "Who said he wanted to?" says the old man.

An old man is celebrating his 115th birthday and the local newspaper sends a reporter round to interview him. The reporter notices the old man's house and garden are full of children of all ages playing together. A beautiful young girl aged about 19 answers the door and shows the reporter in. The reporter asks the old man, "So all these youngsters must be your grandchildren." "Oh no," says the old man. "They're all mine." "All of them?" asks the reporter. "Of course," says the old man. "Including the beautiful young woman who showed me in?" asks the reporter. "Oh no, not her," says the old man, "she's my wife." "Your wife?" says the surprised reporter. "But she can't be more than 19 years old." "That's right." says the old man with pride. "But I would have thought it would be difficult for you to have much of a sex life, what with you being 115 and your wife being a teenager." "Are you joking or what?" says the old man. "We have sex every single night. Every night two of my boys help me on top and every morning six of my boys help me off again." "Hang on," says the reporter, "Why does it take only two of your boys to put you on, but it takes six of them to get you off?" "Well, it wouldn't take so many," says the old man, "but I keep putting up a fight."

An old man goes into his doctor's surgery saying that he feels tired. "Have you been doing anything unusual recently?" asks the doctor. "Well," says the old man, "Wednesday night I picked up a 20-year-old girl and we had sex five times. Thursday night, I picked up a 19-year-old and we had sex eight times and then last night I picked up a pair of 18-year-old twins and we had sex twenty times." "My goodness," says the doctor. "No wonder you're feeling tired. I hope you took precautions with these women." "I certainly did," says the old man, "I gave them all a false name."

An old lady from a remote village in Cornwall goes to stay with her niece in Surrey. Nearby is a very well-known golf course. On the second afternoon of her visit, the elderly lady goes for a walk. Upon her return, her niece asks, "Well, Auntie, did you enjoy yourself?" "Oh, yes, indeed," says the old lady. "Before I had walked very far, I came to some beautiful rolling fields. There seemed to be a number of people wandering around them, mostly men. Some of them kept shouting at me in a very eccentric manner, but I took no notice. There were four men who followed me for some time, uttering curious excited barking sounds. Naturally, I ignored them, too. Oh, by the way," she says, holding out her hands, "I found a number of these curious little round white balls, so I picked them all up and brought them home hoping you could explain what they're all about."

An elderly spinster calls her lawyer's office and tells the receptionist she wants to see her solicitor to have her will drawn up. The receptionist suggests they set up an appointment for a convenient time for the spinster to come into the office. The woman says, "You must understand, I've lived alone all my life, I rarely see anyone and I don't like to go out. Would it be possible for the lawyer to come to my house?" The receptionist checks with one of the junior partners and he agrees to visit the old lady at home to draw up her will. The young solicitor's first question is, "Could you tell me what you have in assets and how you'd like them to be distributed under your will?" The old lady says, "Besides the furniture and accessories you see here, I have £40,000 in my savings account at the bank." "Tell me," the solicitor asks, "how would you like the £40,000 to be distributed?" The old lady says, "Well, as I've told you, I've lived a reclusive life, people have hardly ever noticed me, so I'd like them to notice me after I've passed on. I'd like to provide £35,000 for my funeral." "Well," says the solicitor, "for £35,000 you will be able to have a funeral that will certainly be noticed. It's sure to be one that will leave a lasting impression on anyone who may not have taken much note of you before! But tell me, what would you like to do with the remaining £5,000?" "Well, as you know," says the spinster, "I've never married, I've lived alone almost my entire life, and in fact I've never slept with a man. I'd like you to use the £5,000 to arrange for a man to sleep with me." "This is a very unusual request," the solicitor says, "but I'll make some enquiries and see what I can do to arrange it for you." That evening, the young solicitor tells his wife about the eccentric old spinster and her strange request. After thinking about how much she could do around the house with £5,000, and with a bit of coaxing, she persuades her husband to agree to provide the service himself. She says, "I'll drive you over tomorrow morning, and wait in the car until you're finished." The next morning, she drives him to the spinster's house and waits while he goes into the house. She sits waiting for over an hour, but still her husband doesn't come out. In the end, in frustration she sounds the car horn to hurry her husband up. A few moments later, the upstairs window opens up, the solicitor sticks his head out and yells, "Come back and pick me up this time tomorrow. She's agreed to let the council bury her!"

Death And The Afterlife

Joe tells his friend Pete, "My granddad died last night." "Oh no," says Pete. "Yes," says Joe, "he was working late in the whisky distillery, he had to climb up to check in one of the vats but being a bit doddery on his legs now he lost his balance and fell in." "Oh my goodness!" says Pete. "So what happened? Did he drown?" "Yes, after eight hours," says Joe. "Eight hours!" says Pete. "Why so long?" "Well, it would have been quicker," says Joe, "but he had to get out three times to go to the toilet."

An old Jewish woman goes to a travel agent and asks for a holiday in Calcutta because she wants to consult with the Indian mystics. "Oh, it won't be very suitable for a woman of your age," says the travel agent, "How about a nice cruise?" But the woman insists and takes the trip to Calcutta. When she gets there it's very hot and there are flies buzzing round her as she comes out of the airport and boards a ramshackle old bus. She is on the bus for several uncomfortable hours and finally reaches a remote spot, where there is a temple. There is a queue of people waiting to see the guru so she waits and waits and waits until finally she is allowed in. "Now remember," says one of the men at the door of the temple, "You are only permitted to utter five words to the guru." The woman nods and goes in to where the guru sits in a dark corner. She approaches him and says, "Albie, come home right now!"

An old priest dies and is waiting in line at the Pearly Gates. Ahead of him is a man dressed in sunglasses, a loud shirt, leather jacket and jeans. Saint Peter asks him, "What have you done, that I should admit you into the Kingdom of Heaven?" The man replies, "I have been a taxi driver for many years." Saint Peter consults his list. He smiles and says to the taxi driver, "Take this silken robe and golden staff, and enter the Kingdom." The taxi driver goes into Heaven with his robe and staff. Next, it's the priest's turn. He stands erect and booms out, "I have been a priest for the last forty years." Saint Peter consults his list. He says to the priest, "Take this cotton robe and wooden staff, and enter the Kingdom." "Just a minute," says the priest. "That man was a taxi driver and he gets a silken robe and golden staff. How can this be?" "Up here, we work by results," says Saint Peter. "While you preached, people slept; while he drove, people prayed."

We have no reliable guarantee that the afterlife will be any less exasperating than this one, have we?

Noel Coward

No Fools

A little old lady walked into the head branch of a respected bank, holding a large paper bag in her hand. She told the young man at the window that she wished to take the £3 million she had in the bag and open an account with the bank. As it was such a large sum she asked to meet the manager of the bank first. The teller seemed to think that was a reasonable request and after opening the paper bag and seeing the bundles of £50 notes, which amounted to around £3 million, he telephoned the manager's secretary to arrange this. The old lady was escorted upstairs and ushered into the manager's office. Introductions were made and the lady stated that she would like to get to know the people she did business with on a more personal level. The bank manager then asked her how she came into such a large amount of money. "Was it an inheritance?" he asked. "No," she answered. "Was it from playing the stock market?" "No," she replied. He was quiet for a minute, trying to think of where this little old lady could possibly have come into £3 million. "I bet on things," she stated. "You bet?" repeated the bank manager, "as in horses?" "No," she replied, "I bet on people." Seeing his confusion, she explained that she just bet different things with people. All of a sudden she said, "I'll bet you £25,000 that by ten o'clock tomorrow morning, your balls will be square." The bank manager figured she must be off her rocker and decided to take her up on the bet. He didn't see how he could lose. For the rest of the day, the bank manager was very careful. He decided to stay home that evening and take no chances; there was £25,000 at stake. When he got up in the morning and took his shower, he checked to make sure everything was OK. There was no difference; he looked the same as he always had. He went to work and waited for the little old lady to come in at ten o'clock, humming as he went. He knew this would be a good day; how often do you get handed £25,000 for doing nothing? At ten o'clock sharp, the little old lady was shown into his office. With her was a much younger man. When he inquired as to the man's purpose for being there, she informed him that he was her lawyer and she always took him along when there was that much money involved. "Well?" she asked, "what about our bet?" "I don't know how to tell you this," he replied, "but I am the same as I've always been, only £25,000 richer." The little old lady seemed to accept this, but requested that she be able to see for herself. The bank manager thought this was reasonable and dropped his trousers. She instructed him to bend over and then grabbed hold of him. Sure enough, everything was fine. The bank manager then looked up and saw her lawyer standing across the room-banging his head against the wall. "What's wrong with him?" he inquired. "Oh, him!" she replied, "I bet him £100,000 that by ten o'clock this morning I'd have the bank manager by the bollocks."

I went to the cinema the other day and in the front row was an old man and with him was his dog. It was a sad, funny kind of film – you know the type. In the sad part, the dog cried his eyes out, and in the funny part, the dog laughed his head off. This happened all the way through the film. After the film had ended, I decided to go and speak to the old man. "That's the most amazing thing I've seen," I said. "That dog really seemed to enjoy the film. It's remarkable!" "Yeah, it is," said the old man. "He hated the book."

A man, 92 years old, is told by his doctor that he has tested positive for HIV. Distraught and befuddled, he retires as usual to spend the afternoon at the park bench with other senior citizens. He tells his friend: "Can you believe it? I have HIV... at 92." His friend replies, "You think you have troubles? I have IBM at 80."

An old man of 87 went to the hospital to get a radical new surgical procedure done, where they stretch the skin and pull all the wrinkles up onto the top of the scalp, making you appear years younger. On his way out of the hospital, he met an old friend who didn't recognize him at first. "Rob, is that really you?" said the friend. "You look years younger! I didn't know you had a dimple in your chin." "It's not a dimple, it's my belly button," said the old man and his friend laughed. "If you think that's funny, take a look at what I'm wearing for a tie," he continued.

One sunny Sunday in spring, Father Fitzpatrick noticed that there was a smaller gathering than usual for the noon service. So as soon as the final hymn was sung, he slipped out the back way and went along the street to see who was out and about instead of coming to church. The first person he saw was old Mrs O'Neill, sitting on a park bench with her cane beside her. The good cleric sat down next to her and said, "Good afternoon, Mrs O'Neill, why weren't you in church today?" Mrs O'Neill replied: "Well, Father, it was just such a lovely day today I didn't want to be cooped up in that stuffy old church." The priest was a bit taken aback by this blunt answer, so he thought for a minute, then asked, "But Mrs O'Neill, don't you want to go to Heaven?" To his surprise, the elderly lady shook her head vehemently and said, "No, Father." At that, the priest got to his feet indignantly and said firmly, "Then I am ashamed for you." Now it was Mrs O'Neill's turn to be surprised. She looked up at him and said, "Oh, Father, I thought you meant right now."

Jesus returned and ended up by the side of the River Severn in Worcestershire. He confronted an old chap who was sat there fishing. "I am Jesus – I have come to save all from the horrors that be," exclaimed the great one. "Sod off, you're scaring the fish," answered the old one. "No, you don't understand – I have returned to save the Earth, now tell me, where should I start?" The old boy thinks for a while and tells him to perform a miracle, then he will believe that this is truly The Lord. "Walk across the river," he tells Jesus. So Jesus starts walking across the river, and the water is lapping round his ankles – then around his shins, then his knees. This starts to worry him, but he continues, knowing that he can do it. The next thing he knows, he slips and disappears under the water, and nearly drowns. He manages to claw his way back to the shore, and the old man says to him: "There you are, see, you're not Jesus, you can't walk across water." Jesus responds, "Well, I used to be able to do it until I got these holes in my feet..."

Never Too Old For...

Two elderly men are sitting at the bar, watching the young girls go by. One says to the other: "You know, I'm still sexually interested in women. In fact, I always get excited when I see the young girls walking by. The real problem is that at this age, I don't see so well any more."

Old age and treachery always beats youth and talent.

Their respective spouses having died, a couple in their late sixties decide to marry and move to Bournemouth. In preparation for this they talk through the sharing of household expenses and various other matters. Jane asks Harold what they should do about their present houses. "Well, we ought to each sell our home and then we can each fund half the purchase price of our new home." Jane agrees. Harold then asks Jane what she'd like to do about the grocery bills. She suggests: "Neither one of us eats very much, so maybe we ought to split that bill on a monthly basis." Harold agrees. Then what about the utility bill? Again, they decide to share. Then Jane asks Harold what he wants to do about sex, to which he replies: "Oh, infrequently." Jane looks at him and asks: "Is that one word or two?"

There were these three catering students driving along an country road one day when they saw a farm. So they pulled in, and knocked on the old farmer's door. The farmer answered the door and the three students introduced themselves and said: "We were just passing by and saw your field of buttercups, and were wondering if we could go and get a bucket full of butter." The old farmer scratched his head and said: "You boys ain't gonna get no butter from buttercups, but you're more than welcome to try." About an hour later, the three came back, thanked the farmer and drove off with their bucket full of butter. The farmer once again scratched and shook his head, mumbled under his breath and went on about his business. About three months later, the same three students came up to the farm, knocked on the door and asked the old farmer if he remembered them. He chuckled and asked what he could do for them this time. One of them said: "We were just driving by and happened to see you now have a field of milkweed and we were wondering if we could go out and get a bucket of milk?" Once again, the old farmer chuckled, shook his head, scratched it and sarcastically said: "You boys go on out there and get your milk from my milkweeds." Once again, about an hour later, the three came back with their bucket overflowing with fresh milk and drove off. This time, the farmer was really confused, but just a little less sceptical. It was about three or four months later when the three agricultural students came back and again knocked on the old farmer's door, this time saying that they were driving by and saw the field full of pussywillows. This time, the old farmer went with them.

If you reach 90, you can help advance medical science. There isn't much we know about sex at that age. Rats don't live that long...

Drink And Drugs

There's a bar where all the regulars are really into body-building. The owner is a body-builder and he only employs body-builders as bar staff. The walls are covered in body-builder photos and they are always having body-builder competitions. On the wall behind the bar is a sign that says, "Win €1,000: Beat The Bartender." Written below it are the rules of the competition: "The bartenders are so strong that, after any one of them has squeezed a lemon with his bare hands, nobody can ever squeeze anything else out of it: anyone who can will win the prize." The space around the bar is filled with photos of people who have tried to win the competition, but failed. One day, a skinny, sad-faced little old man walks into the bar and announces he'd like to try for the prize. It is a Saturday night, the bar is packed and everybody starts to laugh. The guy's head is about the size of the bartender's hand, and he's over 60 to boot, and nobody believes he has a chance. The bartender picks up a lemon and starts to squeeze it. The juice gushes out quickly, but after a few seconds it stops as the man squeezes everything out: juice, pips, pith and even squashed rind. The bartender then hands the lemon husk to the tiny old man. The man puts his hand around the wizened, almost unrecognizable lemon and starts to squeeze. To the astonishment of everyone present, juice begins to drip from the fruit and before long seven, eight, nine, and then ten full drops have been squeezed!

Everyone starts to cheer and the bartender coughs up the money. "That's amazing – really amazing," says the bartender. "Are you a secret body-builder? Are you a martial arts expert? How did you do it?" "That was quite easy actually," says the old man, looking modest. "I work for the Inland Revenue."

An old boy sits down in his local and asks the barman, an old friend, for a drink. The old boy is wearing a big, old-fashioned stovepipe hat, a black jacket and waistcoat, and a false, square beard. The barman serves him a drink and says, "You off to a party tonight, then?" "Yup," says the man, "I've come as my love-life." "What are you going on about?" asks the barman. "You look like Abraham Lincoln." "Indeed I do," says the man, "my last four scores were seven years ago!"

Two little old ladies are sitting outside their nursing home having a smoke because it's a no-smoking establishment. It begins to rain and one of them pulls out a condom, cuts the end off and puts it over her cigarette, keeping it nice and dry. The other lady asks her what that thing is. "It's a condom," the little old lady replies. "And where do you get them from?" her friend asks. "Any chemist will sell them to you," the lady replies. The next day, the woman's friend goes off to her local chemist and walks up to the counter. "I'd like some condoms, please, young man," she says to the man behind the counter. "Yes, ma'am," he says, giving her a funny look. "Would you like any particular brand?" "Not really," the little old lady replies, "as long as they'll fit a Camel!"

An old boy walks into an Irish bar in New York with a small dog under his arm. He walks straight up to the bar and puts the dog on it. The barman tells him that animals aren't allowed in the bar and that he'll have to leave. The man says this dog is special, that it can talk and that if anyone wants to bet him $500 he'll take them on. The bartender laughs, but decides to indulge the old guy anyway and takes him up on the bet. So the guy turns to the dog and says slowly, "Now, Jock, what do we call the thing on top of this bar that keeps the rain off our heads when the weather's bad and the sun off our heads when the weather's good?" The dog shakes his head and then barks, "ROOF!" The barman looks at the man and bursts out laughing. "I'm not paying for that crap – you must be joking!" So the man says, "OK, OK, I'll show you again," and he turns to the dog and says slowly, "Jock, who was the greatest baseball player of all time?" The dog shakes his head and then barks, "RUTH!" The bartender hops over the bar, picks up the dog and the old man, then throws them both out. As they both lie on the sidewalk the dog looks up at the man and says sheepishly, "Should I have said DiMaggio?"

With Age Comes Wisdom. Apparently

A woman went to the surgery. She was seen by one of the new doctors, but after about four minutes in the examination room she burst out, screaming as she ran down the hall. An older doctor stopped and asked what the problem was, and she explained, obviously in shock. The older doctor marched back to the first and demanded, "What's the matter with you? Mrs Johnston is 67 years old. She has four grown children and seven grandchildren, and you told her she was pregnant?" The new doctor smiled smugly as he continued to write on his clipboard. "Cured her hiccups though, didn't I?"

Four people were travelling in the same carriage on a French train. There was an old, distinguished lady wearing a fur coat and a haughty expression; what was probably her granddaughter, a stunning 20-year-old of Playboy calibre; a highly decorated elderly General and a soldier fresh from boot camp. They spend the time chatting about trivial things, and then entered a very long tunnel. While in the tunnel, the sound of a kiss was distinctly heard, followed by the unmistakable sound of a hand slapping a cheek. Silence followed, as all were lost in their respective thoughts. The old lady was thinking: "Isn't it wonderful that, in this day and age, there are still young people ready to defend a young woman's honour?" The young woman was thinking: "How strange that he'd want to kiss that old hag beside me. I'm far more attractive!" The General was thinking, while rubbing his stinging cheek, "It's an outrage that any woman could think I would try to sneak a kiss in the dark." The soldier had a big grin on his face and was thinking: "Isn't it great that someone can kiss the back of their own hand, then smack an old General in the face and get away with it?"

A young naval student was being grilled by an old sea captain: "What would you do if a sudden storm sprang up on the starboard bow?" "Throw out an anchor, Sir," the student replied. "What would you do if another storm sprang up after?" "Throw out another anchor, Sir." "And if another terrific storm sprang up forward, what would you do then?" asked the Captain. "Throw out another anchor, Sir." "Hold on," said the old Captain, holding up his hand. "Where are you getting all these anchors from?" "From exactly the same place as you're getting your storms, Sir."

Size Isn't Everything

For years, a little old lady had two monkeys as pets. One day, one of them died of natural causes. Overcome with grief, the second monkey passed away two days later. Not knowing what to do with the remains, she finally decides to take them both to the taxidermist and have them stuffed. After telling the owner of her wishes, he asks her, "Do you want them mounted?" "No, holding hands will be fine," she said, blushing.

There's this really vain surfer type. He jogs and he lifts weights, and he stretches and he tones. He's admiring himself in the mirror one day and he notices that all of him looks great apart from his willy – it is the only part of him that doesn't have a tan. So he tries instant tan from all sorts of places and tanning booths, but nothing works. Eventually he goes to see a doctor, who tells him that because of the sensitive nature of the skin, he will only be able to tan his willy in proper sunlight. So the man goes to the beach. Sadly, there are no nudist beaches near where he lives, so he goes to a normal one and tries to get himself a tan without anyone noticing. He can't manage it, so he develops a plan: he digs a hole big enough to hide in and buries himself, apart from his willy, which he leaves sticking out, and leaves a straw up so he can breathe. He puts on suntan lotion and falls asleep. A few minutes later, a couple of little old ladies walk past and one of them notices the willy in the sand. She prods it a couple of times with her walking stick and gets it to wake up a little bit. Then she sighs and says to her friend, "There's no justice, is there?" "What do you mean, dear?" her friend replies. The lady says, "Well, I've spent my life being curious about willies, enjoying them, asking for them, hoping they'll get bigger, and now here I am, 80 years old, and they're growing wild on the beach!"

An old man walks into a bar using a cane and carrying a crocodile. The barman says, "Sorry, mate, no animals allowed in here – especially dangerous ones like that." The man says, "Oh, go on: my croc can do a fantastic trick and it'll have people coming from miles around to see it. Let me show you…" "Well, OK then," says the barman, "but if I think it's crap, I'm going to chuck the pair of you out." So the old man says something to the croc, who gets up on his hind legs and opens his mouth. The man then drops his trousers and puts his pecker into the croc's mouth. The croc shuts its mouth tight around his pecker. The crowd in the bar all gasp out loud, but then the man picks up his cane and raps the croc's head with it three times – tap, tap, tap! The croc opens its mouth and the old man's pecker is there – still attached – without even a scratch on it. Everyone in the bar starts clapping and cheering the old man. "Now," says the old man, looking around the bar, "Does anybody else think they're up to this fantastic trick? Would anyone else like a go?" There is silence and all the men look to the floor. Suddenly an old lady pipes up, "I'll have a try, but you only need to hit me on the head once!"

An ageing farmer is having trouble with his prize stud bull, which has a herd of 300 cows to sort out. It won't do what is required of it, so the farmer takes it to the vet. Without even examining the animal, the vet hands the farmer a small bottle of pills and says, "Grind one of these into its feed, stand back and watch it go!" Two weeks later, the farmer returns to the vet and says, "Veterinary, that was truly incredible. I did what you said and as soon as he'd eaten the feed, he leaped over the fence and screwed all 300 cows in less than an hour!" The vet says, "So, what's the problem then – why are you back?" The old farmer says, "Well, I was wondering: it's a bit personal, but I've got a hot date with a 30-year-old tonight and I could really do with one of those tablets. I'm not really the man I used to be, after all." "Well, I can't really let you have a whole one," says the vet, "but I guess a quarter of a pill wouldn't do much harm!" So he gives a quarter-pill to the farmer, who goes off to prepare for his date. A few days later, the farmer is back at the vet's again. "What is it this time?" asks the vet. "Well, the pill worked fine – 40 times that one night," says the farmer. "So, what's up, then?" asks the vet. "Well, now I need something for my wrist," says the farmer. "She never turned up!"

An old man had a dog he just loved but that dog had the nasty habit of attacking anything that moved, including people. His friends told him if he had the dog "fixed", he would lose his aggression and quit this behaviour. Thinking it might be a good idea, the old man had his dog fixed. A few days later he was in his front room when the postman came up the steps. The dog jumped up, went right through the door and attacked the postman. The old man ran out, pulled his dog away and began apologizing. "I am so sorry," he said. "I don't know what to do or say. My friends told me he would quit attacking people if I had him fixed, but it didn't work. I just don't know what to do." The postman picked himself up and said, "You should have had his teeth pulled: I knew when he came through the door he wasn't going to hump me."

It was a dark, stormy night. The young soldier was on his first assignment – guard duty. The old General stepped out, taking his dog, a healthy-looking, very strong German Shepherd, for a walk. The nervous young soldier snapped to attention, made a perfect salute and shouted: "Sir, good evening, Sir!" The General, out for some relaxation, returned the salute and said, "Good evening, soldier: nice night, isn't it?" Well, it wasn't a nice night, as it was raining and the soldier had only the standard coat on, while the General had a waterproof overcoat and a pair of gloves, but the Private wasn't going to disagree with the General, so he replied, "Sir, yes, Sir!" The old General continued, "You know, there's something about a stormy night that I find soothing: it's really relaxing. Don't you agree?" The soldier didn't really agree, but then the soldier was just a soldier, and responded, "Sir, yes, Sir!" The General, pointing at the dog, said: "This is a German Shepherd, the best type of dog to train. Very intelligent, very sensitive and very faithful." The private glanced at the dog, saluted yet again and said: "Sir, yes, Sir!" The old General continued, "I got this dog for my wife." The soldier simply said: "Sir, good trade, Sir!"

Money, Good Looks...

An old soak is looking for a whorehouse and stumbles into a chiropodist's office. He walks up to the front desk and is directed to one of the inspection rooms. Without looking up, the receptionist waves him over to the inspection table and says, "Stick it through the curtain." Thinking, "How cool is this?', the drunken old duffer pulls his plonker out and sticks it through the middle of the curtain. "That's not a foot!" screams the doctor on the other side. "Well, lah-di-dah," says the drunk, "I didn't know there was a minimum!'

There once was a beautiful young woman who wanted to use her good looks to get rich quick. So, she started to hang around older men in the hope of netting one for herself to marry and to shag him to death on their wedding night. Pretty quickly, she found herself a rich 80-year-old, who looked frail, and their romance went quickly and effectively. Three months later it was their wedding day. All went well and in the evening they found themselves in a five-star hotel in Paris. Both retired to their separate bathrooms and she emerged first, seductively dressed, as she slipped between the satin sheets of the huge bed they were about to share. The man's bathroom door opened and he walked out sporting a condom over a 12-inch erection. He was carrying a pair of earplugs and some nose plugs, too. The young woman's heart sank and she began to suspect something was up. Tentatively, she asked, "Er... what are those for, dear?" The old man replied, "These take care of the two things I can't stand the most: the sound of women screaming and the smell of burning rubber!"

A couple have been married for years and years. On their 60th anniversary they decide to go on a second honeymoon. "Let's go to all the same places that we did just after our wedding," the wife says. "Sure," says the husband. "And let's do the same things that we did after our wedding," the wife says. "Sure," says the husband. "And we'll make love like we did after our wedding," the wife says. "Sure," says the husband, "only this time it's me who gets to sit on the side of the bed crying, 'It's too big, it's too big!'"

Car Trouble

Tiger Woods was having a quiet holiday far away from the sport paparazzi, driving around North Wales in his Volvo. One evening, noticing that he was almost out of petrol, he stopped at a station to fill up. An old man came out from behind an antiquated counter and approached the car. "Fill her up," Tiger Woods said, getting out of the car to stretch his legs. As he did so, a tee fell from his pocket and landed at the feet of the old timer. The attendant picked it up, turned it around in his hands, obviously puzzled, for a full minute. Then, defeated, not able to figure out what it was, he turned to Tiger

Woods and asked: "Say, what is this, young man?" "Oh, this is called a tee," the champion golfer answered. Seeing the lack of comprehension in the old timer's eyes, he elaborated: "It's to rest my balls on when I'm taking long drives." The man looked him up and down, then glanced at his car and said admiringly: "They really think of everything at Volvo."

An middle-aged woman had been driving for a marathon 16 hours straight when she decided she'd had enough: she was still at least 6 hours away from her destination, it was almost seven o'clock in the morning and she had dozed off and nearly crashed into a telegraph pole. She decided to pull on to a side road and rest for a bit before carrying on. She turned off the car and closed her eyes... drifting off to sleep, precious sleep... All of a sudden an old man in a bright blue jogging suit knocked on her window, scaring her half to death. "Sorry to wake you," he huffed, jogging in place. "But can you tell me what time it is?" The woman glanced at her watch. "7:15," she said through the glass. "Thank you," the jogger said, and left. "Just my luck," the woman muttered angrily. "I'm parked on someone's jogging route." She considered driving off and parking somewhere else, but she was too tired, so she settled back into the seat, trying to re-capture the beautiful dream she was having... Suddenly another jogger knocked on her window. "Hi, do you have the time?" he said. The woman sighed and looked at her watch. "7:19," she said. "Thanks," the jogger said, then trotted off. She looked down the road and saw more joggers coming her way. Irritated, she retrieved a pen from the glove box and scrawled "I DO NOT KNOW THE TIME" on the back of a magazine. She jammed the hastily-constructed sign in the window with her shoulder and settled back to sleep. Another old jogger knocked on the window just as she started dozing off. The woman pointed at the sign and shouted, "Can't you read?" "Sure I can, madam. I just wanted to let you know that it's 7:27."

A Dog's Life

A butcher is leaning on the counter towards the close of day when a wee dog with a basket in its jaws comes pushing through the door. "An' wot's this then?" he asks. The dog knocks the basket sharply into the butcher's shins. "You little bugger." As he reaches down to smack the dog, he notices a note and a tenner in the basket. The scribble on the note asks for three pounds of his best mince. The butcher reckons this is too easy. He goes to the window and reaches for the dried-up stuff that's been sitting out all day. The dog growls at him. The butcher turns around and, glaring at the mutt, gets the best mince from the fridge. Weighing out about 2½ pounds, he drops it on the scale with his thumb. "Hmmmmm, a bit shy. Who'll know?" Again, the dog growls menacingly. "Alright, alright," as he throws on a generous half pound. He wraps it up, drops it in the basket and drops in change from a fiver. The dog threatens to chew him off at the ankles. Another fiver goes in the basket. The butcher is quite impressed and decides to follow the little dog home. The dog quickly enters a high-rise building, pushes the lift button, enters the lift, and then pushes the button for the twelfth floor. The dog walks down the corridor and smartly bangs the basket on the door. The door opens, and the dog's elderly owner screams abuse at the dog and then tries to kick it inside. "Hey, what are you doing?" says the butcher. "That's a really smart dog you've got there." "He's a stupid little bugger," says the old guy indignantly. "That's the third time this week he's forgotten his key."

A blind old man with a guidedog at his side walks into a department store. The man walks to the middle of the shop, picks the dog up by the tail and starts swinging it round in circles over his head. The manager, who has seen all this, thinks it a little odd, so he approaches the blind man and says: "Pardon me. May I help you with something?" The blind man says: "No thanks, I'm just looking around."

Given the increase in crime, an old chap goes to a dog-breeder to buy a guard dog, only to be presented with a scruffy terrier mongrel. "What use is that?" he asks. "Ah, but he's a trained killer, this one," promises the breeder. "Watch: Guard dog? That chair!" In a blur of little snappy teeth and yapping, the chair is reduced to splinters. "Amazing!" says the man. "Can I have a go? Guard dog? That box!" In seconds the box is shredded to mere fluff. Delighted, he buys the mutt and rushes home to show his wife. "Look at our new guard dog," he says. "He's a trained killer!" "What, that thing?" she replies. "Guarddog, my arse!"

Fair Trade

The son of a wealthy older lawyer graduated from college and was considering the future. He went to his father, who had a very large office, and asked if he might be given a desk in the corner where he could observe his father's activities. He could be introduced to his father's clients as a clerk. That way, he could decide whether or not to become a lawyer. His father thought this a splendid idea and this arrangement was set up immediately. On his son's first day at work, the first client in the morning was a rough-hewn man with calloused hands, in workman's attire, who began the conversation by saying: "Mr Lawyer, I work for some people named Gonzales who have a ranch on the east side of town. For many years I have tended their crops and animals, including some cows. I have raised the cows, tended them, fed them, and it has always been my understanding and belief that I was the owner of the cows. Mr Gonzales died and his son has inherited the farm, and he believes that since the cows were raised on his ranch and fed on his hay, the cows are his. In short, we have a dispute as to the ownership of the cows." The lawyer said: "I have heard enough. I will take your case. Don't worry about the cows. The cows will be ours." After the tenant farmer left, the next client came in, a young, well-dressed man, clearly a member of the landed class. "My name is Gonzales. I own a farm on the east side of the town," he said. "For many years, a tenant farmer has worked for my family tending the crops and animals, including some cows. The cows have been raised on my land and fed on my hay, and I believe that they belong to me, but the tenant farmer believes that since he raised them and cared for them, they are his. In short, we have a dispute over ownership of the cows." The lawyer said, "I have heard enough. I will take your case. Don't worry about the cows. The cows will be ours." After the client left, the son came over to his father with a look of concern. "My father, I know nothing of the law, but it seems to me that we have a serious problem regarding these cows." "My darling son, truly, don't worry about the cows," said the old lawyer. "The cows will be ours."

There was a country doctor who was the only doctor for miles around. He wanted to go on a fishing trip, so he called the elderly local vet and asked him to look after things while he was gone. The vet asked: "Is anything happening?" The doctor replied, "Mrs Jones is about due, but I don't think the baby will come before I get back. Anyway, if it does, just deliver it. This is her third and the first two went

really easily." The old vet said "OK," and the doctor went on the fishing trip. When he returned, he called the vet. "How did things go while I was gone?" "Pretty good." "Did Mrs Jones have her baby?" "Yes, it was an eight-pound boy. Everyone's doing fine." "Did you have any trouble?" "Well, there was just one little problem." "What was that?" "I had a terrible time getting her to eat the afterbirth."
The merchandizing manager of a large food chain was on holiday. While driving through rural Norfolk he developed a headache and decided to stop in the next town and buy some aspirin. Stopping at a small grocery store, he went in and got his aspirin. While in the store, more out of habit than anything else, he walked around to see how it was merchandized. To his amazement, only about two of the ten aisles in the store were devoted to the basic staples and the other eight aisles were filled with salt. He had never seen anything like this in his life and wondered what caused this huge demand for salt in a small rural town in Norfolk. Seeing the proprietor in the rear of the store, he said, "My God, you sell a lot of salt." The old boy shook his head ruefully. "Who, me? Wurr, boy. I don't 'ardly sell no salt at all, but that lad that sells me salt, he sure knows how to sell salt."

Doctor: "You're in good health. You'll live to be 80."
Patient: "But, doctor, I am 80 right now."
Doctor: "See, what did I tell you?"

Three retired nurses died and went to the Pearly Gates. St Peter asked the first one: "What did you do on Earth that you deserve to get in here? The first nurse replied, "I was an intensive care nurse and I saved hundreds of lives." "Welcome," said St Peter, "come right in. And what did you do?" he asked the second one. The second nurse replied, "I was an emergency room nurse and I saved hundreds of lives." "Welcome," said St Peter, "come right in. And what did you do?" he asked the third one. The third nurse replied, "I was a managed care nurse and I saved the taxpayer hundreds of thousands of pounds." "Welcome," said St Peter, "come right in... but only for three days."

Bits And Pieces

An old man is having problems with his dick, which has certainly seen better times. He consults a doctor who, after a couple of tests, says: "Sorry, but you're just not young enough any more. Your dick is burned out. You won't be able to make love more than 12 more times." The man walks home deeply depressed; his wife is already expecting him at the front door and asks him what the doctor said concerning his problem. He tells her what the doctor told him. She says: "Oh my God, only 12 times! We shouldn't waste that; we should make a list." He replies, "Yes, I already made a list on the way home. I'm afraid your name's not on it."

This successful older guy goes to the doctor for a vasectomy. Unlike the usual patients, he shows up in a Rolls-Royce, and sits in the doctor's office in a tuxedo with black tie. The doctor says, "I've done a lot of these, but I've never seen a Rolls and tuxedo before. What's the story?" To which the man responds, "If I'm going to BE impotent, I'm going to LOOK impotent."

A woman starts dating a doctor. Before too long, she becomes pregnant and they don't know what to do. About nine months later, just about the time she is going to give birth, a priest goes into the hospital for a prostate gland infection. The doctor says to the woman: "I know what we'll do. After I've operated on the priest, I'll give the baby to him and tell him it was a miracle." "Do you think it will work?" she asks the doctor. "It's worth a try," he says. So the doctor delivers the baby and then operates on the priest. After the operation he goes in to the priest and says, "Father, you're not going to believe this." "What?" says the priest. "What happened?" "You gave birth to a child." "But that's impossible." "I just did the operation," insists the doctor. "It's a miracle! Here's your baby." About 20 years go by, and the now-elderly priest realizes that he must tell his son the truth while there is still time. One day he sits the boy down and says, "Son, I have something to tell you. I'm not your father." The son says, "What do you mean, you're not my father?" The priest replies, "I'm your mother. The archbishop is your father."

Three old friends, a Catholic, a Jew and an Episcopalian, all die and reach the Pearly Gates. The Catholic asks to get in and St Peter says, "No, sorry." "Why not?" says the Catholic, "I've been good." "Well, you ate meat on a Friday in Lent, so I can't let you in." The Jew walks up and again St Peter says no. The Jew wants an explanation, so St Peter replies, "There was that time you ate pork... sorry, you have to go to the other place." Then the Episcopalian goes up and asks to be let in, and St Peter again says no. "Why not?" asks the Episcopalian, "What did I do wrong?" "Well," says St Peter, "you once ate your entrée with the salad fork."

The old vicar of a small congregation was trying to find a contractor to paint his church. Because the church fund was low and he couldn't pay very much, he selected the lowest bidder. The contractor decided to make the job pay better by skimping on materials. He thinned the paint with solvent and then only applied one coat. Within months, the poor paint job began to flake away and the church looked worse than it had before the work was done. The old vicar sent a note to the contractor that said: "Repaint, repaint – thin no more!"

A psychiatrist visited a Norwich mental institution and asked a patient, "How did you get here? What was the nature of your illness?" He got this reply... "Well, it all started when I got married, and I reckon I should never have done it. I married a widow with a grown daughter, who then became my stepdaughter. My dad came to visit us, fell in love with my lovely stepdaughter, then married her. And so my stepdaughter was now my stepmother. Soon, my wife had a son who was, of course, my daddy's brother-in-law, since he is the half-brother of my stepdaughter, who is now, of course, my daddy's wife. So, as I told you, when my stepdaughter married my daddy, she was at once my stepmother. Now, since my new son is brother to my stepmother, he also became my uncle. As you know, my wife is my step-grandmother since she is my stepmother's mother. Don't forget that my stepmother is my stepdaughter. Remember, too, that I am my wife's grandson. But hold on just a few minutes more. You see, since I'm married to my step-grandmother, I am not only the wife's grandson and her hubby, but I am also my own grandfather. Now can you understand how I got put in this place?"

There was an elderly Alabama widow who lived in a large mansion. She was feeling generous when it came to Thanksgiving, so she called up the local military base and asked to speak with the Lieutenant. "Please send up four nice young men to eat dinner here on Thanksgiving, but please, don't send any Jews. Please, no Jews." The Lieutenant replied, "No problem, ma'am, and I am sure I speak for the Army when I say we all appreciate your kindness." Well, Thanksgiving rolled around, and the widow went to answer the door when the bell rang. She was surprised to see four of the blackest boys that anyone had ever seen, especially in the south. "But, but, there must be some mistake," she stammered. One of them replied: "No ma'am. Lieutenant Goldstein doesn't make mistakes."

Oddbods

A dotty old boy was bothering the waiter in a restaurant. First, he asked that the air conditioning be turned up because he was t oo hot, then he asked it be turned down because he was too cold, and so on for about half an hour. Surprisingly, the waiter was very patient. He walked back and forth and never once got angry. So finally, a second customer asked him why he didn't throw out the old pest. "Oh, I don't care," said the waiter with a smile. "We don't even have an air conditioner."

Two ageing violinists make a pact that whoever dies first will contact the other and tell him what life in Heaven is like. Poor Max has a heart attack and dies. He manages to make contact with Abe the next day. Abe says: "I can't believe this worked. What's it like in Heaven?" Max replies: "Well, it's great, but I've got good news, and I've got bad news. The good news is that there's a fantastic orchestra up here, and in fact, we're playing 'Scheherazade', your favourite piece, tomorrow night." Abe says: "So what's the bad news?" Max replies: "Well, you're booked to play the solo."

I guess I don't mind so much being old, as I mind being fat and old.

Peter Gabriel

A tourist is sightseeing in a European city. She comes upon the tomb of Beethoven and begins reading the commemorative plaque, only to be distracted by a low scratching noise, as if something were rubbing against a piece of paper. She collars a passing native and asks what the scratching sound is. The local person replies: "Oh, that's Beethoven. He's decomposing."

I'm 59 and people call me middle aged. How many 118 year old men do you know?

Barry Cryer

Age And Charm

There was a Cornish girl who finally found a good job in the city. One night, shortly after arriving in the city, she was invited to a very exclusive party. She didn't know anyone, so she was trying to find someone to talk to when she saw an elegantly-dressed elderly lady standing alone. She approached the lady and said, "Where'm you from?" The lady gave an indignant look and said, "Well! Where I am from, we DON'T end our sentences with a preposition." The young girl immediately replied, "Alright then, where'm you from, bitch?"

Respect old people. They graduated school without Google or Wikipedia.

Two elderly US army friends decide to have a reunion. One decides to visit the other one, who lives in a big town. The visitor gets lost and calls his friend: "Hey buddy, I am coming over, but I'm lost and have no idea where I am." His friend replies: "It's OK, just look at the street intersection, there will be two signs, read them to me." The lost one looks over and then says: "OK, OK, I see them. One says Walk, the other one says Do Not Walk." "Oh good, you're right down the street. I'll come down to fetch you."

In childhood, we yearn to be grown-ups. In old age, we yearn to be kids. Wouldn't be wonderful if we didn't have to celebrate our birthdays in chronological order.

Robert Brault

A woman in her late fifties arrives home after a shopping trip, and is horrified to find her husband in bed with a pretty, firm young woman. She is about to storm out of the house when her husband stops her by saying, "Honey, before you go, at least give me one chance to explain how on earth this happened!" The woman decides that she owes him this much at least, so stops to listen to his story. He begins, "Well, I was driving home in the pouring rain and I saw this poor thing at the bus stop, soaked. There's a bus strike on, so I offered her a lift and it turned out that she was really hungry. So I brought her home and gave her some of last night's leftovers. I noticed her clothes were shabby so I offered her that jumper you wore once and didn't like and those trousers that don't fit you any more. I noticed her shoes were full of holes, so I gave her a pair of your shoes that you never liked, too. Anyway, just as she was about to leave she asked me, 'And is there anything else that your wife doesn't use any more?' So here we are!"

An old guy walks into a bar and orders a double whisky – straight. As he begins to drink he reaches into his wallet and pulls out a photograph. He takes a quick peek at it and then puts it back quickly in his wallet. He then finishes his whisky, calls the barman over and orders another. He begins to drink it, and as he does so, he reaches into his wallet and pulls out the photograph again, looks at it and then puts it quickly away. He continues doing this for about an hour. Eventually the barman asks him, "Hey mate, what's with the photo? I'm not worried by the amount you're drinking, I'd just really like to have a look at the picture – what on earth is it?" The old man replies, "It's a photograph of my wife. When she starts to look good, I know it's time to go home!"

It's a beautiful day in County Kerry and people all over the county are sitting outside the pubs enjoying stout by the pint. In a cosy pub, one old chap turns to his friend and says, "You see that old boy over there?" His friend nods. "Have you noticed that he's the spitting image of me? It's bloody uncanny, that's what it is, to be sure. I'm going to go over there and ask him a few questions: after all, 'tis not every day that you get to meet someone who could be your exact double, now is it?" And off he goes to see the man he is talking about. He taps him on the shoulder and says, "Excuse me, I couldn't help noticing from over there that you look almost exactly the same as me. I was thinking what an incredible coincidence that was!" "Me too, me too," replies the man, "I noticed you earlier and I was just about to come over and talk when I saw you coming over anyway. 'Tis an incredible thing, to be sure. So whereabouts are you from?" he asks. "Well, I'm from Galway, originally," says the first old man. "No, that's incredible!" says the second, "Me too! It's just unbelievable. What street did you live in?" "Why, I lived in Moher Street for 20 years, so I did," comes the reply from the first man. "No! I can't believe it – I did, too," says the second. "And what number in that street was it?" he asks. "Why, I lived in number 20." "Unbelievable," comes the reply, "that's the number I lived in. And what were your parents' names?" "Ruari and Siobhan," comes the reply. "This really is uncanny," the first man says, "those are the exact names of my parents, too!" At this point, the bar staff turn up for the next shift. The new guy asks, "Anything happening?" and the guy who is about to go replies, "No, not really; just the Rix twins being drunk again!"

Doctor, Doctor

An old man goes to the doctor with a strange problem. "Doctor, whenever I break wind there is no smell at all. It's really strange, and no matter what I eat, I get the same result – no smell whatsoever!" The doctor has a cursory investigation and then asks the man if he can possibly break wind there and then. The old man drops his trousers and pants, and farts extremely loudly. The doctor sniffs at the air a couple of times and immediately says, "Oh yes, this is a common one. I know exactly what the problem is," and he walks out of the room. He comes straight back with a six-foot pole with a large brass hook on the end. "Doctor! What the heck are you going to do with that pole?" asks the old man. "I'm going to open the window," says the doctor. "You've got a blocked nose!"

An ageing man goes to a doctor and, twitching his fingers and stuttering, finally manages to say, "Doctor, I have a... er... sexual performance problem. Can you help me?" "Oh, that's not a problem for us men any more!" announces the proud physician with a broad wink. "This new pill just came out – a new wonder drug called Miagra. That does the trick! You take a few of these and it's the end of your problems!" So the doctor gives the man a prescription for a packet of Miagra and sends him on his merry way. A couple of months later, the doctor runs into his patient on the street. He's pleased to notice that the man is looking slimmer, better-groomed and all-round happier. "Doctor, doctor!" exclaims the man excitedly, "I've got to thank you! This drug is a miracle! It's wonderful!" "Well, I'm glad to hear that," says the physician, rather pleased with himself. "And what does your wife think about it?" "Wife?" says the guy with a silly grin on his face. "I haven't been home yet!"

A rather embarrassed 50-something man goes to see his doctor and tells him: "Well, I have this problem. You see, I can't get it up for my wife anymore, if you know what I mean." "It's quite all right," the doctor says. "Get undressed and we'll see what the problem is." He does so, but can find nothing wrong with the patient. "Come back tomorrow," he advises. "Bring your wife with you. I'd like to examine her, too." The anxious patient turns up the following day with his wife, as promised. The doctor has a quick look at the woman, then asks her to take her clothes off. "Mmm... I see... Now turn around, please. Mmmm... Can you crouch down for me? That's it. Gooooood, now get on all fours on the carpet. Yes, this way... Mmmm... It's OK, you can put your clothes back on." While the wife is getting dressed, the doctor takes the husband aside and tells him: "You're perfectly healthy. Don't worry. Your wife didn't give me an erection either."

An old man says to his doctor: "Doctor, I lost my memory!" "When did this start?" the Doctor says. The old man replies: "When did what start?"

Old Dogs

Jake moves to Australia after working all his life in the City. He buys a farm in the remotest part of the Outback he can find. His post arrives once a week, his groceries once a month and he can call the Flying Doctor on his radio if he has an emergency. One night, after six months of this, Jake is finishing his dinner when he hears a knock on the door. He walks up, opens it and sees a huge, grizzled old outbacker standing in front of him. "G'day, mate," says the outbacker. "I'm your nearest neighbour, Bruce Sheldon, from 20 miles east. I'm having a party Saturday night and I thought you might like to come along, mate." "That'd be great," says Jake. "I haven't really spoken to anyone for six months. Thanks a lot." Bruce is about to turn away, but instead says, "I think I'd better warn you, though: there'll be some serious drinking going on." "Not a problem," says Jake, "I like a couple of pints myself." Bruce is about to turn away again, but instead says, "Better warn you, though, there'll probably be some fighting, too." "Not a problem," says Jake, "I know how to keep out of trouble." Bruce is about to turn away again, but instead says, "Better warn you, though, there'll probably be some pretty wild sex, too." "Not a problem," says Jake, "I've been alone for six months, remember? Now, what time should I show up?" Bruce turns once more and says, "Whenever you like, mate. There's only going to be me and you there anyway!'

The old General arrived at his office on a Sunday morning and discovered that none of his private aides was there. Grimly, he remembered it had been one aide's birthday party the previous evening and he had no doubt as to what condition they were in. At around ten o'clock, five aides arrived, unshaven and dressed in rather piteous attire. They saluted as smartly as they could and braced themselves for the old General's grilling. "I presume you were at Smith's birthday party last night, weren't you?" "Sir, yes, Sir," one aide answered. "And you couldn't get up early enough this morning to get to the office because you were too drunk!" thundered the General. "Er, no, Sir," the aide said timidly, looking at his friends. "So what is your excuse, young man?" the old General wondered, sitting down, with a dangerous, vicious smile on his lips. "I can explain. You see, we did run a little late, I admit. We ran to the bus but we missed it; we hailed a cab but it broke down; we found a farm and bought eight horses but they dropped dead; we ran ten miles, and now we're here. It's just a logistical problem, really, General, Sir!" The General eyed him suspiciously, but as he hadn't heard such a good one for a long time, he let the men go. An hour later, the last aide showed up, in the same dishevelled state. "Sorry, Sir," he said. "I ran late; tried to catch a bus but missed it; I hailed a cab but..." "Let me guess," the old General interrupted. "The cab broke down, so you bought a horse in a farm but it died on you, so you ran for ten miles. Do you really think I'm going to swallow this?" "Er, no, Sir. You see, there were so many dead horses on the way that it took forever to go round them."

Four retired friends decide to go golfing. One of them pays the fees, while the other three go up to tee off. They are all bragging about their sons. The first man says, "Well, my son's in construction, and he's so successful that he gave one of his friends a brand-new house for free." The second man says, "Well, my son's a car salesman, and he's so successful that he gave one of his friends a Porsche for free." The third man says, "Well, my son's a stockbroker, and he's so successful that he gave one of his friends a share portfolio for free." At this point the fourth man arrives on the scene and they tell him, "We were just discussing how our sons are doing. Is yours successful?" The man says, "Well, my son is gay, and he's an erotic dancer in a gay bar." There is a silence as the others look embarrassed for the man. "I'm not really thrilled about the dancing, but still," the man continues, "he does pretty well anyway. His boyfriends recently had a bit of a competition among themselves and gave him a share portfolio, a Porsche and a brand-new house, all for free!"

An old man has been on a desert island for twenty years. One day, while he is knee-deep in the sea spearing a fish, he notices a strange movement in the water. A few minutes later, a few feet away from him, a gorgeous woman in a tight wet suit stands up. Dumbfounded, he simply watches her approach, dripping with water, teeth flashing, hips swaying. "How long has it been since you last had a cigarette?" she asks in a throaty voice. "My dear, it's been decades," the old chap answers in a shaky voice. The woman diver opens the zip of her breast pocket and fishes out a packet of cigaretes and a lighter. She places a cigarette in his mouth and lights it. She lets the man take a drag and then asks: "How long has it been since you last had a nice Scotch?" "A long, long time," the old man replies, holding his breath. The woman pulls down the front zip of her wet suit, just enough to reach down and bring out a bottle of whiskey. She places her hands around the neck and gently twists the cap open. She takes a swig, licks the liquid on her lips and passes the bottle to the guy and then asks, her finger toying suggestively with her front zip, "Tell me, how long has it been since you last played around?" "My God," breathes the old boy. "Don't tell me you have golf clubs in there, too!"

Nikos, a wizened old Greek man, was sitting in a bar talking to a young tourist. "So," he says, "you see that wall out there in that field?" He points to a huge stone wall separating two fields. "Can you see how well it's built? I spent three years of my life moving stones from down in the valley up to those pastures and carving them so they fitted. That's the strongest fence between here and Athens! And do they call me Nikos the wall-builder? No, they do not!" Then he continues, "So, you see the bar here? The one you are leaning on, right now?" and he raps it with his knuckles. 'Can you see how well it's built? I spent a year of my life cutting, sanding and waxing this bar. This is the finest bar between here and Athens! And do they call me Nikos the bar-builder? No, they do not!" Then he continues, "So, you see the pier out there in the water?" He points to a long, solid pier that stretches out into the deep, deep water. "I spent five long years of my life putting that pier together. I cut down the trees, I nailed the boards and I dug the holes for the poles. It almost killed me, and it is the finest pier between here and Athens! And do they call me Nikos the pier-builder? No, they do not!" Then he looks around and checks the bar before he continues, "So, I screw one lousy goat...!"

A man is confused about sex and the Sabbath day. He just cannot work out whether having sex on the Sabbath is a sin or not, because he doesn't know whether it is work or play. He goes to see his local priest and asks him for his opinion on this question. The priest gets his Bible down and flicks through it, reading a passage here and a passage there. Eventually he tells the man, "Well my son, after consulting the Good Book, I have decided that sex is probably closer to work, and therefore you should not practise it on the Sabbath." The man thanks the priest, but as that wasn't really the answer he was looking for, he decides to go and see the local minister, who is married and may see things a bit more his way. He asks the minister the question and, to his disappointment, the minister gives him the same answer as the priest, "No sex on the Sabbath." The man decides to go and see another type of holy man – the wise old local Rabbi. The Rabbi is asked the question and he ponders it over. Eventually he says, "Well my son, I have come to the conclusion that sex is definitely play so therefore you can have sex on the Sabbath." The man says, "That's great, Rabbi, but how do you come to that conclusion when so many others disagree?" The Rabbi thinks a little and then says quietly, "If sex were work, my wife would get the maid to do it!"

In the Czech Republic, some drunken friends accidentally drank their grandfather's ashes mistaking them for instant coffee. They realised their mistake when they noticed that the coffee tasted of Werther's Originals.

A reporter was interviewing an 104-year-old woman: "And what do you think is the best thing about being 104?" She simply replied, "No peer pressure."

Youth Is Wasted On The Young

We all know kids can be cruel, and nobody respects their elders anymore, but these tasteless jokes at a wrinkly's expense take the biscuit, even if they are hilarious:

A young man was at a cash machine when an old lady came up to him and asked him to check her balance. So he pushed her over.

"My granddad's like Spiderman, a young boy proudly announced one day at school. "He hasn't got any super powers though – he just finds it difficult to get out of the bath."

"Give me all your money now, you old cow, or you're geography!" shouted a young man as he tried to mug an old aged pensioner. "Don't you mean history?" the old lady replied. The mugger said, "Don't try and change the subject."

A young man asks his grandma one day, " Granny, have you seen my pills, they were labelled 'LSD'?" His granny replies, "Sod the pills, have you seen the dragon in the kitchen!"

Wrinklybook

Some wrinklies revel in being on Facebook, Twitter and other popular social media sites, if only so they can spy on their sons, daughters and grandchildren. But you can spot a wrinklies' Facebook 'update' from a mile off! If you want to appear cool to all your new 'followers' and 'friends', keep clear from these cringeworthy wrinkly 'tweets' and 'posts':

Just received an email from a prince in Nigeria. Sent him some money. Good deed for the day done!

Just baked a moussaka. Tasted nice. Needed more salt though. @Wrinklie

Dear Facebook, how do I Google something on Yahoo?

I forgot what this thing # is called? A hash brown? @Wrinklie

Glad that Deidre and Ken have finally sorted things out. For now!

Popping out now to buy some bread. @Wrinklie

Wrinkly TV

Some television shows are aimed purely for the silver foxes. Stay young – and avoid these TV programmes:

8 Out of 10 Naps

Game of Bones

Mock The Weak

Only Stools and Hearses

Blackbladder

Granddad's Army

Father Dead

Sleeping Up Appearances

Last of the Summer Whine

The Boil Family

The Wrinkly Lads

The Old Ones

The End

There is no pleasure worth forgoing just for an extra three years in the geriatric ward.

John Mortimer

Life would be infinitely happier if we could only be born at the age of eighty and gradually approach eighteen.

Mark Twain

Life is like a roll of toilet paper. The closer you get to the end, the faster it goes.